FIFTH EDITION

Written and researched by
David Bramwell
and Tim Bick

The Cheeky Guide to Brighton 5th edition

Created by David Bramwell and Tim Bick

Comments, suggestions or enquiries: david@cheekyguides.com
ISBN 0953611086
Published in 2009 by Cheekyguides Ltd
PO Box 243, Brighton BN1 3XT
www.cheekyguides.com

Thanks to the following contributors:

Fred Pipes for *Open Houses* (p48) and *Weird Cycle Lanes* (p309); **Curtis Tappenden** for *Sketching* (p49); **Dave Mounfield** for *Things To Do in Hove* (p52) and *Restaurant Toilets* (p144); **Cath Quinn** for *Love in Brighton* (p54), **Dan Parkinson** for *Murmuration* (p59); **Sam Benkle** for *Orb360* and *In Vino Veritas* (pp60 & 132); **Marcus O'Dair** for braving those cold Brighton waves which can tower over 100cm high in *Surfing in Brighton* (p67); **Andy Roseman** for record shops (p69); **Annabel Giles** for *Girlie Shopping* (p87); **Jonny Young** for *Red Mutha, Shoppun*, and *Harvey's Beer* (pp86, 95, 166); **Lisa Wolfe** for *Dressing Properly* (p90); **Brian Mitchell** for *Greasy Spoons* (p114); **Rachel Blackman** for *Coffee Corner* (p105); **Steve Morley** for *Cafe One Ten* (p109); **Joseph Nixon** for *Vegetarian Brighton* (p118); **Michael Kemp** for *Posh Nosh* (p145); **Owen Chir** for *St James Tavern* (p161); **Letitcia** for *Brighton Sex Tour* (p253); **Emily Dubberly** for *Sex Tips* (p261)

Special thanks to Rachel Blackman, Emma Ridley and Matt Preston.

Photo credits

Matt Preston (www.mattprestonphotography.com): Phoebe's grave, pebbles, yeti, Jane Bom-Bane, seagull, Two Wrongies pp9, 11, 12, 125, 143, 191; **Alexis Maryon**: naked boys p17; **Peter Chrisp**: snowman p34; **Barry McFarlane**: Volks Railway p41; **Brighton Swimming Club**: pp65, 66; **Brian Gittins**: 3 and 10 p189; **Toby Amies** (tobyamies.com): Drako and fairy pp211, 247; **Clive Andrews**: birdlady p216; **Dean Stockings**: Dolly Rocket p218; **Katherine Griffin**: furry things p237; **Eric Paige**: Storm men p243; **Cathy Teesdale**: Letitcia p253.

Illustrations

Huge thank yous as always to **Lisa Holdcroft** for the cover, maps and innumerable cartoons that appear in this book. She is Brighton's answer to Rolf Harris (but not quite as hairy) and can be contacted at *lisa.holdcroft@ntlworld.com/(01273) 705658.*

Editing

Thank you eagle-eyes **Eve Poland** for showing us the error of our ways with erroneous commas, apostrophes and occasionally whole paragraphs.

Printed By Grafica Veneta S.p.A., Trebaseleghe (PD) – Italy

Cheeky Profile #1: MR TIM BICK

Since winnning a Katie Price lookalike contest at the Hanbury Ballroom in 2009, Tim has commanded nothing but love and respect from this celebrity-obsessed town. And with the real Katie still tied up in his loft, he continues to make a handsome living out of guest appearances at local events, though he nearly got rumbled at The Pussycat Club recently when, mid-way through a pole-dancing routine, he inadvertently 'popped out'. A typical Piscean, Tim collects tinned meat products and exotic underwear, and has an irrational fear of fish and chips.

Lives in: Brighton's fashionable 'Muesli Belt' better known as Hanover
Best feature: inner ear
Favourite metal: tungsten
Cheeky fact: for the fourth edition of this book, Tim single-handedly reviewed over thirty Brighton clubs in less than two weeks and has only recently started to 'come down'.
Not many people know that: Tim's tongue is *so* long, he could wear it as a large scarf in winter, though he chooses not to.
Most likely to say: 'I'm sorry, I'll clean it up.'

Cheeky Profile #2: DR DAVID BRAMWELL

A medical man and drunkard by profession, Dr Bramwell turned to guide book writing when – owing to his notoriously shaky hands – a routine operation left a patient missing both nipples. Having lived in Brighton for nearly twenty years now David still recalls those halcyon days when the beach was sandy, traffic wardens helped you double park and Chris Eubank hadn't been invented. A typical Aries, he enjoys shouting, wrestling woodland creatures and going 'brrrr'.

Lives in: Brighton's unfashionable district of disgruntled teachers; better known as Hanover.
Best feature: coccyx
Favourite metal: zinc
Cheeky fact: David is so dedicated to the guide that he once took part in a four-hour naked cycle ride just to get a good photo, and has only recently started to sit down again.
Not many people know that: David collects stuffed animals and has two bum holes.
Most likely to say: 'I do apologise, I had cabbage for lunch.'

CONTENTS

In the beginning there was only Herring...

1500s Brighton starts life as a prosperous fishing village, paying the government 400 herring a year in taxes.

1783 The town becomes a fashionable health resort when the noted Dr Russell declares that drinking seawater will get rid of boils and put hairs on your chest. Not advisable today unless you want to get rid of your hair and sprout boils on your chest instead.

1790s Brighton's first massage parlour is opened by self-styled "*Shampooing surgeon to His Majesty, King George IV*" Sake Deen Mohammed. It is in actual fact, a ***genuine*** massage parlour, unlike the ones advertised in the back of *Friday Ad*, but that doesn't stop a flood of missives from lonely gentlemen seeking 'relief'.

1823 The Prince Regent has the Royal Pavilion built as somewhere he can bring back a few mates after the pubs have closed.

1930s Torsos start turning up in boxes around the town, heralding the reign of the infamous trunk murderer. Police are on the lookout for a male with a long grey nose and extra-large stools.

1939 Movie star Johnny Weismuller opens the brand-new lido at Saltdean with the immortal line *"Me Tarzan, you Saltdean Lido"*.

1940 The West Pier is chopped in half by the War Office to prevent (and I quote) "*a German invasion via the ice-cream kiosk*".

1960s Brighton is host to the 1964 *It's a Knockout*, featuring Mods and Rockers battling it out on the seafront. The town remains a popular choice for deckchair rage for the next twenty years.

1972 Sir Laurence Olivier campaigns fiercely for kippers to be returned to the menu on the Brighton Belle railway line. He succeeds (for a while).

1974 The Eurovision Song Contest is held at the Dome Theatre. Swedish supergroup Abba scoop this prestigious award with *Waterloo*, while neighbouring Norway again scored "*nul points*" with *Yes, We Have No Roll-Mop Herring.*

1979 *Quadrophenia* is released and Sting has his equity card revoked. Scuffles start up again on the beaches for a while as all the Mods completely miss the point of the movie.

1984 Lady Thatcher visits the bathroom and survives the IRA bombing of the Grand Hotel. Others are not so lucky.

1989 Hundreds of packets of cocaine are found washed up on the beach at Peacehaven. Police cordon off the area when Julie Burchill arrives for a closer look.

1992 Local cult The Temple of Psychic Youth join hands around the Pavilion and attempt to levitate it, but are stopped at the last minute by police. Apparently their founder, Genesis P.Orridge, had dropped 20p and just wanted to check that it hadn't rolled under there.

1995 The West Pier is declared an independent state by a bunch of squatters but after two weeks they run out of Rizlas and abandon their plans.

1998 A chip-pan fire causes the Albion Hotel on the seafront to burn down. *"Meester Fawlty, is fire! Is fire!"*

2001 Brighton achieves city status after 1,000 cyclists ride all the way to Downing Street to present Mr Blair with several compromising photographs taken during the Labour Conference here in 1992. The photos are said to feature the then Prime Minister, a horse, an egg whisk and three blonde Swedish students at a well-known Waterloo Street bordello.

July 2001 The citizens of Brighton awaken one morning to discover a huge army of uniformed zombies patrolling the streets. The council claim they are traffic wardens, sent to improve parking conditions, but the townsfolk are unconvinced, especially after one of them is spotted devouring the flesh of an elderly couple from Hove.

Revellers at the now legendary Fatboy Slim beach party

July 2002 A quarter of a million people turn up for a mass piss-up on the beach. The Fatboy Slim gig isn't bad either.

January 2003 Brighton Pier catches fire. Nothing is damaged except the ghost train, which needed repairing anyway. Convenient that.

March/May 2003 The West Pier burns down and, overnight, 20,000 starlings are made homeless.

December 2005 Carbon monoxide emissions in Brighton go down a staggering 60% after Chris Eubank is declared bankrupt and forced to drive his monster truck for less than 14 hours a day.

February 2006 Brighton is judged to be Britain's healthiest city, with more fruit and veg sold here than anywhere else in England. The cause turns out to be record sales of cucumbers and courgettes at the little grocer's next to the lube shop on St James's Street.

September 2007 The statue of Steve Ovett disappears from Preston Park. All that remains is his foot. Police rule out a possible case of stolen-to-order art theft but admit they're baffled why anyone would want to vandalise this ugly, emaciated lump of crap.

2009 The credit crunch hits Brighton. Things get so bad that the Overpriced Kitsch Tat Shop in the North Laine closes its doors for the last time.

2010 Brighton celebrates 200 years of being ***the*** cultural centre of the South with a huge fireworks display and twinning with Chas from Chas and Dave.

2011 The Marina declares itself an independent state, with its own sailing-boat navy which employs champagne corks as ammunition. The entire enterprise collapses three weeks later when they run out of chunky knitwear.

BRIGHTON MYTHS

HIPPY STUFF

New Age legend has it that a stone circle once stood in the Old Steine but was smashed up by the Victorians and used to form the base of the big fountain there. This feature is actually claimed by some as the source of all Brighton's energy and weirdness. It is interesting to note that Old Steine means 'old stone'. Give Julian Cope a ring: he'll put you straight.

PHOEBE HESSEL

Phoebe Hessel, a local trader of fish, pincushions, gingerbread and apples, was a local celebrity in Brighton during the late eighteenth and early nineteenth century, and lived through six different monarchies to the glorious old age of 107. She was a celebrity, however, not for her longevity and comestibles but thanks to her heroism and love. The story goes that when her lover, Samuel Golding, prepared to leave Brighton and join the army, Phoebe was unwilling to desert his side and so accompanied him disguised as a man. The two continued to serve in the army for 17 years and even fought and were wounded at the Battle of Fontenoy!

OK, so the fact that Phoebe lived to a ripe old age certainly gave her plenty of time to embellish her tale, and I am inclined to wonder how she hid her boobs for all those years, but the story does have a happy ending, as the two finally returned and got married.

Her grave can still be found in the churchyard of St Nicholas halfway up Dyke Road, where it is surrounded by a small metal fence to keep out dwarves.

THE HAND OF GLORY

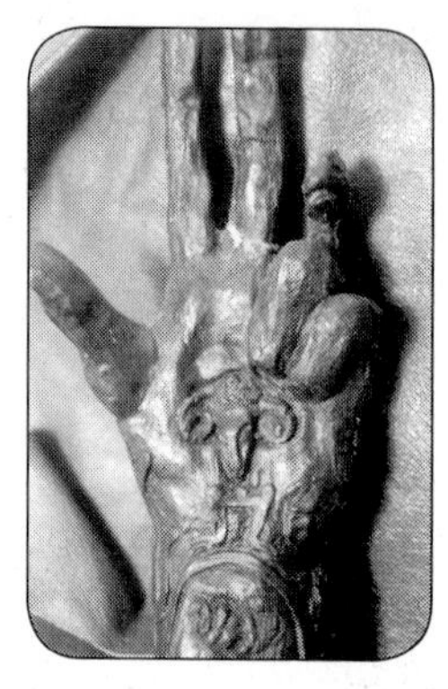

A charm believed to cure lumps on the throat once carried the name of the Hand of Glory. This involved a number of gruesome things including the severed hand of a recently hanged man, which was rubbed on the offending article or made into a candle (!). The last hanging to take place in Brighton was at the Steine in 1834, where a woman with a gammy neck is said to have run from the crowd, taken the dangling hand of the dead man and joyously rubbed it all over her affliction.

THE UBIQUITOUS EUBANK TALE

This short and simple tale comes in many forms but the basis of it is that Chris (*wherever* he is) is making a big public display of the fact that he's got a mobile telephone and is making a real show of taking important calls from important people when, to his utter embarrassment, the phone starts ringing in his hand. Now several people I've met lay claim to this one and seem to get a bit annoyed when I suggest it's an urban myth, even though I've heard countless versions, ranging from Chris shopping in the Lanes and Chris jogging along the seafront, to Chris sitting in a bath of baked beans in Lust.

SUBTERRANEA

Perhaps it's down to childhoods filled with Blyton-esque stories of bookcases that swivel round when you pull on the curtain rope, to reveal secret staircases disappearing darkly down, but virtually every long-term Brighton resident has a tale of some underground tunnel or other. Some of the most popular stories are of those under Queens Road whose purpose is lost to the mists, and a vast network of tunnels emanating from the Pavilion, used by Prinny for everything from visiting Mrs Fitzherbert's pad on the Old Steine, to puffing on a pipe in a Western Road opium den, to riding his horse back and forth from the stables across the road. There really is a tunnel under the Pavilion gardens, built during the Prince's latter-day publicity-shy era (Regency paparazzi were of course notoriously slow off the mark with their easels but very good at drawing from memory), although I'd recommend a Shetland pony as your mount if you don't want to bash your bonce on the doorframes.

THOSE PEBBLES

Possibly one of the most curious (and certainly most persistent) Brighton myths centres around the origin of the pebbles on our beaches. Some of the most sensible Clarks-shoes-wearing friends still swear blind that the stones were deposited here in the 20s to prevent beach erosion and that Brighton actually once had sandy beaches. Where this story originated is a mystery but it does throw up a few interesting questions for the plethora of believers of this myth, such as: where are the photos and newspaper stories about such a mammoth undertaking? Where were the stones from? And don't the stones run for more than 100 miles of coast? What kind of loony would pebbledash 100 miles of glorious sandy beaches? And besides, what's a groyne for anyway?

MURDER MYSTERY

Take one of the tours during the festival and you will learn about some of the gruesome murders that happened in the 20s and 30s here. There are many accounts of body parts deposited around town in trunks, and a bagged, severed head is said to have been left once in the Horse and Groom bar in Hanover (which, if you've visited the place, isn't all that surprising).

One year, a friend Jason decided to do the murder tour and left his house to walk down to Bartholomew Square where it was starting. The guide introduced the tour by saying:

"We'll commence by visiting the location of probably the most gruesome murder Brighton has ever known," and proceeded to walk the group back to Margaret Street, where Jason lived.

"Hey this is the street where I live!" he thought, with growing alarm.

"And it was in this house that the body was dismembered and stored in a cupboard for two weeks..." said the guide, pointing at Jason's bedroom window.

Jason now lives in America.

THE BRUNSWICK WATER YETI

"An unusually large, naked hairy man-creature scuttled across Hove Lawns then did disappear into the brine, pausing but to empty his bladder of such sulphurous liquid as did make mine eyes burn." Or so claimed seawater enthusiast Dr Russell, back in the 1760s. Whether he'd been gulping down too much saltwater is anyone's guess, but thus the legend of the Brunswick Water Yeti was born. This mythical beast has been described by terrified eyewitnesses as immense, hirsute, demonic, weak-bladdered and *"a bit like Bob Geldof"*, while local punk band Anal Beard famously took their name from the creature's excessively hairy backside.

In the 80s, Brighton's legendary protester and naked-swimming enthusiast Brian Behan was twice mistaken for a water yeti, as has been Hove crooner Nick Cave, despite his pushing a baby buggy and smoking a fag at the time. The only witnesses who have claimed to have heard the call of the water yeti are Ron Stanson and Roger Crunt, visiting the city in 2004 for a *Dr Who* convention. While both agreed they heard an unearthly cry, Ron swore it was *"Zygonesque"*, while Roger declared it to be *"definitely more Sontaran-like"*.

Said to dwell in a deep cave underneath the West Pier, the water yeti is thought to have survived for a century on dead starlings, chips, lollies and cigarette butts dropped over the side of the West Pier by visitors, but since the pier's closure in the 70s reported sightings have increased as the creature has been forced to scavenge the shores and streets of Old Brunswick, feeding on rodents and small mammals.

Until the yeti is caught police recommend all owners of children under five foot to keep them locked up at night and have issued a ten o'clock curfew for Brunswick residents Leo Sayer, David Van Day and Prince.

Photo by kind permission of Carl 'Yeti Hunter' Vincent

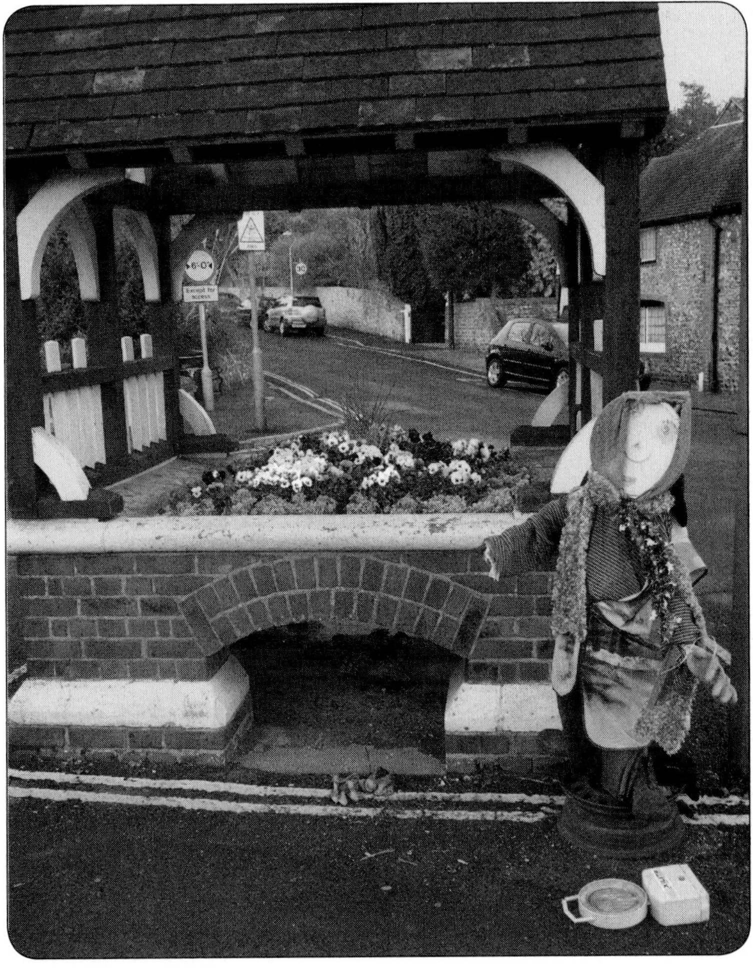

PATCHAM MAN

If you've ever driven out of Brighton past Preston Park up to the roundabout you will undoubtedly have noticed a strange dwarfish creature standing by the edge of Patcham village dressed in a fluorescent jacket, and sporting a round metal head and bizarre attire. It's been there for years; so who created it and why? Some locals will try and tell you it was put there to slow motorists down, by making them think it's a small policeman. Others claim it is yet more evidence that voodoo is being practised in the nether-regions of Brighton in an attempt to keep the Brunswick Yeti away. And while neither of these claims can be substantiated, it has to be said that, to this day, no sightings of the Yeti have ever been reported in Patcham.

Here, There & Everywhere

NORTH LAINE

www.northlaine.co.uk

As Brighton's official bohemian quarter, North Laine has some of the best shops, pubs and cafés in town. Glamorous, young, posey, vibrant and pretentious it may be, but Cleethorpes High Street it is not: this colourful area does its best to be Haight Ashbury, Carnaby Street and Greenwich Village, all squeezed into just a handful of streets.

Many of the independent shops here are kitsch, retro or shamelessly glitzy. From Borderline and Cissy-Mo to Revamp and Blackout, if it's CDs by the Chocolate Watch Band, silver thigh-high platforms, a kimono or a Ganesh ashtray you're after, you'll be spoilt for choice. And while some of the shops' merchandise seems perfectly normal to long-term Brightonians it can appear a tad bizarre to new visitors – see Wildcat's urethral vibrators, Cybercandy's scorpion lollies, Pussy's range of offensive greetings cards (including one with the caption "*Jesus Loves Everyone. Except for You, You Cunt*") and pretty much anything in the Guarana Bar.

Unsurprisingly, North Laine is a posers' paradise. From 60s retro to cyberpunk, every fashion gets a look-in. Walk down Kensington Gardens in full KISS make-up with cream crackers stuck to you and few heads will turn.

The shops in North Laine are also a good starting point for checking out what's going on in the clubs and venues, as the streets visibly sag under the weight of posters and flyers in every window. In fact it can feel like you're in a ticker-tape parade as they are handed to you on street corners and thrown from the tops of buildings. Stand around in the same spot for too long in Kensington Gardens and someone will bill-poster you.

Priding itself on its café culture, North Laine really blossoms during the summer months when balconies heave with milkshakes and suntanned legs, and tables and chairs start to sprawl across the roads. It's a pleasure then just to hang out in some of the cafés here and watch the world and its dog go by. The Dorset, Kensington's and Pavilion Café are especially good haunts, though if pornographic displays of food are more your thing, Bill's is not to be missed.

While it would be remiss of me not to mention the gentrification that has been happening here in the past few years, resulting in the arrival of such unwelcome retail titans as Tesco and Starbucks, the truth is, it'd take more than a few trendy eateries and chains to spoil things. The old adage "*in North Laine anything goes*" is as pertinent as ever, so don't be surprised if after an afternoon's visit you end up going home with a leopardskin suit, pierced genitals and a live monkey: it's just another typical day for North Laine.

North Laine curios

- It's almost impossible to buy anything of practical use here.
- The Bonsai Shop in Sydney Street has mysteriously remained open for twenty years despite the fact that no-one has ever seen a customer buying a bonsai, let alone entering the shop.
- The sorting office on North Road has a strict policy of only employing heavily tattooed rockabillies, lesbians and Dennis Waterman lookalikes.
- There are more hairdressers per metre here than in the whole of Wales.
- The lighting embedded in the New Road benches is proximity-sensitive, so at night you can actually create your own light show by somersaulting along the seating.

A SPOTTER'S GUIDE TO THE MISCREANTS & QUADRUPEDS OF NORTH LAINE

1. Big Ian standing outside Immediate Clothing on Sydney Street having a fag.
5 points

2. The Slow Cowboy (the thin guy who walks as if on broken glass and is always sporting the most outrageous wardrobe, ranging from dayglo suit and mohican to looking like he stepped out of *Yellow Submarine*)
10 points

The Slow Cowboy, at a standstill

3. The passive aggressive smiley bloke with thinning hair who hangs around Gardner Street and carries an old ghetto blaster (if you ask nicely he'll play a CD of your choice).
4 points

Simeon shares another hilarious joke with a customer

4. The Steve Marriott-a-like mod sitting on his scooter outside Jump The Gun on Gardner Street – don't try to photograph him though, he's shy.
6 points

5. Simeon the cat lolling around in Brighton Books on Kensington Gardens.
8 points

6. Terry, the Dockerill's tapir.
12 points

KEMP TOWN

Cross over the Old Steine from the bottom of North Street and you'll find yourself in Kemp Town, a haven of B&Bs, cafés, restaurants, some good shops and home to much of Brighton's gay and lesbian community, not to mention its eccentrics. Buy your strawberries next to a drag queen in Somerfield, stumble across the guy who sports a sparkly top hat and decorates himself with posters of his guru, Maitreya, or witness (as I have) two guys rolling around on the street half-naked at three in the morning singing *"the hills are alive with the sound of music"*. Kemp Town may not be a part of Brighton that has been dressed up for visitors, but it is the rough edges that actually provide much of the appeal. Perhaps in truth this is the part of Brighton that ***truly*** deserves the label 'bohemian'. Where else in the world would a local charity shop (the Sussex Beacon) have an annual sale of second-hand rubberwear and bondage gear?

To explore Kemp Town simply take a walk up St James's Street and keep going: you'll discover restaurants, cafés, second-hand shops, healthfood stores, barbers, pubs, gay-lifestyle boutiques and innumerable bars. There's even Doggy Fashion, should you be caught short needing a t-shirt and bow tie for your pooch, or the big pink flea market for retro booty. Venture down the side streets that run to the sea from St James's Street and you'll soon discover where the bulk of Brighton's B&Bs and hotels are to be found.

True, this part of St James's Street has taken a downturn in recent times with the closure of several restaurants and shops and the controversial imposition of a Starbucks, but the arrival a few years ago of Bom-Bane's and the Tea Cosy on George Street show there's life in the old dog yet.

Follow St James's Street far enough and it eventually becomes St George's Road. Here Kemp Town begins to feel more like a village (it ***is*** actually known as Kemp Town Village). Continue further

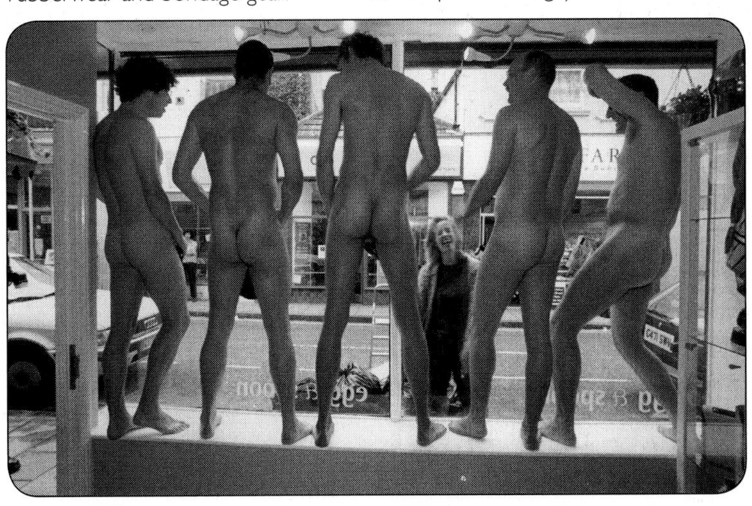

A shopper peruses the available wares in Kemp Town's red light district

BRIGHTON PEERS

by Cool CHEESE

DAY TRIPPER

LIVES: CROYDON

SPOTTED: PARADING UP AND DOWN THE SEAFRONT. IN ALL THE AMUSEMENT ARCADES

A couple of happy poofs

and, after a mini pub crawl between such classic boozers as the Hand in Hand, Sidewinder and the Barley Mow you'll reach Sussex Square and Lewes Crescent. These stunning white flats are occupied by some of Brighton's most affluent bohemians, and have housed their fair share of celebrities – Lewis Carroll, Cate Blanchett, Gaz Coombs, Kevin Rowland and Howard Marks, to name just a few. If you want to head back into Brighton you can simply turn on your heels and go back the way you came. Alternatively, you could take a stroll along the seafront, though (depending on your tastes) you may have to turn a blind eye to the crowds of men enjoying a bit of rough and tumble in the bushes at Duke's Mound.

KEMP TOWN VILLAGE

www.kemptown-village.co.uk

Nowhere in Brighton will you find a more pleasant, active and friendly community than the stretch of shops, pubs and food outlets on St George's Road in Kemp Town. Not only do these places have a convivial, supportive and easygoing spirit, but they even try and outdo each other every year with an over-the-top window-display competition.

In recent years the Kemp Town Village community has also organised an annual June carnival and winter festival, when St George's Road becomes pedestrianised for the day and the street is filled with stalls, food, live music and entertainment.

With such fabulous shops and venues as Kemp Town Books, Pardon My French, the Barley Mow and the Hanbury Ballroom, Kemp Town Village harks back to the good old days when pub landlords left a bowl of water by the door for your dog, shopkeepers were friendly and only sailors had tattoos.

WEST STREET

With its amusement arcades, nightclubs for the under-twelves, theme pubs and burger bars this is Brighton's answer to Las Vegas. But without the glamour. And more violent. Hang around here of an evening and, chances are, you'll get into a fight with a seventeen year old. Stick around too long and her boyfriend will have a go as well. Look for the giant translucent cones in the middle of the road, originally intended as sealed performance spaces for mime artists.

THE (OLD) LANES

A series of wonderfully confusing narrow passages and cobbled streets make up this antiquated corner of Brighton, steeped in history and stories of smugglers, ghosts and randy nuns. The passages are known locally as twittens (an old smugglers' term for 'thin street with over-priced shops') and are enclosed by West Street, East Street and the seafront. You should enjoy wandering around here and perusing the shops – and don't worry if you get lost, even long-term residents still do from time to time.

The Lanes is renowned for its abundance of jewellers, antiques shops, cafés, restaurants and expensive clothes boutiques and, though relatively conservative compared with fashionable North Laine, at night the busy restaurants and pubs such as the Cricketers, the Hop Poles and the Victory give it a new lease of life.

At the centre of the maze lies the dolphin sculpture in the fountain at Brighton Square. It is an old Brighton custom to run around it twice, throw your trousers in and make a wish, though for the more prudish a coin will suffice. If you head past Rounder Records from here, have a look at their back wall to see which album they have spraypainted on it this month. As a reference point, you'll be on your way to East Street.

If you haven't got long in Brighton, you should definitely make a stroll round here a priority; choose from any

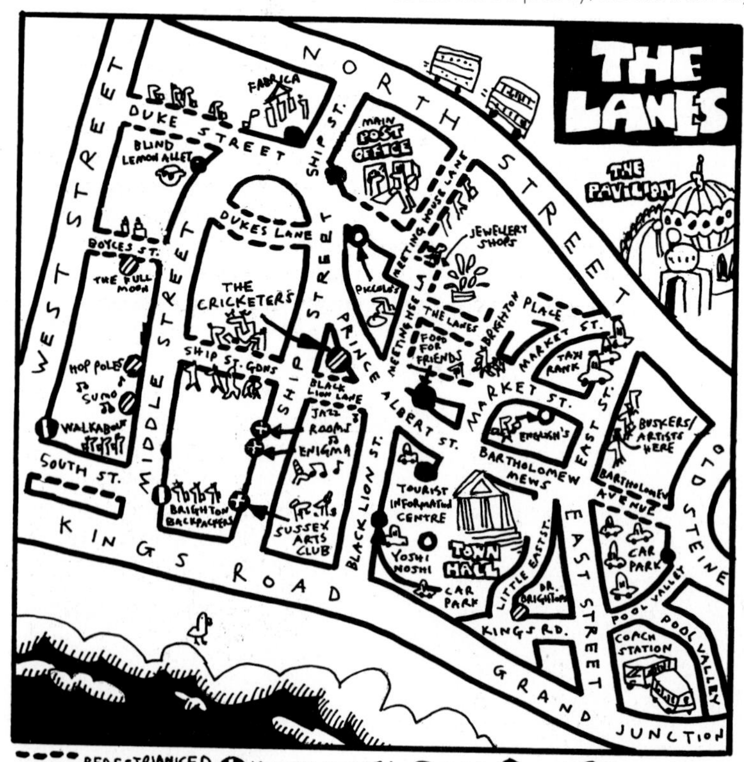

number of enticing restaurants such as Terre à Terre, Northern Lights or English's, and don't leave without eating a doughnut at the Mock Turtle and poking your head in at Fabrica Gallery on Ship Street to see what current dazzling art installation they have in this beautiful building.

In summer this is also a popular area for street entertainment. On East Street you'll find jazz bands, performance artists and tarot readers. Once I even saw a girl busking with a rat. She kept it on her shoulder while playing her guitar, and now and again she let it drink from her mouth. Eurrrgghh!

Really though, the best time to visit the Old Lanes is at dawn when the noise of the seagulls and the light of early morning pierce the empty alleyways. At times like this, eerie folk tales and ghost stories about the area may no longer seem like a load of old cobblers. In fact the Northern Lights restaurant has long claimed to be haunted by the ghost of a dead fisherman, while Jack the Ripper was said to have once stayed at the Cricketers pub. But if you ***are*** wandering the Lanes late at night and feel the ground rumbling and shaking below you and hear an ethereal voice calling out: *"yeth, tith I"*, don't be frightened – it's just Eubank greeting his minions from his monster truck, as he returns home from another night at Hotel Du Vin celebrating the opening of an envelope.

The Spider-Cat

Scaling the wall on the corner of a building on the Old Steine, close to the entrance of Pool Valley, there's a small black cat that's been there almost forever. Rumour has it that it's a witch who had a heart attack midway through her animal transmogrification process and became as the stone she clung to. Local wiccans frequently gather here in homage, though as it's very close to a bus stop they may simply be off on a trip to the country to gather enchanted moss or something.

THE SEAFRONT

"The beach washes away the ills of mankind." Dr Richard Russell

Stretching from the nudist beach by the Marina across to Hove and beyond, this is one of the key inspirations behind all that is Brighton. In summer the seafront is ***always*** swarming with life – families with kids, groups of foreign visitors, young couples engaging in heavy petting and the obligatory loony with a metal detector.

Hey, I found another ring-pull

And when the sun is out you'll want to join the crowds down here, brave the sea for a swim, kayak, hang around the cafés or indulge in a spot of sunbathing.

The most popular stretch lies between the two piers. Here you'll find clubs, amusement arcades, the Fishing Museum, Jack and Linda's (for a fine drop of fish soup), the Carousel, the Artists' Quarter, palmists and an assortment of outdoor entertainment during summer. If you want a good walk, follow the seafront path all the way to the multi-coloured beach huts in Hove and stop for some grub

at the Meeting Place Café. The area between the piers is also a hotspot for some of Brighton's best-known clubs – the Honey Club, Funky Buddha Lounge and Digital are all here – and on summer evenings you can expect the clubbing crowd to be out in force, particularly around the Fortune of War and other seafront bars.

East of Brighton Pier is a stretch of seafront known as Madeira Drive. While this whole area of the seafront is in need of rejuvenation it does come alive when there are car and motorbike rallies which, in summer, seems to be every other weekend. The loopiest of these is the coach rally, where identically dressed white-shirted drivers in black tie, replete with 'steering bellies', demonstrate their skills at parking and slaloming their lurching behemoths between sets of cones. Apart from two (not very) crazy golf courses and the Concorde 2, there isn't much in the way of entertainment here, though the very lack of development does mean that in summer the stretches of beach here are mercifully quieter than between the two piers. And for kids, of course, running along this stretch of the seafront all the way to the Marina is the miniature Volks Railway – a reminder of how much smaller people were in the old days.

If you do take a wander east of Brighton Pier, look out for the strange old house set into the promenade just beyond the Concorde 2. The story goes that before the promenade was built, all the houses along the front were sold and demolished, apart from one belonging to some stubborn

old guy, Carl Vincent, who refused to sell up. The council couldn't move him, so in desperation they built the promenade over his house and it's still there today. Beyond here is the Nudist Beach, once controversial, now mainly populated by the gay community and a character known as Windmill Man. I'll leave you to figure out how he got his nickname.

Whichever part of the beach you prefer, sometimes, when it's a warm night and you're in the mood, it's good to bypass the busy bars and clubs. Just find a quiet spot, get some beers and food, and bring some friends to watch the sun going down.

If you're still around after all the clubs have cleared, the beach does *eventually* get pretty empty, although there's always the odd clubber who's crashed out after too many pills, and a guy still looking for his contact lens. In fact, even in the cruellest winters you will find little pockets of life here, like lone penguins on an iceberg.

And, finally, it's time to come clean. Yes, it's true, I'm afraid: there is no sand, only pebbles. According to Dr Malcolm Cornwall at Brighton University, around 100 billion to be precise (he also reckons it'd take 2,500 years to count them all at the rate of one per second!) and not a decent one for skimming but, as a small compensation, when you take your picnic down the beach and the wind whips up, at least you won't be crunching your way through a tuna-and-sand ciabatta…

PARKS & GARDENS

Let's face it, Brighton is not renowned for its greenery. Down on the seafront the council seem to have done everything in their power to remove all traces of the stuff, while the town centre boasts little more than a bit of grass and a few flowers outside the Pavilion. But all is not lost. Head inland and Brighton has a modest selection of parks and open spaces to keep even the most ardent picnickers, tree-huggers and Ultimate Frisbee teams happy.

Preston Park

London Road

Brighton's largest park is located a little way down Preston Road about half an hour's walk from the seafront. It's a great spot for cycling – you can use the professional track at the top of the park and then race back down over the bumpy road or simply cycle around the park's perimeter. There's also a café in the middle and loads of space for big sports games.

Although it's a good place for a picnic, the ever-present noise of cars from the main road can sometimes spoil a tranquil afternoon here so it's best to plonk yourselves further up the hill if it's peace and quiet you're after.

If you do visit, look out for Steve Ovett's right foot at the bottom of the park, facing the road. There used to be a full statue of him running in his skimpy satin shorts, before some lunatic made off with everything but his foot.

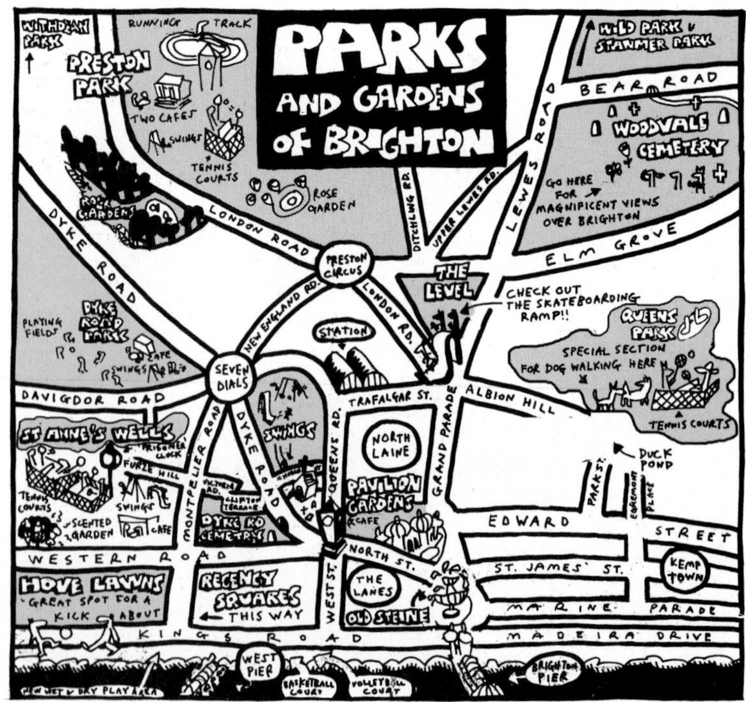

Before...

...after

St Ann's Well Gardens

Somerhill Road, Hove

This small, pretty park in Hove has a scent garden, a newly refurbished family-friendly café, a few picnic areas and tennis courts. It's a popular spot for mums out with the young-uns and has a resident old lady called Madge, who'll engage you in conversations about boxing given half the chance.

The park's most curious feature has to be the strange clock on a pole that overlooks the tennis courts and bowling green. It's straight out of the 60s cult TV show *The Prisoner* and, in keeping with the spirit of the programme, never, ever, ever tells the right time.

Queen's Park

Between Kemp Town and Hanover

Queen's Park may be a bit of a hike if approached from the town centre or seafront, but you'll soon forget those aching corns and bunions once you arrive at this beautifully sculpted park with its sloping hills, large green areas, lake and tennis courts.

Approach from the sea up Rock Gardens and Egremont Place and you'll find it. If you've got kids, hunger pangs or a dicky belly you'll find an excellent kids' play area, café and toilets on the western side of the park as you enter. If you've come to escape kids/crowds etc, head around the lake (formerly a rollerskating rink in the 60s) and up the hill to discover such curiosities as the tiny waterfall, the scented garden by the eastern entrance, and the 'Wildlife Area' full of butterflies, birds and wild fennel in the summer. Such features as this small overgrown wilderness demonstrate that Brighton council can be surprisingly inspired sometimes (though equally it could just be a ploy to save on pruning expenses). Other features to look out for are the park's carved wooden benches and strange old monuments.

When you've had enough of the chaos and trendiness of the beach and city centre, it's good to know there's somewhere you can have a picnic, climb a tree, feed the ducks, play hide and seek in the bushes or simply curl up under an old oak for the afternoon with a good book and a treacle sandwich.

Woodvale Crematorium

Lewes Road/Bear Road

Hidden away down the Lewes Road, Woodvale Cemetery is one of Brighton's best-kept secrets. The largest expanse of greenery in the whole of the city centre, it is in turn mysterious, spooky and beautiful, particularly in spring when everything is in bloom.

Wander round its spacious and hilly terrain and you'll stumble across the columbarium, the memorial gardens, strange mausoleums (there's even one where you can peek through a crack in the door and see the dead bodies inside) and the little paths that disappear off into the undergrowth. If you want a quest you can look for the graves of Lance Schumacher (one of Custer's men) or the original Mr Hannington, though they might take a good couple of days to find.

Come on a cold overcast February and it can feel a little sinister, particularly with the hospital high up on Elm Grove towering over like some dark satanic mill. If *Buffy the Vampire Slayer* lived in Brighton, she'd doubtless spend most of her evenings here, as in the gloom it can't help but inspire thoughts of the supernatural. When it's warm, however, the crematorium is the perfect place to clear the cobwebs, draw inspiration, picnic, meditate or simply enjoy a bit of peace in a town that never stops.

The Pavilion Gardens

After a morning's shopping in North Laine, these gardens behind the Pavilion make an ideal spot for a bit of lolling around in the sun. Sure, it gets busy here in summer, with groups of foreign students, picnickers, snogging couples, pigeons and that bloke who's always there playing the sax, but it's a pleasant alternative to the concreted seafront and the closest Brighton gets to the cosmopolitan atmosphere of a city-centre square like those in Amsterdam or Rome. It's also one of the rare spots in Brighton with a bit of decent greenery and has a commanding view of the Pavilion to boot.

If you're in need of refreshments the café here offers drinks, hot snacks and those famous rock cakes. Look for the photos on the café history noticeboard on the side of the hut. They sure had big ears in those days.

HOVE... AN APOLOGY?

Dear Readers

Over the years I have offended tens of people by not including Hove in the title of this book, as officially Brighton & Hove come as a package these days. Of course, unless you're a hardcore Hovestrian, you're probably wondering what all the fuss is about. I mean, after all, you say, isn't it just a poor man's Brighton offering sheltered accommodation for right-wing old ladies who spend their time making jam and writing angry letters to The Argus, and Nick Cave? In fact, you shout, rising to your feet in indignation, come on, there are hardly ***any*** decent pubs and the only sources of entertainment are the goth night at Babylon Lounge and colonic chanting classes at Revitalise.

And while you'd be right in such matters, Hove ***has*** got a few tricks up its sleeves, hence I'm devoting the rest of this letter to no fewer than ten amazing Hove facts!

Hove fact number one: Hove begins at Boundary Passage (the longest alleyway in Brighton, opposite Little Western Street) and continues most of the way to Dorset.

Hove fact number three: Hove is home to some of the city's most dazzling architecture, including Brunswick Square, Adelaide Crescent and Blatchington Road.

Hove fact number four: Cycling is prohibited on Hove promenade, unless you're riding a penny farthing.

Hove fact number seven: Hove is the birthplace of cinema, hip hop, croissants and Jackie Chan.

Hove fact number eight: Hove rhymes with cove.

Hove fact number ten: Hove is very, very close to the magnificent city of Brighton.

Curiously, there is an age-old joke that Hove should be renamed Hove Actually owing to the countless times its residents, when asked if they live in Brighton, reply with snooty indignation - "No, Hove actually". As a catchphrase it has, however, become as drab and tiresome as "Ooh, I could crush a grape", "Shut that door" and "Turned out nice again". Oh god, now I'm really showing my age. Perhaps I should move to Hove…

Your humble servant

Dr Bramwell

Brighton, obviously

BRIGHTON EMBARRASSMENTS

THE MARINA

Mercifully hidden away on the outer reaches of Brighton seafront lies the Marina – a concrete jungle of factory shops, casinos, an Asda, a drive-through McDonalds, the world's largest multi-storey car park and a really tacky Walk of Fame for such Brighton celebrities as er… Leo Sayer and er… *The Argus*. The antithesis of Brighton's saucy, seedy, devil-may-care spirit, the Marina resembles some god-awful nautical theme park crossed with Moss Side. The best solution for this place would be for the council to throw its hands in the air, say "*Oops*" and send in the bulldozers.

THE AQUARIUM TERRACE

When the old Concorde and go-kart track opposite Brighton Pier were demolished a few years ago, did the council use the opportunity to add a bit of much-needed greenery to the seafront, or install something fun like an open-air pool? No, of course not! Instead it opted for the Aquarium Terrace – a monstrous, neon-lit white blob that has bizarrely remained empty for ***more than ten years!!*** Currently home to one café, a Burger King, an amusement arcade and twenty For Rent signs.

THE LONDON ROAD

Dirty, smelly and unsightly, London Road is the home of the discount meat store, boarded-up shops, Brighton's grimmest pubs and the occasional dead body. The visual equivalent of waking up after a heavy party to discover that someone's emptied an ashtray into your mouth.

WESTERN ROAD & CHURCHILL SQUARE

While no worse than any other city-centre high street for its bland selection of chain stores and coffee franchises, it is the *endless* stream of buses that makes Western Road particularly unpleasant on the eye, ear and nose, not to mention the huge weekend crowds which fill the narrow streets.

What is especially tragic about Churchill Square is that this area was once home to row upon row of beautiful flint fishermen's cottages and cobbled streets, until they were flattened to make way for a 70s shopping arcade. And though the refurbishment in the 90s was a remarkable improvement, that's still like saying drinking hot wee is preferable to drinking it cold.

THE LIBRARY CAFE

Well, the lack of one to be precise. We used to have one before the library moved. A place where you could go and read the paper, slurp on a cuppa, eat cake and have a natter with other library folk. Then a brand spanking new library was built with a big empty building next to it, which, we were promised, would be the café. Instead it's a fast-food chain selling pizza.

ANSTON HOUSE

Sitting opposite Preston Park on the main A23 route into the city, nothing says "*welcome to Brighton*" like a big derelict 60s office block surrounded by nine-foot-high security fencing. Until a couple of years ago the building was partly shielded by beautiful, mature, officially protected trees, before an unscrupulous developer decided to chop them down, turn the adjacent green wasteland into a bomb site, stick up an ugly metal fence and then lose interest entirely. Still, it's only been empty for 22 years, what's the rush?

Lose loads of money at the American-style Casino.

Marvel at the American-style bowling alley!!

See the stunning American-owned Asda and its huge concrete carpark!

Enjoy an American-style in-car meal at our drive-through McDonald's.

MARINA

Brighton's architectural masterpiece

See all the latest American movies at our multiplex cinema. Over 300 screens and no subtitled foreign shit.

Have fun, take a driving test!!!

BRIGHTON DRIVING TEST CENTRE

Baggage FACTORY

Enjoy our factory-outlet shops offering Dynasty style blouses for the modern lady and knitwear for rugged men.

Take the Hollywood-style Walk Of Fame with such stars as The Argus and the Hove Greyhound Stadium!!

Weird & Wonderful Things To Do

MUSEUMS & LANDMARKS

The Pavilion

Old Steine (01273) 290900
10am-5.15pm October-March,
9.30am-5.45pm April-September
Adults £8.80, children £5.10
www.royalpavilion.org.uk

If you have a pathological hatred of dreary stately homes full of rooms that all look the same, with weird shiny-faced waxwork dummies like Des O'Connor in awkward poses and hordes of people gawping at a four-poster bed where King Steve IV died of consumption, then you, my friend, are not alone. And while it's true that the Pavilion does have that familiar set-up with those awful little rope chains and hordes of American tourists giving "*oohs*" and "*aaahs*" in every room, it cannot be denied that this building is nothing short of astonishing. An Indian palace in a small English seaside town with a stunning and surprising interior modelled on a top-of-the-range oriental brothel, carpets that would shock the most outré Vegas casino and heaps of gold leaf. Surely that's got to be worth a look? And it is. Not only is the Pavilion Brighton's most famous landmark but the very emblem of the place. Could you really visit Paris and not go up the Eiffel Tower?

Step inside and be prepared to enter a labyrinth of bamboo, impressive sculptures, fire-breathing dragons and the most outrageous chandeliers in the universe. *"George clearly had a lot of gay friends,"* as a friend of mine wryly commented. And where to begin with the Music Room and its secret

doorways and crazy carpets? *"All designed to delight and unsettle you,"* the audio guide whispers in your ear. And it will. And yet, surprisingly, it all works extremely well, despite being the ultimate in 18th-century bling. While upstairs is less dazzling that the ground floor's banqueting hall, kitchens, foyer and sitting rooms, it ***is*** rich with good stories about the extravagances of the 22-stone prince. It is well documented, for example, that the Prince Regent was renowned for his love of women and food. He had two secret doors installed in the bedroom, one for his midnight rendezvous with Mrs Fitzherbert and the other for a bloke selling seafood in a basket. Legend has it that the prince got so drunk some nights he'd get them mixed up and end up eating Mrs F's handbag while making love to the seafood guy, but then this was Brighton after all.

Dreamed up and partly designed by Prinnie in 1823 as a weekend retreat, this stately pleasure dome helped establish Brighton as a fashionable place to be seen. One hundred and eighty years later, the Prince's devotion to art, music, extravagance and philandering seems to have left an indelible impression on the town. Holiday cottages do not come more exotic than this. A must see.

Top tip: Come as early as possible in the morning to avoid the crowds of foreign language students standing around with sketch pads and questionnaires and, if you're feeling flush, splash out on the Basement to Bottle tour (see later in chapter) and get to journey through the hidden passageways and corners of the building not normally open to the public.

Brighton Pier

The epitome of cheesy seaside fun. Not only Brighton's most popular attraction but the UK's top tourist spot to boot. Experience life on the ocean waves with the famous Dolphin Derby, see the Isle of Wight from the top of the Helter Skelter (on a clear day), sing Elvis at Horatio's Karaoke Bar, wolf down some fish and chips, scream your head off on the big dipper, yawn your way through the ghost train, lose your car keys down the gaps in the floorboards, have your palm read by an Australian backpacker called Gypsy Kevin and get absolutely soaking wet on the log flume. Brighton without Brighton Pier would be Tommy Cooper without the fez.

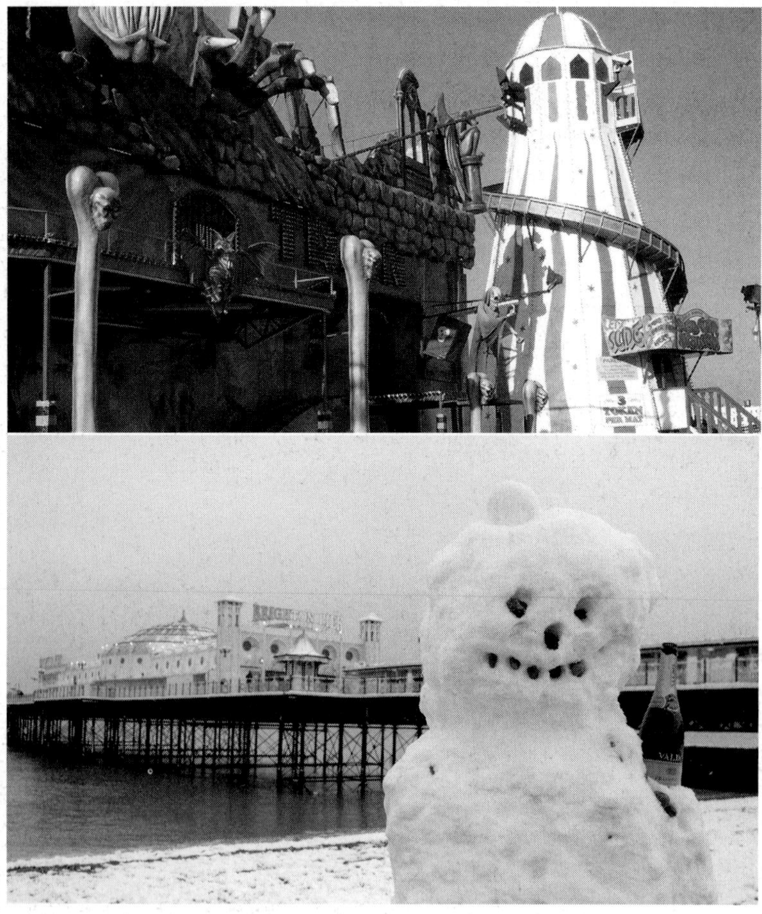

THE WEST PIER

A tragedy of epic proportions, the West Pier was cock of the town until it was marooned by a storm in the 70s and left to rot like Miss Haversham's wedding cake. Then in late 2002, over the space of a few months it endured a further storm and two suspected arson attacks which pretty much destroyed everything. And yet! There, like a small beacon of hope, much to everyone's surprise and delight, the little fortune-telling kiosk bravely hung on. Against all odds it survived. Oh how it cheered our hearts to see it waving the flag of courage when all around was desolation and despair. Then, at the end of 2005, it fell off too.

A few years later, and with the cost of removing the skeleton currently estimated at over a million pounds, no one seems in any hurry to clear up the remains. But some (myself included) have grown to love this spinach-encrusted birdcage. If nothing else, it serves as a costly reminder to keep a watchful eye on the things we love in this town and never to allow anything else to fall into rack and ruin. With the exception of the Marina, of course.

Brighton Museum and Art Gallery

Church Street/Royal Pavilion Gardens
(01273) 290900
Tues 10am-7pm, Wed-Sat 10am-5pm, Sun 2pm-5pm
Admission free
www.brighton.virtualmuseum.info

Re-opened in 2002 after a much-publicised refurbishment, Brighton Museum is a place to be cherished: it's modern, spacious, beautifully lit, packed with imaginative displays, has a sweet little café and is totally free.

On the ground floor much of the space is given over to the town itself, covering its social history from sport, work and religion to leisure and even, er, England's last cork shop. Wander round and you can watch old videos of Brighton, listen to recorded voices, feel the mystery objects (a dead seagull and a 'Prince Albert'), peruse the paintings of Sake Deen Mohammed and Dr Russell, and learn all about the mods and rockers. You're not meant to sit on the scooter in the far-left corner, but it makes for a terrific photo so go on, be a devil. Thankfully they've not shied away from Brighton's historical penchant for dirty weekends either. From the 'lick my melons' calling card of a 90s brothel to club posters, Brighton's unashamed association with hedonism is well documented. In fact so ***much*** so that, conversely, the town's long history of alternative/unusual medical practices and as a health resort is almost completely overlooked.

New to the ground floor are the two Egyptology rooms, opened in spring 2009, and with plenty to keep the kids happy. If you're feeling brave you can even have your face made up in Egyptian style (don't worry, the paint comes off after a couple of weeks). Upstairs are the Brighton History Centre full of books, old newspapers and microfiche, the café (unchanged since 1856) and the museum's exhibition space. Hats off to whoever chooses the exhibits – the themes over the past fifteen years

have been consistently fascinating and innovative. Personal highlights have included fetishism, paintings by Captain Beefheart, carnivalesque and the history of cinema in Brighton and Hove. The remains of the second floor are given over to the history of fashion, containing the Prince Regent's enormous breeches handmade by High and Mighty, and a rather brilliant section on the human body. Again in keeping with the residents' rampant narcissism, it covers themes of flesh, skin, body modification, spectators and performers. Keep a look out for presidential candidate Barbie and Glenda Jackson as you've never seen her before!

And finally, if you've haven't visited for years and need to see a familiar face, beloved Gallet cat Brunel (a giant model of one of the ornamental pair in the cabinet by Art and Design) is still there by the entrance, awaiting a stroke and your donations.

St Bartholomew's Church

Ann Street
(01273) 620491
www.stbartholomewsbrighton.org.uk

Located behind Trafalgar Street and London Road, St Bartholomew's may be off the beaten track but, as the biggest brick church in Europe, is rather difficult ***not*** to find.

Impressive for its size and Italian Gothic design, inside St Bart's is decorated with oil paintings, Italian mosaics and marble archways and could well have been the setting of an old Peter Greenaway film.

It's best visited during Brighton Festival in May when it plays host to a series of concerts ranging from Renaissance choral music to piano recitals.

The Booth Museum of Natural History

194 Dyke Road (01273) 292777
Mon-Sat 10am-5pm, Sun 2pm-5pm, closed Thurs Admission free
www.booth.virtualmuseum.info

Originally opened as a private museum in 1874 by bird-stuffing enthusiast Mr Booth, this building has blossomed into one of the focal points and main archives of natural history for the Brighton area. As well as providing a home to thousands of creatures, skeletons and strange things in specimen jars, it is a resource centre for local schools, while on special days they even do live taxidermy for the public. Should you stumble across any fresh road kill, just *"scoop it up and bring it in"*.

On entering the museum the first thing you'll notice is the smell of mothballs and the wonderfully gloomy atmosphere. Towers of stuffed birds line the walls, while in the centre lie two incongruous but beautiful stained-glass windows.

At this point, if you're in a group, I recommend splitting up and going it alone for maximum effect. Walk down the aisles at the side and enter Hitchcock's terrifying world of *The Birds*. Down the centre you'll find the Victorian parlour, discovery lab – a hands-on science area for kids – and, at the back, an impressive array of skeletons.

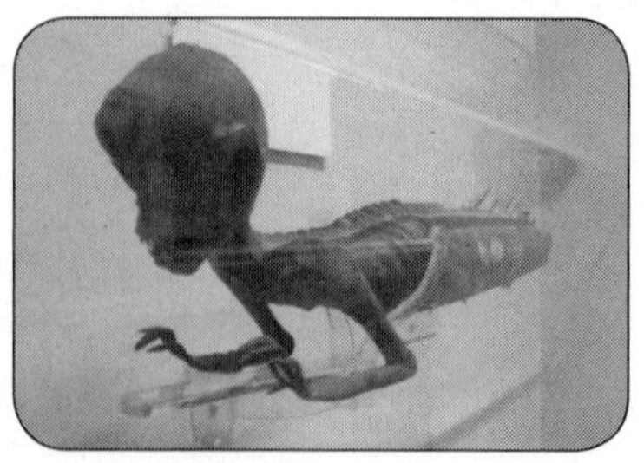

Look out for the sheep that looks like Daisy from the Woody Allen movie, the charred remnants of a (half-eaten) dodo, the remains of a dog from Stanmer Park, the *Harry Potter* owls and the famous 'toad in the hole'. I bet you won't find the warthog's head though.

What you see in the museum is, however, only a small percentage of what's been collected over the years as, owing to lack of space, they're unable to display everything. With special permission though, you can get a behind-the-scenes tour. I have been lucky enough to experience this and thoroughly enjoyed wandering through dusty old badger-lined corridors where they've got everything from the reindeer that defunct department store Hanningtons used to borrow every Christmas, to a scorpion found by a guest in the Grand Hotel.

"If you find odd things in your sandwiches they'll end up here," declared Keeper of Biology Gerald Legg. Later he took me into a room with a large metal worktop and muttered: *"I've had a tiger*

on that table".

To find the museum, follow Dyke Road from the Clock Tower and you'll find it opposite the tennis courts after about a fifteen-minute walk.

Warning – check first for kids' visits, if you're childphobic they could spoil your experience. Could you spend the night here on your own, though? I swear they all come to life then.

Brighton Toy & Model Museum

52/55 Trafalgar Street (01273) 749494
Tues-Fri 10am-5pm, Sat 11am-5pm
Adults £4, children/oldies £3
www.brightontoymuseum.co.uk

While not in the most glamorous of locations (housed under a damp railway bridge below Brighton Station), what this museum lacks in setting it makes up for with its pristine collection. There are more than 25,000 exhibits, beautifully displayed and all clearly the pride and joy of founder Chris Littledale.

Model railways make up the bulk of the collection and – unlike their full-scale counterparts upstairs – actually

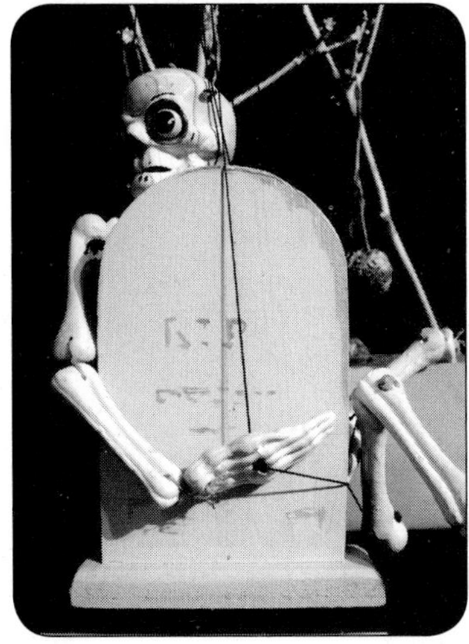

run. In fact, once a year in October they go mad and set off ***everything*** for the day – it's like a scene from *Toy Story 2*. While internationally renowned for the extensive collection of 1930s model trains, there's plenty more to see here, including a toy theatre and puppet section, model cars and Japanese dolls.

Curios to look out for include the old Punch and Judy stand (with the baker hanging in the gallows), the pantomime horse underneath the model railway in the far right-hand corner, the Dribbler Train (also known as the Piddler), Edwina the wicked witch in the theatre and puppet section and – my favourite – the old Drunkards Dream machine (a drunk lies inebriated in a liquor basement, and if you stick in 10p you get to see his hallucinations, which range from scurrying rats to the devil, who pops out of a beer barrel!).

Children, trainspotter types and anyone with an interest in old toys and models will love this place. Weekend revellers will not. Watch out during schooldays, though: like the Booth Museum you may be surrounded by gangs of schoolkids trying their best to knock over all the little figurines in the cabinets.

Top tip: Since 2009 this place has also doubled as a tourist information point.

Hove Museum

19 New Church Road, Hove
(01273) 290200
Tues-Sat 10am-5pm, Sun 2pm-5pm
Admission free
www.hove.virtualmuseum.info

Long gone are the psychedelic carpets and cardboard cut-out of Ringo Starr, but the 1970s teashop still remains (thankfully) in this beautiful old museum in deepest darkest Hove. Downstairs is an exhibition space that changes seasonally, while upstairs the Wizard's Attic and History of Cinema are, alone, worth the trek here.

The Wizard's Attic is a room that children (and adults) will thoroughly enjoy. The low-level lighting creates a wonderfully spooky atmosphere (to go with the attic theme); there are toys hanging from the ceiling, little cubbyholes with fairground mirrors, a tin bath full of soldiers, a clock that runs backwards and even a painting where the eyes follow you around the room. And dare you put your hand in the hole below the box full of creepy-crawlies?

Further on, the History of Cinema section tells the history of Hove's (little-known) role as the birthplace of the British film industry. Exhibits range from old zoetropes and magic lanterns to a tiny six-seater cinema, which shows three short films every half-hour. In *Professor Heard's Magic Lantern Show* a talking skull guides you through a magical journey in which ghosts and goblins rise from a witch's cauldron. Another, *On and Behind the Seafront*, has some classic footage of a bygone Brighton, including the fabulous open-air swimming pool at Black Rock and a troop of elephants wandering down Trafalgar Street. Look out also for the seven or eight old films that are constantly running in the room next door – the footage of people cycling off the pier into the sea is wonderfully silly.

And once you're through horsing around, make sure to pay your respects to Hove's loveable grannies and Mrs Doyle types by popping into the tearooms for a big wedge of cake and a nice hot cuppa.

Hove Museum's fossilised merkin inspires awe in today's plucked generation

SEAFRONT ATTRACTIONS

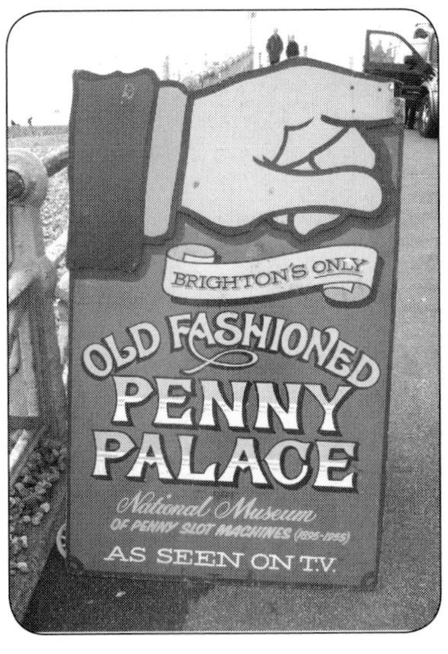

Victorian Penny Arcades

Brighton seafront
Open *"when it's nice"*

Situated between the Palace Pier and the Doughnut, these places open, close, open for a while, close for good, re-open under new management, close for winter, open again... you get the picture. If either happens to be actually open when you're passing (and it's much more likely in the summer months) they're good fun. For a quid you get a handful of those big old pennies to spend on mechanical Gypsy fortune tellers, What the Butler Saw machines and more besides. Sadly the kids can't play 'Win a Ciggie' any more but they will enjoy the early pinball-style games and watching the vicar being haunted in his graveyard. A perfect slice of old-school seaside charm (though if the guy behind the counter is less than charming, don't worry, he's always like that).

THE VOLK'S RAILWAY

Easter until mid-autumn *www.volkselectricrailway.co.uk*

The Volk's opened on 4 August 1883, making it the oldest electric railway in the world (you'll find it in *Guinness World Records*, sandwiched between the world's biggest pair of shoes and a photo of a man with four-metre long fingernails).

On its official opening day the railway's creator, Magnus Volk, invited a number of civic dignitaries for the first ride but, owing to their combined weight (civic dignitaries were notoriously portly in those days), they managed to break one of the planked pedestrian crossings that ran across the track. The train's first ever journey came to an undignified halt and the dignitaries were unloaded, to the jeers of a group of hostile cabbies, who believed it would take away their custom. They really needn't have worried.

The Sealife Centre

Marine Parade, opposite Brighton Pier
(01273) 604234
Mon-Sun 10am-6pm
Adults £12.95, children £9.50
www.sealifeeurope.com

When I think back to our very first review of the Sealife Centre in 1999 ("a couple of kippers and a dead dog floating in the shark tank") it's hard to believe how much the place has been transformed. Once a shabby and embarrassing tourist attraction, the Sealife Centre is now nothing short of sensational. And while its prices are not for the faint-hearted (take the whole family and it'll cost you a kidney), whether you're entertaining the kids or looking for somewhere unusual for a blind date, you will not be disappointed. Housed inside a beautiful cavernous Victorian building, the Sealife Centre is packed with a whole range of European sea life in huge tanks, and offers feeding opportunities, glimpses "inside the lab" where stuff is nurtured and grown, and a Jules Verne Nautilus room where you can look down on the sharks and Lulu (the marine turtle, not the pint-sized Scottish singer). And, of course, the payoff at the end is the underwater tunnels where you get to see them all swimming overhead. *"Look it's waving,"* said my nephew Alex on our last visit, as a stingray flapped by.

But that's only just the beginning of your adventures – new sections include Sea Serpents (still being built when we went to print) and Amazonia, a cross between a hall of mirrors, the Eden Project and a dimly-lit tropical fish shop. If you've got very young kids, be warned, they ***might*** find this genuinely scary in a hiding-behind-the-settee-while-*Dr Who*-is-on kind of way. They are also prone to walk into the mirrors – which is hugely entertaining to watch, provided it's not your own kids.

While you're there keep a look out for the seahorse tank, which is home to an utterly ridiculous creature with a long snout, and don't miss the chance to go on the Submarine Adventure, not least to watch little kids' faces as they genuinely think they're submerging.

With its shadowy corners, X-Files style soundtrack and well-considered displays, the Sealife Centre is fun, entertaining and surprisingly kitsch-free. Don't you love a happy ending? **Top tip:** Check online first for offers that'll save you cash.

Fishing Museum

201 Kings Road Arches (01273) 723064
9am-7pm Free

Worth a visit if you're wandering between the piers. There's a beautiful old fishing boat in the centre of the exhibition and plenty of ephemera, old photos, and memorabilia from Regency days and beyond. They also run a twelve-seater passenger boat, Skylark, over summer when the weather's good.

Volleyball

Yellowave Beach Sports Venue, 299 Madeira Drive (opposite the Concorde 2)
(01273) 672222
www.yellowave.co.uk

A few years ago I got a call from a friend who was looking for people to make up numbers for a volleyball game. A few hours later and I was hooked, not least by the fact that I was running around barefoot in real sand on Brighton seafront for the first time ever and for a couple of glorious hours genuinely felt I was on some exotic Mediterranean beach. Sand envy aside, Yellowave has been a fantastic addition to Brighton seafront. There's a very welcoming vibe down here; if you've never played before you can get lessons, join a beginners group and hang out afterwards for a beer at the café. Still not convinced about the name though, particularly with the absence of toilets down on Brighton seafront...

A Cheeky Tale

Back in 2003, local comedian and prankster Guy Venables made the headlines when he took a skinny-dip in the shark tank here. Posing as a cleaner, he hung a sign on the Nautilus Room door saying "Closed for Cleaning", stripped off and dived in with the turtles and sharks. When interviewed about it, he said, "*it wasn't the sharks I was worried about, more the stingrays. If you're naked and get hit by a stingray in the 'wrong place', that can be disastrous. Although the water* **was** *very cold so the target shrank quite considerably!*"

Like the Tardis, it's much bigger on the inside

UNUSUAL TOURS

Sewer Tour

(01903) 272606
www.southernwater.co.uk/homeAndLeisure/daysOut/brightonSewerTours

Usually booked up aeons in advance for the Brighton Festival, this Southern Water-run tour offers a first-hand experience of the sites and smells of Brighton's magnificent Victorian sewers. It all begins underneath the Palace Pier with a few dos and don'ts (no smoking, no swimming) then it's hard hats on and into the murk. The highlight is undoubtedly walking the 200 metres or so through the main sewer that finally brings you up at the Old Steine via a manhole cover. The chaps leading the tour will tell you everything and more about the design and where your poos go; the smell is surprisingly mild considering what's down there and, if you're really lucky, you might catch a glimpse of the Brunswick Yeti skulking in the shadows.
Top tip: Forget trying to get on this tour during the Festival. Instead, call them direct on the number above or book via the website and be prepared for a ***long*** wait.

Ghost Walk of The Lanes

www.ghostwalkbrighton.co.uk

This 70-minute tour of all things ghoulish and ghastly in the Lanes is a perfect blend of melodrama, high camp, humour and the odd entertaining prop, performed by actor Rob Marks. Gather outside the Druids Head pub in Brighton Place, then into the dark alleyways and twittens for grizzly tales of ghostly nuns and gruesome murders, and a final nightcap at the (also haunted) Northern Lights restaurant. And speaking of which, for those hungry for more, Rob can sometimes be found in different guises upstairs there, donning fake beard or 'tache and spooking the audience with yet more ghastly tales...

At time of going to print, tours were running Thurs-Sat 7.30pm outside the Druids Head pub. Best to check website for current times.

Basement to Bottle Tour

03000 290901 By appointment only, £23
www.royalpavilion.org.uk/visitor_services/specialistguidedtours.asp

If you've ever wondered what's inside that enormous dome atop Brighton's famous Pavilion (quite a lot of entertaining 19th-century graffiti as it turns out) and what else normal visitors never get to see, this tour will slake your curiosity as well as provide some magnificent bird's-eye views of the building. You also get to poke around the servants' corridors, explore secret doors and dusty staircases from the Prince Regent's bedroom, and, finally, the pièce de resistance that I've been waiting years to see, the mysterious tunnel under the gardens. Be on your best behaviour down here though, as due to an oversight with the paperwork this bit remains Crown

property and technically they are permitted to shoot you for certain transgressions, including wearing "*dress ill-befitting a gentleman*". The main function rooms are all covered too, and your entertaining guide knows enough about the history and construction of the Pavilion to do a specialist round on *Mastermind* without the need to say "*pass*". A bit of a treat.

Old Police Cells Tour

Town Hall, Bartholomew Square
(01273) 291052
Tours 1st May-1st Nov Tues, Thurs, Sat 10.30am, first Sat every month in winter
Free/donation

Hard to believe that the basement of Brighton's town hall once came complete with its own law courts and police cells. In fact they were used right up to the late 60s and in 1964 would have been found crammed with the 70-odd mods and rockers who were arrested for brawling on the seafront and having "*irritating Cockney accents*". Shocking also to discover that in 1844 the 'Inspector of Nuisances' came to a sticky end with a poker across the back of the head here. Brighton remains the only place in the UK where a chief constable has been murdered on duty in his own station. I know these things courtesy of retired policewoman Carol Pople, who runs free tours of the old station here and chairs the museum.

Besides hearing stories of famous murders you'll see plenty of uniformed waxworks and even a 1938 photo of the occasion Brighton's football team played Germany, with the latter performing the Nazi salute. And if anyone can figure out what lunatic dreamed up the exhibition "knitted home of a famous murderer" (an example of which can be found in the basement), do let us know.

Carol also throws in a few curious facts about the building itself, like how the council failed to give planning permission ***to itself*** for completion of the town hall (the design of which is meant to be based on the Greek cross). If you're looking for a tour with a difference or fancy something a little creepy and can't face the smell of the sewers, this donation-funded one-hour tour might be just the ticket.

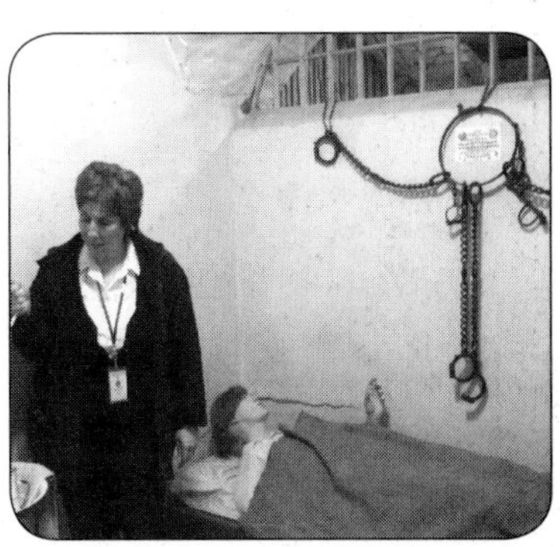

The Old Police Cells - also available for hourly rental as an S&M dungeon

ARTY FARTY

The Phoenix Gallery

10-14 Waterloo Place (01273) 603700
Mon-Sat 11am-6pm, Sun 12noon-4pm
Admission free
www.phoenixarts.org

Over the past twenty years the Phoenix Gallery has transformed from a grotty squat to a thriving art gallery with exhibitions changing on a monthly basis. They also organise a wide range of workshops, ranging from tapestry and ceramics to Super-8 moviemaking, and run open days where you can have a good old nose round the artists' studios. I encountered an installation piece here once that was a telephone down which a pre-recorded computerised voice would give you relationship advice – I managed to convince a room full of inebriated people that it was actually Stephen Hawking on the other end of the line and within seconds there was a mob clamouring for a go on it.

Permanent Gallery

20 Bedford Place (01273) 710389
Thurs-Fri, Sun 1pm-6pm, Sat 11am-6pm
www.permanentgallery.com

If it hadn't been for regular weekly trips to the old Taj Mahal on Bedford Place for coriander and ghee (a favourite sandwich filling) I'd never have known about this place. Thankfully its relative obscurity hasn't resulted in a swift demise, as for lovers of underground art and DIY culture it's a rare gem. This is first and foremost an exhibition space for original and challenging artists and art – it's always worth dropping in to see what the latest exhibition is. One year the guys at the gallery created a huge Brighton Memory Map, removed all the place and street names and encouraged people to write their experiences onto it instead. It was hugely popular and by the end had lines like: "*where mother's ashes were scattered*", "*lost my virginity*", and "*I went*

for a job as a receptionist in a brothel here. What was I thinking?" Get on their mailing list and you'll also find out about live drawing opportunities in the gallery, rare film nights, discussion forums and regular talks from artists.

The unsung hero of the gallery though is the bookshop. It's an outlet for people making exceptional publications and sells hundreds of unique zines, illustrated books and CDs. It's mainly local work on sale but there is some stuff from farther climes. The zines from American artist Sophie Mol are particular favourites, as are the beautifully packaged CDs from local bands like Hamilton Yarns.

Fabrica

40 Duke Street (01273) 778646
Wed-Sat 11.30am-5pm, Sun 2pm-5pm, closed Dec-April due to lack of heating
Admission free

This converted church is a gallery space for installations and contemporary art, and is an essential drop-in spot when visiting the Lanes in summer. They do four main shows a year, offering the public a chance to see new commissioned works from artists who over the years have done everything from growing a wildflower meadow to building a giant shell.

The Artist Quarter

Kings Road Arches

Tucked away down on the seafront between the two piers and below the kissing sculpture, this small stretch of the beach has been home for nearly twenty years now to a collection of local artists whose colourful workshops and galleries are permanently on display to the public. Originally owned by fishermen, these little rooms would once have been used for descaling fish (to be sold where the carousel now stands), which still accounts for the occasional odd whiff.

Far more in keeping with Brighton's bohemian nature than the plethora of café-bars found down here, the Artist Quarter captures the creative and communal spirit of the town. Open all year round, even in the most improbable gales, this is London gallery quality at half the price, with work ranging from cards and paintings to exotic furniture and puppets.

The Big Green Bagel

Brighton seafront

This sculpture arrived about fifteen years ago and was a gift from the Mayor of Naples (we gave his city a large bronze herring). Officially entitled Il Grande Bagel Verde, but known locally as the Seasick Doughnut, it has survived five storms and several demolition attempts by local art puritans.

Brighton (and Hove) has probably more artists per square metre than anywhere else in the known universe. Every May and December you can go and nose around their houses and gardens when they hold free weekend mini-exhibitions, known collectively as the Artists' Open Houses. In 2009 there were more than 200 houses and studios, containing the work of over 750 artists and craftspeople. Most houses are grouped geographically into Trails, which originally had their own brochures. They are now all gathered together into one handy brochure, with maps. As well as the visual arts (paintings, drawings, prints and sculpture) you'll also find ceramics, furniture, jewellery, stained glass, clothing, cards and more on sale direct from the artist or designer at cheaper-than-gallery prices.

The oldest Trail is Fiveways, named after the road junction, which started in 1982 when Ned Hoskins (109 Stanford Avenue) opened his house to the public during the Brighton Festival. This Trail also has the distinction of its own pub, the Open House, on Springfield Road. Over the railway tracks, south of London Road station, is Beyond the Level, founded in 1996. Trails further afield include Rottingdean, Prestonville, Hove, Portslade and Shoreham, while in the middle of the city are Central Brighton Artists, The Hartington Trail, Hanover Art Trail, and Seven Dials Artists.

One outstanding feature of the Open Houses is the cake. Many houses offer home-made refreshments of a high standard, often in their gardens. Best house for cake is Kate Osborne's house at 32 Stanford Avenue, part of Fiveways, and the best place for Open House virgins (but no cake) is The Dragonfly House, 48 Ditchling Rise (Beyond the Level). The houses do change from year to year, so check the brochure or www.aoh.org.uk before setting out.

Make sure you add your address to their guest books when you visit: that way you'll be invited to next year's private view and be given lots of wine. Or try your chances on the Friday night before the first weekend on May.

Alan (Fred) Pipes

An artist's guide to sketching Brighton

by Curtis Tappenden

It's a fact: there are more artists and illustrators per square mile in Brighton than pubs. These diligent loners can be found nestled in North Laine bars, scrawling images of seagulls in raucous courtship rituals in their sketchbooks or seducing punters during the Brighton Festival Artists' Open Houses. It's a have-a-go place with a noble heritage: Turner, Gillray and Piper to name but a few. So how about it? Begin where your art is. Cake and a cuppa in the Royal Pavilion Gardens sketching buskers or out-to-lunch locals against the Onion Palace. Next, take your line to the end of the line on Volk's Electric Railway by Brighton Pier. This magnificent Victorian invention gently rocks as a stiff easterly blows into your face – challenge enough to scribble incomprehensible doodles, but hey!

Disembark at Black Rock, relax into a deckside seat at the Marina and regard moored yachts bobbing gently in the glistening Riviera-style harbour. This could be St Tropez… but it isn't. No bare flesh of the life-class, just tightly buttoned-in bodies keeping warm – an ideal chance to perfect rippling watercolour reflections.

Bike or blade west along the promenade, select a midday pitch from an array of beach bars and cafés, then take inspiration from the thriving artistic community under the arches and visit Castor + Pollux modern artworks gallery. Passersby will throw coins at you; some will even suggest you take up painting for a living. Keep focused, it's flattery of sorts.

Continue west to reacquaint yourself with bold colours by making swatch studies in your journal using Hove's gaudy beach hut façades as a template.

Round the trail off in one of the city's fabulous parks. Paint Preston Park's bowling greens or the 300-year-old elm; sniff out St Ann's Well Gardens' beautiful scented blooms; or try a hand at moving bird studies on the lake at Queens Park.

Your final haunt: Brighton's extensive hillside graveyards. The Extra Mural Cemetery on Lewes Road is the resting place of Dickens's illustrator, Hablot Knight Browne (Phiz). Draw the rare oriental shrubs and be stunned by heavenly panoramic views of Brighton & Hove. To die for! Happy sketching.

Skulking around town with sketchbook, pen and watercolour box, ***Curtis Tappenden*** *is a local author and illustrator of 17 books including three popular Sussex titles published by Snake River Press. For more information on sketchbooking or painting in Brighton & Hove email him at curtis.tappenden@gmail.com.*

The spotter's guide to

When in 2000 the Brighton and Hove Bus Company had the idea of daubing the names of more than 50 famous people with local connections on their buses, it gave celebrity spotting in this town a whole new twist.

No longer are you obliged to spend two hours in the rain outside the Brighton Centre just to catch a glimpse of Robbie Williams' flabby arse. All you need now is a pencil, a copy of this guide and a rudimentary knowledge of public transport. Just five minutes on Western Road and you could see Norman Cook, Winston Churchill or even Leo Sayer streak by and nearly knock you over.

We've only included our favourite fifteen here, but serious spotters can find the rest listed at *www.buses.co.uk*.

When you've spotted all fifteen tear out this page, send it to us with all the boxes neatly filled in, and the first five we receive will each win a special Cheeky cagoule and a year's subscription to *match.com*.

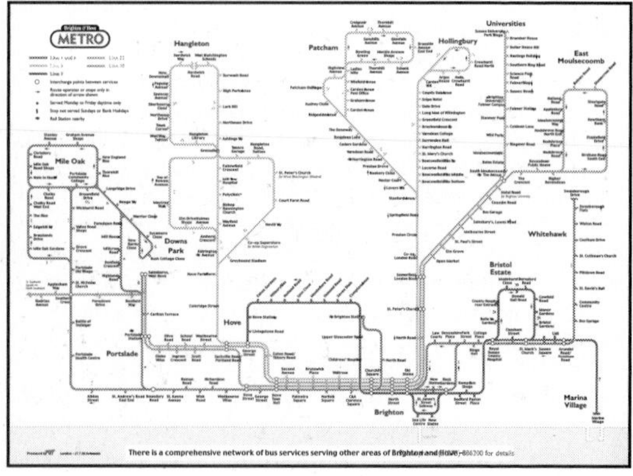

The territory of the Brighton & Hove bus

Brighton & Hove buses

- *John Wisden* (Bus number 863) – single-handedly kept the word almanac in use
- *Lord Olivier* (817) – grumpy kipper-obsessed luvvie
- *Jimmy Edwards* (648) – dead comedian with a moustache big enough to hide loaves of bread in
- *Sir George Everest* (848) – had a mountain named after him
- *Adam Faith* (649) – hiccuppy singer responsible for discovering Leo Sayer (down the back of his sofa)
- *Sir Winston Churchill* (825) – The Greatest Briton Ever (as voted by you the great British public) whose policies included "experimenting with chemical weapons on Arabs" and "the sterilisation of the feeble-minded"
- *Dusty Springfield* (865) – perma-beehived singer with a liking for the ladies
- *Ivy Compton-Burnett* (621) – racy novelist with a hatred of Hove
- *Rudyard Kipling* (869) – you've eaten the cakes, now read the book
- *Prince Regent* (803) – a swimming pool in town*
- *Charles Busby* (824) – small yellow man who spent much of his time hanging precariously from telegraph wires
- *John Nash* (811) – celebrated country-and-western singer, whose hit *A Cowboy from Whitehawk Buggered up my Patio* made him a superstar. I think.
- *Stanley Deason* (827) – one-time maverick mayor who, in the early 70s, famously elected Frank Zappa as the King of Hove
- *Carl Vincent* (845) – notorious birdwatching nut who spent a year living as a herring gull on Telscombe Cliffs
- *Charles Dickens* (828) – had a mate who knew someone in Brighton

The male and female of the species

AMAZING BUS FACTS

- Often seen gathering in flocks at Churchill Square or North St.
- Predators: trucks and taxis.
- Prey: Cyclists, dozy tourists and prams.

*not sure why this one is here.

Things to do in Hove when you're (not) dead

By Dave 'BN1' Mounfield

While Hove is now officially part of Brighton - and we're all meant to be one big happy family - it unfortunately remains the straightlaced and disapproving maiden aunt who tries to ignore sleazy old Uncle Brighton being sick under the sideboard at family get-togethers. Nevertheless, this "small piece of Rhodesia on the South Coast"*, as Pete McCarthy once described it, does have some saving graces, so indulge us, if you will, as we endeavour to pick out a selection of interesting activities and places to visit in this civic equivalent of the afterlife. But beware, gentle reader. In Hove, no-one can hear you scream.*

Kings Lawn and Brunswick Lawn

The only bit of grass left on the seafront that the council hasn't dug up and ruined. And lovely it is too. This long stretch of lawn is ideal for picnicking, frisbee throwing or just lolling around. And when you get a bit peckish, the Meeting Place Café is nearby for a hot cuppa and a slice of cake.

Marrocco's

8 Kings Esplanade, Hove
(01273) 203764

Situated next to the soon-to-be-demolished-and-rebuilt-as-the-Empire-State-Building-once-King-Kong-finished-mauling-it King Alfred Centre, this family-run seaside café is endearingly chaotic and resolutely un-designer, with some very fine homemade Italian-style ice cream, a job lot of pine fittings and some pretty good basic Italian dishes gracing its otherwise fairly standard café fare.

To have a late-afternoon perambulation along this stretch of the front, ending it here with a knickerbocker glory and coffee while watching the staff run around in a permanent frenzy of Italian disorganisation, is a real pleasure.

Gwydyr Salon

Top end of Palmeira Square,
by the Floral Clock, Hove (01273) 732923

Remarkably, this establishment is the oldest barbers in town, having kept it short and neat for 125 years non-stop. It is also the only barbers in the city with no vowels in its name (well, the first bit anyway), and the only place I know where gentlemen can come for a 50s-style close shave. Situated in the basement of Gwydyr Mansions, there are some nice steps down to a spiffingly old-fashioned window display for pomade-type products. Enter its portals and you will be delighted by the original 30s decor, with black-and-white tiles and green vitriolite. A very pleasant and humorous gentleman gave me a good cut on my visit, made all the more pleasurable by his heavily ironic use of the word *"sir"*. As in *"does* ***sir*** *think that?"*

They've even had a book of poetry written about them by a poet in residence, which you can buy while you're there. It's not bad either.

Hove Floral Clock

This civic wonder at the top of Palmeira Square is a clock, made of flowers!! How crazy is that?! For many Brightonians it stands as a gateway marker, beyond which lies the cold, blasted wasteland of Hove proper or Darkest Hove, as it is known. Even in the spring, when it's cheery, the hands point to (usually) the wrong time, as a kind of mute memento mori, insinuating *"It's only a matter of time, Brightonian, before you grow old and must perforce cross the shadow line, into Hove, and the arms of Death"*. It's very pretty though.

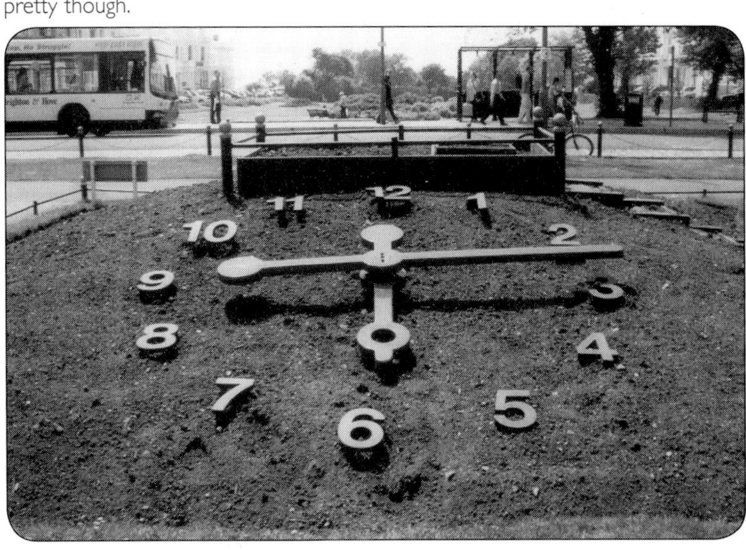

FINDING LOVE

Brighton might be the place where marrieds head to settle and gays head to wed, but the truth is, half the town seems to be single and looking for love. So, with the words of the Great Bard, "faint heart never won fair ladyboy"*, ringing in your ears, and the advice of the lovely (but not single) Cath Quinn below, you'll have no excuses now for not bagging yourself a dream partner. Unless, that is, you still live with your mum...*

Pubs & clubs

While you're pretty much guaranteed a cheap fumble in the bars on West Street, for more serious connoisseurs of romance, The Bee's Mouth, The Eagle, The Open House, The Globe and The Sidewinder are friendly, flirty drinking establishments, while cocktail sophisticates will find hidden gem Valentino's a likely place to rub shoulders with singles. Brighton's nightclubs are roughly divided into those where customers drink themselves into a frenzy of orgiastic mayhem and those where far too many drugs are consumed for sex to be considered at all. Skating the line in the middle are the likes of Casablanca and club nights at Komedia, which offer pulling opportunities to all ages no matter what their narcotic preferences.

Classes

For those who have waved a sad farewell to mash-up nights on the pull, and are seriously looking for a relationship, Brighton has many, many ways to meet people and learn a thing or two at the same time. Whether you want to make pots, spin poi, dance the tango, meditate on a transcendental level, indulge in 'laughter' yoga, or train in gender alteration surgery there's a class here for you. Good starting points include Evolution and Phoenix Gallery.

Speed dating

As the most efficient way to write off vast swathes of the local population, speed dating certainly has its uses. But for most the novelty value of having your two-minute date bark their accomplishments at you in chronological order (for girls) or spending the entire evening awaiting your two minutes with the only hotty in the room (guys) soon wears off. That said it's a great way to meet potential friends and/or assemble guests for an upcoming party. There are several events around the city, all mercifully in the kind of venues where you're unlikely to bump into colleagues or exes.

Websites

Brightonians are a sophisticated bunch on the whole so if you give the lonely-hearts sites a go, expect applicants to be web optimised, photographed in achingly cool accessories, with descriptions packed full of humorous asides and allusions to little-known authors, designers, fashionadas, gurus, bands etc. In terms of where you should be signing up, we do have our very own *lovebrighton.com*, and *www.mysinglefriend.com* is great fun too, but for the biggest collection of local daters it's rather telling that *The Guardian*'s Soulmates site *dating.guardian.co.uk* remains the best for an enormous selection of residential daters who won't drone on about *Hello* magazine and football all night. If that appeals, however, try *match.com*...

HAVE A SURREAL AFTERNOON IN BRIGHTON

1. Put on your silliest hat, pack up some fish-paste sandwiches and head off to number 64 Elm Grove, where you will need to part with a few quid to discover what the future holds from Mystic Margaret. Try not to be frightened by her make-up and listen carefully to the nuggets of wisdom she imparts to you.

2. Wander up to the top of Elm Grove and reward yourself with a quick cuppa at the café at the very top where you can pretend you are in a Mike Leigh film or, if it's a ***really*** good day in there, a David Lynch.

3. From here cross over and follow Tenantry Down Road as you pass through Brighton's shantytown. The curve of houses you can see far below are Roundhill Crescent, where notorious baby-eater Genesis P.Orridge used to live, while the strange little huts on either side of you are occupied by Brighton's flourishing Amish community. Keep your mp3 player well hidden at this point or you may have a bloodbath on your hands.

4. At the end of the road take a left and look for the entrance to Woodvale Crematorium – the chosen resting place of infamous occultist Aleister Crowley. This vast graveyard is remote and enchanting: if Buffy ever came to town, this would definitely be her hangout.

5. Leave by the main exit at the bottom, and head into town. Your afternoon can be made complete with a pint in the Basketmakers pub, tucked away at the bottom of North Laine. Search the tins on the wall to see who can find the strangest message inside, and then leave one of your own. After that it's either home for tea or popping to Organic Shamanic at the Open Market for some fly agaric and ayahuasca and flying to Neptune on the magic swan.

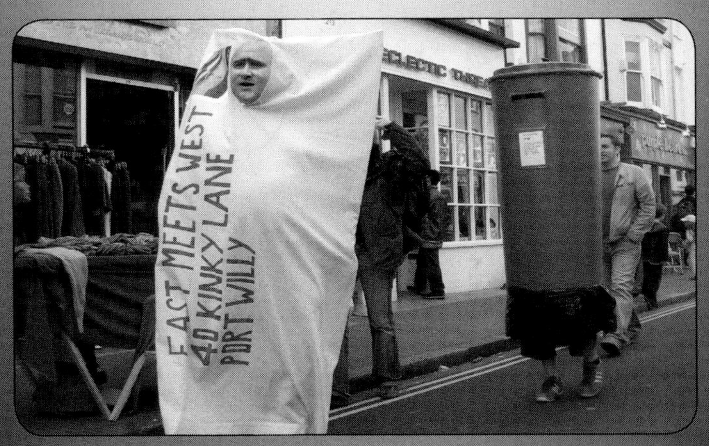

ANIMAL MAGIC & The Great Outdoors

BEASTS

Dolphin and seal spotting

Contact Stephen Savage 0777 361 0036 (the Dolphin Hotline)
www.seawatchfoundation.org.uk

There has been an increase in sightings of dolphins along the coast, in particular bottlenose dolphins and harbour porpoises. To spot one is rare but the best time to see them is high tide between March and September. Between the two piers and around the Marina are your best viewing spots, and the website is there to help with identification. The most celebrated dolphin ever seen in Brighton was dubbed Smurfy because of his unusual iridescent colouring and large white floppy hat. If you do see one (a dolphin, not a Smurf) phone this chap above and make him very happy; he's currently tracking all dolphin, whale and seal activity along the south coast.

Rockpooling

Past the Marina on the Undercliff Walk to Rottingdean you'll find some good rockpools with edible spider and shore crabs, sea anemones and other saltwater goodies. If you're in the car, drive to Rottingdean (just follow the coastal road heading towards Eastbourne), head to the seafront and turn right. From Brighton Pier it'll take ten minutes to cycle or 30 minutes to walk.

Llama trekking

Ashdown Forest Llama Park
Wych Cross, East Sussex
(01825) 712040
www.llamapark.co.uk
£40 per llama

Every couple of years or so the llama farm seems to change location. Once it was on the Downs and now it's drifted all the way to Ashdown Forest, which means it shouldn't really merit inclusion in a book about Brighton but as we're suckers for something a bit out of the ordinary, we've decided to overlook the fact. And for lovers of large hairy quadrupeds what better way to spend an afternoon than taking a stroll with one of these gentle creatures? Worth noting however is that you can only ***walk*** with the llamas, not sit on them. And galloping around the woods on them naked is right out.

Drusillas Zoo

(See *Kids* chapter)

Shepherding

countryside@brighton-hove.gov.uk
Lookerer application courses run Aug-Oct

If you've ever fancied standing around on the Downs with a piece of straw struck between your teeth while tending your flock, Brighton Council now has its own sheep and welcomes volunteer shepherds (known as 'lookerers')! It's free and you can apply by emailing the address above or checking out the council website. If selected you'll be sent on a one-day training course at Stanmer Park to learn about sheep ailments, legal aspects of grazing, and how to handle a sheep and ward off randy Welshmen. Once qualified you'll be required to give up one hour a week to keep a check on your flock, though the temptation to stand around all day in a smock shouting "get orf my land" at ramblers and paragliders will, I'm sure, be overwhelming.

BIRDS

RSPB

(01273) 775333

Apart from the gulls, pigeons, starlings and occasional curio in local parks, you'll have to get out of Brighton to enjoy some really good twitching but there's plenty on offer in surrounding areas. You'll find purple sandpipers at the Marina, a whole host of rarities regularly blown in at Beachy Head, and an RSPB reserve in Pulborough. What Brighton does offer, however, are various birding events in the local area, courtesy of the RSPB. We even have our own RSPB expert Dan Parkinson, who, if asked nicely, will demonstrate the mating ritual of the great crested grebe with you. Just remember to bring a change of trousers.

The starlings

Between the piers, one hour before sunset

Only the most hard-boiled individual could fail to be moved by this spectacular display of nature at its most playful. And like all the best things in life, it's free. No, I'm not referring to Windmill Man, but Brighton's long-established murmurations of starlings. Every night before sunset more than 50,000 of these beautiful shining creatures congregate around the piers in an amorphous swooping mass. It is truly astonishing. Watch for long enough and you'll be hypnotised by the pulsating throng of birds. Dedicated watchers swear that during the winter and summer solstices the birds briefly take the form of Phil Collins in the twilit heavens and tweet out a wobbly rendition of *Sussudio*, but this is of course nonsense. It's clearly *In The Air Tonight*.

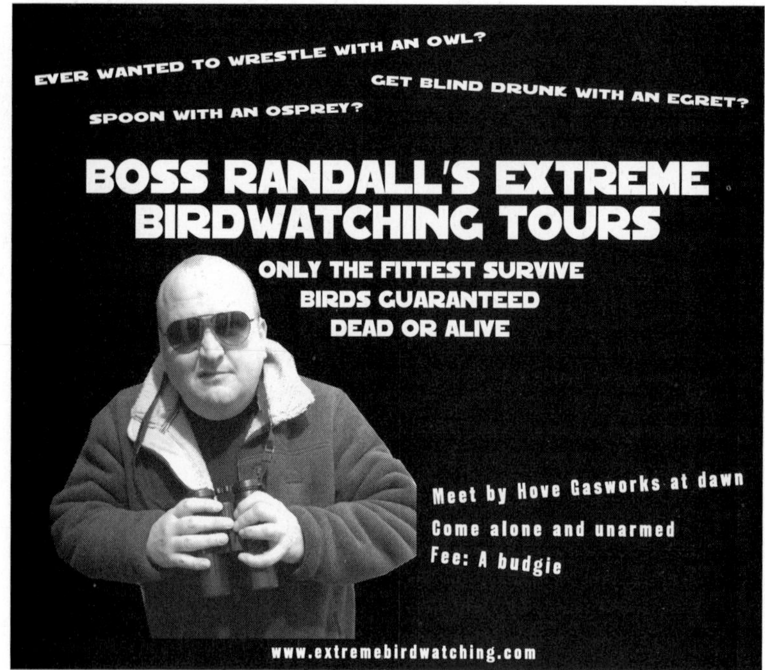

A MURMURATION EXPLANATION

By the RSPB's Dan Parkinson

There are many complicated theories as to what goes on during the murmuration. I think that the starlings are communicating. But they don't make any noise while they fly around – they just look at each other. They can tell which ones have had the best feed that day just by looking, and want to stay with one of those in the roost so they can follow it to the best feeding ground the next day.

Is there one leader that the rest follow? I don't reckon so. They are all trying to keep away from the edges of the flock. The edges are dangerous, because passing sparrowhawks or peregrine falcons will swoop and try to pick off any loose birds. So basically, the starlings need to watch each other, stick with the healthy looking ones, avoid bumping into each other, stay away from the edge and not drop out of the sky.

That's my theory, but once I met a lady at the library who was the spitting image of the guitarist from the *Muppet Show* band. She had her own ideas about the starlings – there are ley lines, she said, that cross at the end of the West Pier and all the magnetic magic messes with their little brains. Could be true. She'd done loads of acid.

I met another guy down on the seafront. He had a can of Superbrew in one hand and a sleeping bag in the other. I think he had a tattoo on his eyelid. His girlfriend was speaking in tongues. He told me that the starlings were spelling out messages from God. To be fair he said they ***might be***. He said the only way I could prove otherwise was to film them and play it

in slow motion and check against all the languages of the world. I never did, so he might be right. It was when *The Da Vinci Code* was big.

Starlings are super social animals too – they feed together, flock together, and go clubbing together. They are the best mimic of any British bird. They're related to mynah birds and can reproduce sounds such as mobile phones, car alarms, doorbells, frogs croaking and other birds. A starling's own call probably sounds like *"cheep cheep cheep"* to you but it would sound totally different to another starling. Our human ears are far too inferior to pick up the real noises.

They are the rude boys of the bird world – they pile onto bird feeders and chase everything else away. If they aren't fighting other birds they'll start on each other. When you see them perched they'll be lined up perfectly, each one about ten centimetres apart, their pecking reach being nine centimetres. They wear shimmery clothes, the boys with blue on their beaks and the girls with pink. They hang out on Brighton Pier and given half a chance they'll shit on you. Imagine if they were a bit bigger – they'd rule the world.

OUTDOOR PURSUITS

Adventure Unlimited

64 Edward Street (01273) 681058
info@aultd.org www.aultd.org

I once spent a brilliant Saturday with a load of friends, clambering over assault courses and playing British Bulldog, hide and seek and lateral-thinking games, thanks to these guys. Not only was it fun and fairly cheap, but we were also entertained by some shameless flirting between my friend and the organiser. They also offer other outdoor-pursuit days including canoeing, raftbuilding, pony trekking and abseiling, as well as a climbing wall at Stanley Deason Leisure Centre. And for the eight-to-eighteen market they run the 818 Club, which offers a mixture of outdoor pursuits and leisure activities. All outdoor events take place outside Brighton and transport is provided, should you need it.

Orb360

0845 643 4360
www.orb360.co.uk
Five minutes' walk from Devil's Dyke carpark
£25 a roll

For the thrill of a lifetime, how about getting strapped into a giant inflatable hamster wheel and hurtling down Devil's Dyke at speeds of up to 30mph? This brilliant company, unique in the South East, offers a multitude of adrenaline-based pleasures, including the Harness Orb, Aqua Orb (yes you guessed, it's filled with water!) to board360, where you get a giant-wheeled skateboard to surf the Dyke. Those of a gentle constitution can always come in summer as a spectator and watch their drag-racing event, where a bunch from Brighton's TV community get togged up to the nines and do their bit for charity. Whatever your choice of activity (and it's fun to do with mates or simply on your own), these guys will really look after

you and ensure you have an aftenoon to remember. And don't forget; you can even arrive in style during summer, courtesy of the Brighton to Devil's Dyke open-top bus. Highly recommended.

OPEN-AIR POOLS

Saltdean Lido

Saltdean Park Road, Saltdean
(01273) 888308
www.saltdean.info/lido
10am-6pm every day, end of May to end of September

This original open-air art deco swimming pool (and cover star of the first Clearlake album, *Lido*) is only a fifteen-minute drive from Brighton and has been restored, repainted and returned to its former glory. Don your best knee-length striped woollen bathing costume and head there on a day with glorious sunshine and you'll have an unforgettable time.

Pells Pool at Lewes

North Street, Lewes (01273) 472334
12 noon-6pm term-time, 12 noon-7.30pm weekends and school holidays, end May to beginning September
www.pellspool.org.uk

This little-known open-air swimming pool in Lewes lays claim to being the oldest of its kind in the country. There's plenty of space for sunbathing on the grass on warm days (and why would you go any other time?) though the presence of snogging teenagers at weekends can be a distraction.

The sea

It's free, there's lots of it, and a visit to Brighton really is not complete without at least getting your feet wet. It's traditional to swim twice around the West Pier before breakfast here, but for newcomers a bit of splashing around will suffice. Be careful when the currents are strong; every year someone gets swept away by a surprising freak tide. For more information see the chapter *The Sea*.

WHERE TO TAKE A GOOD STROLL

The Marina Breakwater

Down near the Marina is a breakwater that extends for about a quarter of a mile out to sea. Go when the sea's a bit rough and it can be a delightfully hairy experience. It'll take you about twenty minutes to walk there from Brighton Pier, and ideally you should try and time it for sunset. Then you could stick around in the Marina for a drink (bad idea) or walk back into town and flop around at the Basketmakers (good idea).

The Undercliff Walk to Rottingdean

From Brighton Pier head to the Marina, find the undercliff path behind Asda, keep going and you'll reach Rottingdean in about an hour. Most of the path from the Marina onwards has been carved out of the imposing chalky cliffs which, together with the magnificent views of the sea, make this walk fairly spectacular. And it's good by bike too as it's completely flat. As you approach Rottingdean you'll start to chance upon rockpools and little coves where people go winkle picking and crab fishing.

Rottingdean is, in contrast to Brighton, one of those classic seaside villages with old-fashioned shops and boutiques. One particular shop, The Cabin (sadly long gone), is said to have been the inspiration behind the Local Shop in *The League of Gentlemen*. In fact years ago one person emailed to tell me, *"I went in to buy a copy of* The Guardian *and the woman said defensively,* 'Oh no. We only stock **local** papers in here…'

Once you've had a good nose around the village you'll need to head back to Brighton, though if you can't

face doing the walk again buses do run regularly back to town.

This really is one of the best and most accessible local walks, whatever the season. In summer there's a café halfway (usually serving Coke and a piece of shortbread wrapped in clingfilm), while in winter you may have your head blown off but if you wrap up warm you can finish it all off with mulled wine in the White Horse.

Glynde to Lewes

Take the train to Glynde and follow the stunning but straightforward walk back over Mount Caburn to Lewes. You can't go wrong (there's nowhere else to walk), you won't see a soul, the scenery is spectacular and when you drop down the hill into Lewes, you are only a short walk from the Lewes Arms for a cheeky pint and a pickled egg.

The Indian Chattri on the Downs

High up on a hill overlooking Brighton is one the town's most curious but least-known memorials, built to commemorate the thousands of Indians who died in Brighton during the First World War. They were brought here because the Royal Pavilion was at that time used as a hospital for the wounded – on the grounds that the soldiers would feel more at home there. Despite these rather misplaced good intentions, the wounded were more than a little bemused at having been stationed in what looked like an oriental brothel and, of course, bringing Sikhs and Hindus from every caste together under one roof meant the atmosphere was not exactly convivial.

Ladies and gentlemen, the Chattri

The 4,000 who died here had their ashes scattered into the sea; the Chattri was built as a memorial to them in 1921 and an annual pilgrimage there is still organised by the Royal British Legion and the High Commissioner for India.

Take the A23 out of Brighton, follow the A273 to Hassocks and go through Pyecombe. Take a right down Mill Lane and follow until you reach the windmill carpark.
From the carpark go past the Old Barn Farm and golf course, and keep following the path until you reach a signpost. Go through the gate, keep the large clump of trees on your right and follow the South Downs Way. (It's probably best to take an OS map, however, as these directions come from some illegible notes I scribbled years ago and it's easy to miss the Chattri, hidden by trees until the last minute. The reference is TQ304111.)

The Sea

Despite the fact that Brighton receives millions of visitors every year, you'd be surprised how few take the plunge and venture – beyond the occasional paddle – into the sea. Is it too cold, is it fear of sharks, jellyfish, toilet paper, or are we all just a big bunch of jessies? In an effort to encourage a few more of you out of the pubs and into the Blue, this chapter gives the facts about seawater quality and explores a few ways to go messing about in the water.

WHERE TO SWIM

Brighton Beach

A lot of people are understandably sniffy about swimming in the sea in Brighton but I have to confess that floating on my back in the water with the sun turning my skin the texture of a leather chesterfield still rates as one of my favourite Brighton experiences. And, of course, it's free. True, you may find yourself in the company of lobster-red revellers standing around up to their waists because they can't be bothered to queue for the (non-existent) toilets, but don't let a little wee put you off. At least it warms the water up a bit.

MCS (Marine Conservation Society water quality rating): Pass

Hove Beach

A lot quieter than Brighton and well-endowed with lawns, benches, grand Regency seafront buildings and charming multi-coloured £500,000 beach huts to have a good old nose into as you stroll casually past. And once you've swum three times round the mouldy remains of the West Pier, you can round it all off with a heart-attack breakfast at the Meeting Place Café.

MCS: Recommended

Shoreham Beach

Just a mile or two beyond Portslade, through Shoreham High Street, over the estuary and a quick burrow through

the residential roads to the left, you'll find a remarkably clean and peaceful beach with sand and only light breezes much of the time. Mostly patronised by bewildered-looking families from southern continents who stand around near the water's edge with all their clothes on, regardless of the weather. And if you get a bit peckish, there's sea kale growing near the high-tide line.
MCS: Not tested

Saltdean

Five miles west of Brighton and relatively quiet. Although the water's fine, the best thing about this place is the Lido, where you can swim unravaged by the sharks that have plagued the area since escaping from some millionaire's underwater fantasy playground a couple of years ago. Allegedly.
MCS: Recommended

And elsewhere

Though more than twenty miles away, Eastbourne and Littlehampton both have Blue Flag beaches, are MCS recommended and are less likely than Brighton to be the victims of inebriated Londoners who treat our beaches as a dumping ground for beer cans, fag ends, crisp packets and their unwanted illegitimate offspring.

WATERSPORTS

Brighton Watersports

185 Kings Road Arches (01273) 323160
All year round (for retail) 10am until *"whenever"*
www.thebrightonwatersports.co.uk
£10 per hour for kayak rental

Found under the promenade between the two piers, these fellows hire out single and tandem kayaks and stand-up paddleboards, as well as organising banana-boat rides and parasailing. They also hire wetsuits, have full changing rooms and showers, and sell beachwear and wakeboarding gear. You can even book parascending and other action sports, both locally and internationally. From experience, kayaking on a warm summer's day, going around the piers, watching the cormorants nesting at the back of the West Pier and seeing Brighton from the sea has got to be the best ten quid you'll ever spend.

Lagoon Watersports

Western end of Hove promenade
(01273) 424842
Feb-end of Nov
www.lagoonwatersports.co.uk

Windsurfing, sailing, yachting and powerboating start at around £45 for a two-hour lesson with an instructor. Their latest activity, stand-up paddleboarding, is proving to be quite a hit too.

Brighton Swimming Club

www.brightonsc.co.uk

Based at Arch 250e down between the two piers, this is the UK's longest-established swimming club, formed in 1860 and still going strong. Many of its hardcore club members meet every morning at 7.30 for a dip before work. Only if the sea "looks suicidal" will they give it a miss. New members are always welcome but are required to wear a coloured rubber cap when going in, which might make you feel like a right charlie but is for your own safety.

Those members who brave the sea when it's below 40° – something that only happens occasionally – can pride themselves on being issued with a club certificate. The late club member Jim Wild, who made it to the ripe old age of 92, used to recall the time the temperature of the sea dropped to below 30° and he returned to the club with icicles hanging from his nipples!

Annual traditions include a big game of water polo down at the Marina, a chilly annual Christmas dip and a Boxing Day race.

SURFING

By shaggy Hawaiian-shirt-wearing blond Marcus O'Dair

Let's face it, Brighton is no surfer's paradise; the waves are infrequent, small and messy, the sea is dirty and the temperatures would send an eskimo running for extra thermal undies. As the title of a film about the Brighton surf scene noted, it's *Not California*.

But Brighton surfers, many of whom have surfed all over the world, are passionate about the local breaks. Yes, the waves are usually small, but they're good enough for several competition-winning Brighton surfers who are out there every chance they get. Yes, it's cold, but people surf in the Outer Hebrides, in Sweden, even in Alaska (the boundary between surfing and masochism being decidedly blurred). And, yes, it's dirty – but hey, what do you expect in Brighton?

The main spots

The two main local breaks are the Hot Pipes and the Marina. The Hot Pipes, near Shoreham Power Station, has a friendly atmosphere and, for once in Brighton, easy parking. This fairly gentle beachbreak is a good spot for beginners.

The Marina, on the other hand, is ridden mainly by shortboarders. It's a fairly fast wave breaking over a shallow chalk-and-flint reef, and suitable for more experienced surfers only. It used to have a reputation as a fairly heavy locals' spot and it's still a good idea to show a bit of respect for the regulars.

Other spots include the West Pier (especially on a groundswell), the Wedge (primarily a bodyboarding break) and Shoreham Harbour. Outside Brighton, check out Littlehampton and Eastbourne and, farther afield, East and West Wittering and Camber Sands.

Shopping

Brighton can be a shopaholic's paradise, particularly for lovers of antiques, fashion, jewellery, music, kitsch, glamourwear, retro clothing and overpriced screenprints of Al Pacino. And with more than 700 independent shops in the centre alone, the town boasts more unique boutiques per square mile than anywhere else in the UK. The most colourful areas with the best shops are definitely North Laine, Kemp Town and the Old Lanes. For the less adventurous, Western Road and the Churchill Square shopping centre have everything that you'd expect to find in a high street (including crowds, concrete and lunatic bus drivers).

North Laine is terrific, not only for its wide selection of 60s/70s clothes and record shops but also for unique boutiques like Wildcat, the world's largest stockist of body jewellery, and Pussy, offering stylish wares for the home as well as a good range of smutty books. Get into the swing of North Laine and you'll find yourself going home with a woolly mammoth ivory nosestud, a mod suit, a chocolate-covered scorpion and a pair of thigh-high boots. And you only popped out for a loaf of bread.

Kemp Town too has an eclectic mix of boutiques, ranging from a wealth of second-hand places to gay clothes stores, poodle parlours and more than 300 shops stocking buttplugs and lube. The Lanes, while a lot less flamboyant than North Laine, are good for jewellery (particularly if trying to track down your great aunt's stolen necklace), antiques, cafés and new clothes shops. Think of it this way: if North Laine was Eric Morecambe, the Old Lanes would be Ernie Wise (with Kemp Town as special guest Danny La Rue).

And finally, before you rush off with your credit cards, don't get up too early! Shops here can open notoriously late (especially in North Laine) and not always at the same time every morning. So, do yourself a favour, have a night on the tiles and get up at the same time as nearly everyone else here – around 11am.

RECORD SHOPS

While every city in England has an HMV store staffed by spotty oiks who insist on playing Scandinavian death metal at full volume, Brighton has some of the best independent record shops outside London, and because of the city's size you can get round them all easily in an afternoon.
There is a long tradition of good vinyl shops down here which, like many of the characterful shops in this town, are an essential part of Brighton's appeal. So come and sample these marvellous enclaves of vinyl/CD and I guarantee you will go home with an armful of goodies, even if it means eating beans on toast till payday.
DJ and vinyl junkie Andy Roseman

Borderline Records

41 Gardner Street (01273) 818611
Mon-Sat 10am-5.30pm, Sun 12noon-4pm

Borderline has consistently stocked an amazing range of music since it opened countless years ago. It may be small but by avoiding chart music and the obvious mainstream fodder, its stock is a carefully selected and extensive range of re-issued jazz, soul, psychedelia, exotica, reggae, latin, soundtrack, electronica, post-rock and indie. Most is on CD but there is a smaller selection on vinyl. Outside there are boxes of cheap CDs starting at £3 and vinyl offers galore. Staff are friendly and helpful and there're always some foot-tapping sounds being played. If you can find a bad record here I'll change my name to Barbara.

Edgeworld

Upstairs above Re-Load, 6 Kensington Gardens (01273) 628262
Mon-Sat 10.30am-6pm, Sun 12noon-4pm

Easy to miss, which would be a real shame, especially for anyone with a passion for small independent labels or with tastes that lean towards *Wire* and *Plan B* magazines. You'll find lo-fi, mellow country, post-rock and electronica here, and offerings from labels such as Pickled Egg, Drag City and Domino. There's also a fair selection of CDs, though the stock doesn't seem to change that often. If you want to hear some of the music on offer there's a tiny listening area in the corner for vinyl or simply ask the friendly (and refreshingly unpretentious) staff, Colin and Dave, to play whatever you fancy. Edgeworld is also a good spot for finding out about some of the more low-key gigs in Brighton. They'll even stock your own CDs as well, if properly packaged. Mine's been sitting there for years.

The Punker Bunker

Below Immediate Clothing, Sydney Street
Mon-Sun 11am-6pm (but *"you can knock a couple of hours off either side, owing to the fat bloke upstairs being late"*)
www.punkerbunker.co.uk

Run by Just One Life promoter Buz, this tiny basement shop caters for anyone with a passion for ska, two-tone, metal, rock and underground punk rock. Hanging on to those old punk-rock ethics, Buz is an eager promoter of live, noisy music in Brighton, sells all his CDs for a tenner or less and discourages nu-metallers from visiting his shop. *"There are certain records I can put on to scare off the nu-metal kids,"* he comments wryly.

You can also buy tickets for all punk-related gigs down here, buy yourself a badge that says Fuck Off, find adverts for local bands and learn all about the scene from Buz. Long may he reign.

The Record Album

8 Terminus Road (01273) 323853
Mon-Sat 11am-4.30pm
www.therecordalbum.com

Up the hill just round the corner from Brighton Station lies the Record Album: the oldest record shop in the country and a must for collectors of rare vinyl.

The shop specialises in all types of deleted recordings and one-offs, especially soundtrack albums, most of which are new or in mint condition, and the records that owner George sticks up in his shop window invariably reflect whatever movies are being shown on terrestrial TV that week. Don't expect to find a bargain: prices start around £10 and go up to £75 or more for that ultra-rare electronic 50s sci-fi B movie soundtrack. George also supplies records to the BBC, theatre and radio and has an extensive mail-order service. It is easy to spend a couple of hours here, simply for the company of its owner – George is impeccably polite and happy to share his passion for music with you. Though ask him why he doesn't stock CDs and George will shudder and say, *"uh, those ghastly little frisbees"*.

Rounder Records

19 Brighton Square (01273) 325440
Mon-Sat 9.30am-6pm, Sun 10.30am-6pm

A first-class record shop offering discount CDs, a 50-50 split of dance and indie, the cheapest vinyl in town and staff whose discerning tastes you can trust. Rounder is also ***the*** place to come for tickets to local gigs and, if you subscribe to their 'weekly' e-mail, not only will you be treated to the acerbic wit of Steve Sexton and co but you'll also be kept up to date on the best gigs in town. Remember to look out for the constantly changing graffiti round the back of the shop. It's all the handiwork of Warp/Skint musician Req.

Wax Factor

24 Trafalgar Street (01273) 673744
Mon-Sat 10.15am-5.30pm
www.thewaxfactor.com

There is an unwritten law in Brighton that all good record shops be run by blokes called Alan. The good news is Wax Factor is not only run by Alan Senior, who has been in the business 25 years and is a mine of information on everything you ever wanted (or didn't want) to know about rare vinyl, but his son Alan Junior trades here too. Alantastic!

CDs are on sale but it is the vast stock of (mainly) 50s to 70s vinyl that is so impressive: the walls are adorned with extremely rare and very tempting records of bygone days, many of which would cost you a kidney or two should you wish to take them home and give them a spin.

Sure, they know the value of what they've got but there ***are*** bargains to be had and they frequently clear out stock for a quid upwards. The two Als will also keep you abreast of new stock if they know your tastes and will endeavour to get you something no matter how rare or bizarre, though they draw the line at animal porn and Sting records.

Next door there's even a 50s-style café complete with jukebox and diner furniture. The ideal spot to have a cuppa and bacon butty as you drool over your finds.

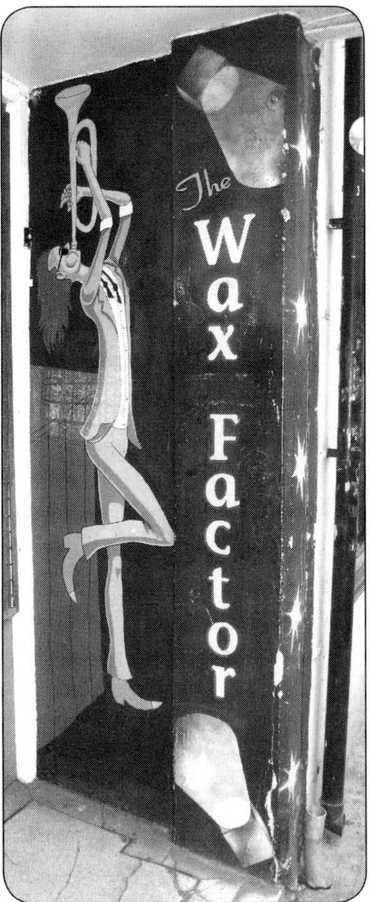

BOOKSHOPS

BIG GUYS

Borders

Churchill Square Shopping Centre, Western Road (01273) 731122
Mon-Sat 9am-7pm, Thurs 9am-8pm, Sun 10.30am-5pm
www.borders.com

When the rest of us are dragging ourselves out of bed, making strong coffee, lighting cigarettes and smearing marmite on the cat, these guys are up and open. Didn't anyone tell them that in Brighton no one even thinks about getting out of bed before 10am, never mind shopping? Still, that's crazy Americans for you*. They do, however, stock a fine array of books and CDs, have a small café upstairs, and the ***very best*** selection of magazines and spoken-word tapes in town. Also a good place for seeing small music performances and book readings – keep a look out for their monthly flyers for details.

**Saying all that, I've just noticed Waterstones opens at 9am too…*

British Bookshops (Sussex Stationers)

194 Western Road (01273) 206606
37 & 37a London Road (01273) 691626
Mon-Sat 9am-6pm, Sun 10am-5pm
www.britishbookshops.co.uk

Don't expect to find the latest occult offering from Julian Cope about elf magic or the history of shoelaces written in Esperanto, but if it's the most popular works of fiction/non-fiction you're after you'll find them here with discounts to rival even those rotten supermarket chains.

Waterstones

71-74 North Street (01273) 206017
Mon-Fri 9am-7pm, Sat 9am-6pm, Sun 11am-5pm
www.waterstones.co.uk

The Brighton branch of Waterstones has always felt more like a friendly local bookstore than a chain, owing much of its success and popularity to its lovely staff, who work hard to ensure that the stock here, as far as possible, reflects the true spirit of the town. Many seem to have their finger on the pulse of what Brighton readers are looking for, demonstrating that with a little care and passion, a chainstore can still have a heart.

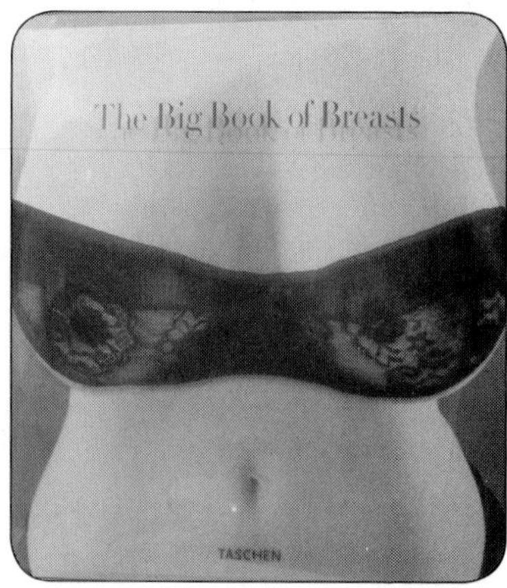

LITTLE GUYS

Brighton Books

18 Kensington Gardens (01273) 693845
Mon-Sat 10am-6pm, occasionally Sun

As well as offering a large selection of rare and unusual second-hand hardbacks (£90 for the collected works of Madame Blavatsky) and cheaper paperbacks (usually sitting in boxes at the front of the shop), Brighton Books is home to some legendary Brighton characters. There's Simeon (the last of the famous Brighton shop cats), a friendly black tom who will greet you at the counter and rub himself against your chest to entice you into making a purchase and – on some days – king of charity shopping, Mr Stephen Drennan. If he's wearing a badge, playing a bizarre record and sporting a black rollneck, you can rest assured that all is well with the universe.

City Books

23 Western Road (01273) 725306
Mon-Sat 9.30am-6pm, Sun 11am-4.30pm
www.city-books.co.uk

Brighton's biggest independent bookshop and a favourite haunt of Nigel Richardson (author of *Breakfast in Brighton*). The kind of place you wander in to buy the latest McEwan and end up having a natter with the owner for half an hour about existentialism, City Books is a local bookshop that cares about its customers and seems to make an extra-special effort in properly representing Brighton through its choice of stock and window displays. Twice shortlisted for the Independent Bookshop of the Year award. What more do we need to say?

Colin Page

36 Duke Street (01273) 325954
Mon-Sat 9am-5.30pm

This former 19th century baker's is officially Brighton's oldest bookshop and comes complete with all the trappings of the dusty, antiquated variety once frequented by JR Hartley, including a marvellous old spiral staircase at the back. Set up in 1975 by John Loska and his twin brother Stephen, the shop specialises in antiquated and rare books but, for the general buyer, always has a box of interesting paperbacks outside and a basement of hardback fiction and factual books ranging from history to the occult. It's also a popular haunt when the luvvies are in town. The likes of Stephen Fry and Simon Callow are regulars, as are old-school politicians (*"the ones who still read,"* quipped Stephen) like Denis Healey. A treat for the serious book collector.

Kemp Town Books

91 St George's Road (01273) 682110
Mon-Sat 9am-5.30pm
www.bookroomartpress.co.uk

One of only two remaining independent bookshops left in the city, Kemp Town Books has been here for more than 35 years, and run by the affable Darion Goodwin for the past fifteen. Charming, personable and peaceful, this is the very antithesis of *Black Books* and even has a little café upstairs that occasionally plays host to evening courses in poetry, life drawing and other workshops. Priding himself on a fast-order service, Darion personally guarantees next-day delivery for 90% of orders (faster than Amazon!) or a free pint and cheesy chips from the Barley Mow next door.

Also worth a note is the Bookroom Art Press, another of Darion's ventures, which offers a variety of beautiful limited-edition prints from such artists as John Nash, Eric Ravilious and Vanessa Bell, which can be seen framed around the shop.

Two Way Books

54 Gardner Street (01273) 687729
Mon-Sat 9am-5.30pm, closed half-day Wed, just like they did in olden times

Frozen in time since 1982, this singular bookshop must be the only place in England still selling Paul Young and Van Halen annuals. If pictures of David Lee Roth in spandex pants aren't your bag, they also do a nifty selection of old comics ranging from *Dr Who* to *Tractor Weekly*. Mix that with more bizarre stuff like shelves of Mills & Boon, Giles compilations and a few discreet piles of porn and you'll probably wonder how they make a living. Barbara Cartland or back issues of *Razzle* anyone?

Wax Factor

24 Trafalgar Street (01273) 673744
Mon-Sat 10.15am-5.30pm
www.thewaxfactor.com

If second-hand books on the occult, drugs, philosophy, sci-fi, eastern mysticism and music are your bag then this is the place for you. The window display alone should be enough to pull you in as you drool over all the Crowley, Philip K Dick and Burroughs books. They have a pretty good selection of general fiction here too, which is just on your right as you enter. More importantly perhaps, they stock one of the best collections of second-hand CDs and vinyl in Brighton, with seven-inches and CD singles in the basement (See *Record Shops*).

West Pier Books

Underneath the West Pier (what's left of it)
Fri-Sun when the sun is shining

At weekends, when the weather is good, you'll find these guys down on the seafront. Run by cultural connoisseur Mark Keeble and "I Predict a Pop Quiz" Pete, West Pier Books holds a good collection of second-hand paperbacks with a slant towards cult fiction. Brighton's answer to *The Persuaders*, the duo can be seen at country fairs or whizzing around Brighton in Mark's black 70s Jag blasting out easy-listening music.

CHEEKY BOOKSELLER OF THE MONTH

West Pier Books' Mark 'Crusher' Keeble

CUT OUT AND KEEP

GROOVY GIFTS, COOL THINGS FOR THE HOME & FUNKY FIREARMS

Blackout

53 Kensington Place (01273) 671741
Mon-Sat 10am-6pm, Sun 11am-5pm
www.blackout-uk.com

Off the beaten track in North Laine, Blackout still gets long-term Brightonians stumbling through the doorway for the first time going "*ooh, are you new?*", despite having been here for more than fifteen years.

The shop's unique angle is kitsch-fashion-folk art and religious imagery and it has cornered the market in Tibetan baby carriers, fluorescent loo brushes, Virgin Mary ashtrays, plastic Hindu gods, recycled-tyre tables and tribal jewellery.

Their policy of selling nothing black (hence the name) received a knock recently when I discovered a black candlestick in here, although staff member Sally insisted that it was just *"very, very dark purple"*.

Castor & Pollux

164-166 King's Road Arches, Lower Promenade (01273) 773776
Mon-Sun 11am-5pm, winter months Fri-Mon 12noon-4pm
www.castorandpollux.co.uk

Named after the Roman gods of seafarers, C&P is an attractive beach-house boutique selling stylish books (*Girls Guide to Surfing* anyone?), furniture, art, flowers, pottery and (increasingly) beautiful prints from artists such as Quentin Blake and Rob Ryan. Owner Mike clearly has a taste for quality; more places like this down on the seafront please!

C&H Weston Ltd

12 East Street (01273) 326338
Mon-Sat 9am-5.30pm, Sun 10.30am-4.30pm
www.chweston.co.uk

Among the sea of over-priced clothes boutiques and jewellery shops in the Lanes these guys remain a curious anomaly. One of the oldest shops in Brighton, C&H Weston started out as gunmakers back in 1819 and while they no longer knock up firearms in the back room, they do stock a huge range of air rifles and pistols, as well as Barbour jackets and the like. While air guns start at £30 and go up to as much as £10,000, you can bag a plastic crow and magpie for a fiver or a giant-sized plastic owl for scaring away seagulls and mad aunties for £20.

NB: To buy an air rifle you need ID that proves you are over eighteen. To buy a Barbour jacket you will need to complete the *Daily Telegraph* crossword in less than ten minutes in front of the staff.

"Point that thing at me and I'll be straight on the blower to the RSPB."

The Lanes Armoury

26 Meeting House Lane (01273) 321357
Mon-Sat 10am-5.15pm
www.thelanesarmoury.co.uk

Souvenir firearms and armour from all periods of history. Get your granny that old Vickers submachine gun she always wanted or maybe a Luger for young cousin Donald. They also have Kentucky rifles, Zulu war shields, Napoleonic swords and even a helmet from the Iraq war. A Tudor suit of armour would set you back around £20,000, though the less affluent can buy a cap badge for only £3. If the Ronnie Reagan picture isn't up then nag them to get it back on display as there's a good story behind it.

Painting Pottery Café

31 North Road (01273) 628952
Tues-Sat 10am-6pm, first Thursday of the month late night
www.paintingpotterycafe.co.uk
Prices start around £5 for tiles and eggcups

As well as holding workshops where children and adults can learn to throw pots and make clay sculptures, the Painting Pottery Café is a place where, for a £5 studio fee, you can try your hand at decorating plates, mugs, eggcups and tiles. They will ply you with coffee, hot chocolate and teas for as long as you want, and will even glaze and fire your finished masterpieces. The late-night Thursday sessions are especially worth attending, as food is laid on and you can bring your own booze. So, men, don't be surprised if after fourteen cans of Special Brew you wake to find eight new eggcups sitting on your kitchen table, each crudely adorned with pictures of your own genitalia.

Pardon My French

15 St George's Road, Kemp Town Village
(01273) 694479
Mon-Sat 10am-5pm
www.pardonmyfrench.co.uk

A cornucopia of luxurious boudoiresque items created by our garlic-loving friends over the seas and specially selected by owners Stephanie and Sandra. The whole shop is jam-packed with curious and wonderful items from French nightwear and Provençal plates to old enamel signs with such messages as "*Chat Gentil*", "*Lapin Lunatique*" or (my favourite) "*Attention! Chien Bizarre*".

Top tip: If you visit the shop wearing a beret and carrying a string of onions they give you a special discount. If that's ***all*** you're wearing however, you might get arrested.

Cuddly unthreatening Hattifatteners

Pussy Home Boutique

Little Pussy, 3a Kensington Gardens (01273) 604861
Big Pussy, 3 Bartholomews (01273) 749852
Mon-Sat 10am-6pm, Sun 11am-4pm
www.pussyhomeboutique.co.uk

Cross the sexy glamour of Bettie Page and the slick design of Frank Lloyd Wright with the cool sounds of Goldfrapp and you're beginning to get an idea of Pussy. Often imitated in Brighton but never equalled, this stylish and saucy boutique boasts a wonderful selection of cool furniture, chic and erotic books (*Big Book of Lesbian Horse Stories* anyone?), jewellery, crockery, exclusive Paul Frank, Tatty Devine, AussieBum pants and t-shirts. Pussy also stocks, without doubt, the best cards in town. How could you resist their offensive range which includes captions like *"You smell of wee-wee"* or *"Jesus Loves Everyone. Except for You, You Cunt"*?

Owner Nicky also has a great talent for predicting trends. Spot something unique in Pussy and, chances are, you'll see it in next month's issue of *Vogue*. It must be said however, that in the past few years Nicky has (unashamedly) gone Moomin crazy and hopes to *"retire to Moomin Valley one day"*. Now you can pop in and buy the books, mugs and plates, put your hand up a Moomin's bum or even buy yourself a furry Hattifattener or six.

Pussy have two shops in Brighton: Little Pussy (the original) in North Laine and Big Pussy in the Old Lanes, which has more of everything and a range of glamorous furniture in the upstairs room. Highly recommended.

Scandecor

20 Castle Street (01273) 820208
www.artdeco-sofas.com

As the eagle-eyed reader may have spotted, this guide tends not to bother mentioning soft furnishings, those things that you spend half your life lolling about on. Let's just assume for a second though that you are in need of a sofa or comfy chair and can afford to purchase (gasp) new. Step in here sir, I'm sorry, madam, and allow me to show you our range of art deco repro soft furniture, made to order in Brighton to designs created by buying originals and pulling them apart to see exactly how it was done. Been at it for over 40 years we have. Yes, they are utterly utterly beautiful aren't they? No, they don't cost any more than a bog-standard mass-produced one from a soulless industrial estate warehouse. We had that Martin Kemp in here the other day you know. Said he's never sat on a DFS sofa in his life...

Timeslip Videos

Bottom of Trafalgar Street, opposite Sydney Street
Open *"eight days a week"* 10am-6pm

Steering away from mainstream, big budget and blockbusters, friendly owner Mick has instead an excellent range of old classics (Hitchcock, Powell & Pressburger etc), cult movies and modern world cinema on DVD and video. And with prices ranging around the £3.50-£12 mark, anyone with good taste in films is going to find something here to take home and cherish.

Yasher Bish

96 Gloucester Road
Tues-Sat 10am-6pm, Sun 12noon-4pm

Specialists in all things Turkish, Iranian and Afghani, from ornate backgammon sets, prayer rugs (£15) and goatherds' bells to a wide range of colourful and very beautiful rugs. Upstairs is packed with original Anatolian pots, some more than 100 years old, but still with that faint lingering smell of olive oil. And back by popular demand – the kitsch classic mosque alarm clocks for only £12!

SPECIALIST CLOTHES SHOPS

From safari suits for him to rubber catsuits for her, Brighton boasts a fine collection of retro, exotic and club-fashion clothes shops, the majority in North Laine. If you want to get kitted out in something especially slinky for a club night or just want something new for the wardrobe, here's a selection of the best places to go.

Andrew Fionda

17 St George's Road, Kemp Town
0797 675 2879

Ladies, if you're in need of cheering up I suggest popping in here. A smiley greeting from Andrew, Parker the gentle chocolate labrador at your feet ready for a good stroke, and before you know it you'll have perked up no end and be ready to splash out on something special as Andrew's 'boudoir' sells some very beautiful, unusual and glamorous vintage dresses. Unless you're Audrey Hepburn these are not the kind of dresses to be slung on for everyday wear but saved for those very special occasions: a prom, wedding, anniversary, big party, Christmas or the passing away of a rich relative.

For the ladies who take their fashion seriously, Andrew's business partner Franck offers a personal shopping service and professional fashion advice. And Parker? Well, what could be more appealing to the ladies than a chocolate-coloured dog?

Boy Parker

6a Kensington Gardens (01273) 687768
Mon-Fri 10.30am-5.30pm, Sat 10am-6pm, Sun 11am-5pm

An offshoot of the Get Cutie empire (see below), this is primarily an elegantly displayed collection of t-shirts that range all the way from pre-ironic to post-ironic, like the one of Kate Moss with blood coming out of her nose (I presume the poor girl had walked into a door or something). There're always a few appealing oddities tucked away in here, be it their two-tone ruffle shirts or a pair of Y-fronts made from towelling.

Dog Parker

Ampwitch

22 Trafalgar Street (01273) 687968
Mon-Sat 11am-7pm, Sun 12noon-6pm
www.ampwitch.com

Popular with the Hobgoblin and alt rock crowd, Ampwitch describes itself "a record shop that doesn't sell records". So while you'll have to go elsewhere for a vinyl copy of the Butthole Surfers' Hairway to Stephen, if it's Southern Lord Records t-shirts, Total Skull merchandise, hand-knitted Angus Young and Hendrix dolls, band mugs or rock mags you're after these guys will welcome you with open arms. And speaking of friendliness, Chris who runs the place seems to have his fingers in various music/promotion pies and is a lovely fellow to chat to about gigs and other events going on in town.

So next time you need a studded belt or new Kiss t-shirt, Ampwitch is a welcome reminder that, unlike Rag Freak by Churchill Square, even if the place is full of all things black and spiky, that doesn't have to include the mood of the staff.

FATBOY SLIM'S

all season fashion tips

Hello! Norman 'Fatboy Slim' Cook here, come to give you some fashion tips! And I reckon I'm a bit of a style guru, because once I was watching What Not To Wear *with Zoe and she said:* "You should be on this programme, Norman," *so she obviously reckons I'd make a better presenter than them! So, without further ado, here's Norm's guide to how to look and feel good, whatever the weather.*

Summer

Summers in Brighton always remind me of being a kid. You know – deck chairs, buckets 'n' spades, weeing in the sea. Nowadays I spend my summers idling on the beach, pottering around the house listening to records, or even making my own, by cobbling together a few R'n'B samples with a drum loop! No, really! It's as easy as that!!!

And what could be more perfect for those long hot, sticky months than to slip into a cool, thin, colourful, 100% cotton Hawaiian shirt? They're comfortable, stylish, eye-catching, and make you look like a real 'Funk Soul Brother.'

Autumn

Now a lot of people see this time of year as an excuse to start sporting knitwear and favouring such autumnal colours as burnt oranges, dark browns and reds. This I believe is a terrible mistake! You wouldn't catch me going out in a snowstorm dressed all in white!!!

Take a tip from me – dare to be different! Why not go for something colourful, and striking? Like a Hawaiian shirt, say! And, when everyone else is turning up to those Halloween parties in black (yawn!), you'll steal the show with a dazzle of colour on your back!!!

Winter

Like many people I tend to suffer from the winter blues, especially during the long months from January to March. If I look out of my bedroom window in the morning and it's cold, miserable and grey outside, my spirits start to flag and, before I know it, I'm comatose in front of the box with a jazz mag in one hand and a joint in the other, watching Kilroy talk to middle-aged housewives about teenage pregnancy. God, do I get depressed!! Until, that is, I remember my faithful Hawaiian shirt! Once I've whipped off my jim-jams and got that cool cotton and splash of colour on my back it feels like a little bit of the summer has returned, leaving me with a rosy complexion and a chance again to face the world with a smile. I recommend you do the same. Magic!

Spring

Now during the 'rainy season', a lot of people favour waterproof coats with hoods. This, I believe, is a terrible mistake. And can be extremely dangerous! Did you know that wearing a hood can reduce visibility by up to 37%?!! If, for example, you were crossing the busy A27 between Worthing and Shoreham, your so-called 'sensible' hooded raincoat might protect you from the wet, but would offer precious little protection when you failed to notice the 30-tonne Juggernaught that was hurtling towards you, smashing into you at a 120 miles an hour and crushing your head like a ripe melon.

So don't be silly. Be safe!! Make yourself visible when crossing the road. Why not go out just wearing something brightly-coloured – something like, say, just for the sake of argument… a Hawaiian shirt?!! Sure you might get soaked, catch a cold, or worse, pneumonia, but at least you'll be safe.

Right – I'm off now;
I've got until tomorrow to write
a new album. Not a problem!!!
Praise you!!!!!
Norm

Dance

27 Western Road
Mon-Sat 10am-6pm, Sun 11.30am-5.30pm

Boots and shoes of every colour, shape and size from thigh-high to glittery DMs, with a nod towards goth culture, fetish and the more unusual. Curiously, I popped in one Christmas to find the owner sat in the middle of the shop with a half-empty bottle of spirits in his hand smoking a fat cigar, listening to music and having a thoroughly good time. In his merry state he did sell me shoelaces that were eight times too big for my shoes, but hats off to a man who clearly knows how to let his hair down at work.

Get Cutie

33 Kensington Gardens (01273) 687768
Mon-Fri 10.30am-5.30pm, Sat 10am-6pm, Sun 11am-5pm
www.getcutie.co.uk

Celebrated for their beautiful prints depicting anything from cowgirls to gothic bats, Get Cutie specialises in handmade 50s-style creations: dresses, skirts and shirts that may be an occasional treat for those on student wages but won't break the bank for the tens of people on decent wages in Brighton. And if you need a pair of knickers with pictures of the Eiffel Tower on them, they'll sort you out. Recommended.

Jump the Gun

36 Gardner Street (01273) 626777
Mon-Sat 10am-6pm, Sun 12noon-5pm
www.jumpthegun.co.uk

The UK's ***only*** exclusively mod shop, Jump the Gun has been established in Brighton for nearly fifteen years now, and is almost as synonymous with the city as sticks of rock, clubbing, Chris Eubank and arson. This well-loved store boasts a handsome collection of suits, shirts, parkas, Dr Martens and coats for the dapper gentleman, all at very reasonable prices (parkas start at £95, shirts £40, suits £175-295). The shop's two owners are brothers Adam and Jonathan, who live and breathe the mod life – arriving to work on Lambrettas, always dressing smartly and nipping up Little East Street every lunchtime for a bit of how's your father. For those not into the scene, Jump the Gun is still worth a visit, for it is as much about proper tailoring, quality garments, good treatment and looking sharp as it is about Mod culture. As Adam puts it, *"We want our customers to go away looking like a cross between John Steed and Sean Connery. But be warned; if you drink too much, you won't fit into these clothes!"*

Passport

108 St James's Street (01273) 621422
10am-4.30pm

Many's the time I've walked past this place and thought to myself, "*Agh! Jesus, my eyes! I'm blind*" for it has to be said that owner Raj is not afraid of a little colour. From the bright pink silky suit in the window to the dazzling array of lurid shirts, waistcoats and ties that hang inside, this is a walk-in-wardrobe for Graham Norton and Jonathan Woss wannabees. A spectacle to behold it may be, but if camp 80s designs are not what Sir desires, Raj does sell some very well-made and well-tailored plain shirts. Be on your guard though – on my last visit he said cheerfully, *"I've got a new delivery coming soon that will be even more colourful!"*

Sunglasses not included

Paul Bruton Army Surplus

Viaduct Road
Thurs-Sat 10am-1pm and 2pm-4.30pm

The two masked dummies that stand guard outside this shop must rank with the Pavilion and the West Pier as the most famous monuments in Brighton. Both creatures have posed with innumerable tourists and even appear on an album cover by some obscure Scottish band. Like Colonel Mike's, the stock in here is immense: you can get kitted out in just about any uniform you fancy, from the pith helmet and khaki shorts style of *It Ain't Half Hot, Mum* to the German guards in *Escape from Colditz*. You'll also find some genuine bargains here: old 1950s coats and jackets for under a tenner, original gas-mask bags for under a fiver, and the most enduring DJ's record bag made of reinforced rubber!

Red Mutha

92 Trafalgar Street (01273) 603976
Mon-Sat 11am-6pm, Sun 12noon-5pm
www.redmutha.com

Once Yamama, now Red Mutha (what is it with the 'mum' theme?), this is one of North Laine's typically quirky boutiques. Specialists in creating one-off, customised, recycled garments for those who dare to wear them, this is not for your Topshop princesses or River Island fashion slaves. Think bits of football shirt, recycled badges, paint splats, hand-drawn images, zips and customised patches. Whether you just buy bits and bobs to go with your more normal outfits (although probably not your work suit) or purchase the craziest 90s acid rave/liquorice allsorts-coloured shirt, this stuff will certainly get you noticed. For individuals (like its owner Red) who want to be really out there, and I mean ***really*** out there.

A GIRLIE DAY OUT SHOPPING IN NORTH LAINE WITH ANNABEL GILES

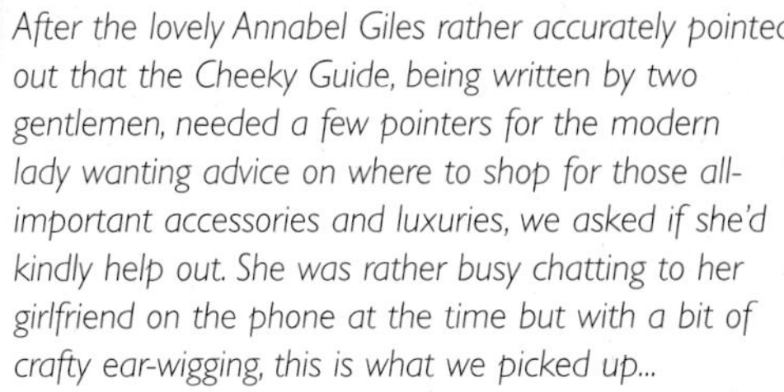

After the lovely Annabel Giles rather accurately pointed out that the Cheeky Guide, being written by two gentlemen, needed a few pointers for the modern lady wanting advice on where to shop for those all-important accessories and luxuries, we asked if she'd kindly help out. She was rather busy chatting to her girlfriend on the phone at the time but with a bit of crafty ear-wigging, this is what we picked up...

"Darling! So thrilled you've got a new boyfriend! Clever, funny, millionaire. No baggage you say? Oh. And handsome too! And he cooks. Good. No, of course I'm not jealous, don't be so silly…

"Anyway, tomorrow I thought we'd try and find you something to brighten up your tiny bedsit first: what about **Velvet,** they do lovely boudoir stuff. Or **Blackout**, for a little colour? How you've managed to lure a man back with that damp patch I'll never know...

"Then I'll need to pop into **lavender/room,** obviously. There won't be anything for you in there – it's mostly I'm-not-that-sort-of-girl silk pyjamas and understated handbags. **Sirène** is for the discerning fashionista, and **Hope & Harlequin** is proper vintage – you prefer 'retro', don't you? **Revamp** might be more your style, actually, it's a brilliant fancy dress shop; and even I have bought huge eyelashes from **Rococo**. You might like to buy one of their wigs, just while your hair's growing out.

"After lunch at **Nia** – there's a very handsome waiter works there but he doesn't fancy me so he must be gay – I need to go to **She Said**, for a beautiful bejewelled vibrator I saw in the window the other day. You can go to **Lick**. For a frozen yoghurt.

"Now I know you're a slavish follower of the Brighton Style, as you seem to wear all your clothes at once, so **Red Mutha** and **Sassy** should be within your budget. And we both might find something in **JuJu**, the shop that doesn't sell zebras, although you could be forgiven for thinking that it does.

"**Anka Beauty** is in a nice quiet spot where they can't hear you scream. I'll have a Brazilian, just in case, and I thought I'd treat you to a medicated clearing facial. Fingers crossed.

"I'd come and help but I'm going out, actually. Yeah, silent speed dating at the **Mad Hatter.** It was my ex-boyfriend's idea…"

RETRO CLOTHES

Hope & Harlequin

31 Sydney Street (01273) 675222
Mon-Fri 10.30am-6pm, Sat 10am-6pm, Sun 12pm-5pm
www.hopeandharlequin.com

Step into a world of old-time sartorial elegance at this vintage ladies' outfitters, with dresses from the 30s to the 60s and more organza than you can shake a stick at. They also specialise in elegant vintage weddingwear that not only does away with all that bouffant dressed-as-a-cake nonsense but chops the starting price down to a remarkably sensible £200 or so. I quite fancy one myself actually but I'm not sure it'll go with three days of stubble.

Shabitat

Lewes Road, opposite The Bear pub
(01273) 677577
Mon-Fri 9am-5pm, Sat 10am-4pm
www.magpie.coop/shabitat.php
www.leftover.co.uk

A dirty great sky-blue warehouse by the Vogue Gyratory might not be most people's first port of call for intriguing second-hand clobber, but the selection in the back room of Magpie Recycling Co-op's HQ is so mind-bendingly cheap you'd be well advised to drop by before you hit North Laine and lash out a fortune on a garish orange tie with an inexplicable stain. Coats are £3, trousers two, and if you've only got a quid you can still get some headgear. There's also a smattering of 'reconstructed' garments by Leftover, giving a new lease of life to sweatshirts and skirts via the clothcutter's equivalent of gene splicing. The remainder of this cavernous barn is given over to

second-hand furniture, the pricing strategy for which eludes me, ranging as it does from £2 for a table to a bizarre painting of Hattie Jacques' disembodied head floating on 60s wallpaper for £200.

To Be Worn Again

51 Providence Place (01273) 624500 &
Sydney Street (01273) 680296
Mon-Sat 11am-7pm, Sun 12noon-4pm

Hidden away just off Trafalgar Street opposite St Bartholomew's church, this is the biggest second-hand clothing warehouse in Brighton. The stock comprises the usual 70s shirts, leather and suede jackets and paisley dresses but as there's so much of everything you're more likely to find something for every member of your Iron Butterfly tribute band. Don't miss the back room with a great selection of coats, including three-quarter and full-length fake furs. It's usually quiet in there,

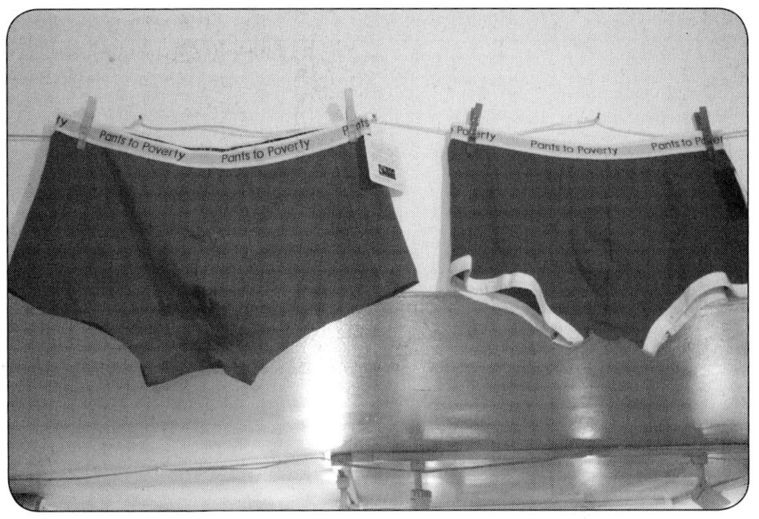

even at weekends: perfect if you're in the mood for trying on loads of things. The shop on Sydney Street also sells trainers and bags, and displays frustratingly not-for-sale vintage kids' toys. So if you really want a scale model of *Stingray*'s Marineville you'll have to build it yourself out of old toilet rolls.

Traid

39 Duke Street (01273) 746346
Mon-Sat 10am-6pm, Sun 11am-5.30pm
www.traid.org.uk

A welcome raspberry to all the trendy clothes stores on Duke's Street, Traid is a sort of upmarket Oxfam whose policy is to favour certain clothes styles for particular areas. While many of their London shops tend to focus on second-hand designer gear, here the emphasis is on retro and sportswear though, to be honest, they seem to have a good all-round selection of fake furs, dresses, jackets and accessories. Their Remade range does the increasingly popular mix-and-match recycling thing with old clothing that you can also find at Red Mutha and Shabitat. On the upside, you will be wearing a unique garment. On the downside, you may not be able to work out whether you've got it on back to front.

HIGH STREET STORES AND DESIGNER LABEL SHOPS

For the ladies there's a wide range of clothes and shoe shops around the Old Lanes including the likes of Designlab, All Saints, Mottoo (for Paul Smith and Nicole Farhi) and Morgan in Duke Street; French Connection, Jigsaw, Monsoon and Coast on East Street; Moist, Ted Baker, Ghost and Oasis in Duke's Lane. If you're looking for Miss Selfridge, H&M and Warehouse you'll find them up by Churchill Square, along with most other predictable high street retailers.

Guys, err... Topman and H&M anyone?

How to dress properly in a slump

by Lady Corinthia Mullard-Frott

Of course, one used to have everything bespoke but hard times have hit, and since Tiger's disastrous Nigerian share-dealing incident, one has become quite an expert at seeking out presentable clothing from second-hand emporia. I'm referring of course to well-made, classic garments and not some Crimplene zip-through A-line frock with diagonal stripes and a Prova label.

My daughter Henry has a weekend villa in Hove and we enjoy a good rummage together. One might find chequered Daks golf slacks for Tiger. or a Joyce Original skirt suit for me. Henry looks for Scottish cashmere, preferably Elgin, and a nice flat brogue by Church's of Kensington. And of course anything with a Utility label is cause for great celebration. So, assuming you have some taste and appreciate that tweed, gabardine, linen and other natural fibres hold sway over this so-called vintage terylene rubbish, one is pleased to share the following recommendations for buying other peoples' old clothes in Brighton and Hove. Enjoy! CM-F (Lady)

Wardrobe: Upper North Street. Clive and Philip's superlative collection of period frocks and jewels. Outrageously expensive but perfect.

Margaret's: Upper St James's Street, Kemp Town. Next to the flea market, an unmarked treasure trove of men's and ladies' clothes, fabrics and trimmings sourced with impeccable taste by the delightful Margaret.

Snoopers Paradise: Kensington Gardens. If you close your eyes going past the goth and new-age stalls, there are a few highly respectable clothing retailers here for men and women. Numbers 52, 31, 22 at the back, and 41 on the far right.

Dirty Harry: Sydney Street. Yes, it is grubby and stocks an alarming number of acrylic cardigans but occasionally has an absolute stunner, and reasonably priced.

Oasis: Kensington Gardens. You'll struggle to find the name or see through the barred windows. The shop is gloomy and cluttered but does have good pieces. Take a torch.

Starfish: Gardner Street. Another overpriced trendy one but worth a pop.

Ivy's: Church Street. Gentlemen readers who mourn the loss of the highly dodgy Rosen's in the same street may want to brave this proper old-school "clobber" outlet.

Apologies to Hove for under-representation but you need to pull your socks up. Do say hello if you see me rummaging – then back away: I'm used to getting what I want and I always carry my riding crop.

SWEETIES, FAGS & THINGS FOR THE DOG

Choccywoccydoodah

24 Duke Street (01273) 329462
Mon-Fri 10am-6pm, Sat 12noon-4pm, Sun 10am-5pm
www.choccywoccydoodah.com

You'll forgive the ludicrous name the second you enter, take in that sweet smell of Belgian chocolate and marvel at the most outrageous, over-the-top chocolate cakes you've ever seen. They've got spiky fetish cakes, ones covered in realistic vegetables (including carrots and cabbage), ones with willies, roses, mermaids and more besides. If you can't afford a cake (their top-notch wedding cakes can cost up to £1,000), they do gold coins and Cuban cigars for under a fiver, though their consistent bestsellers continue to be the chocolate shoes and solid chocolate dogs like Ruby, the bulldog puppy. Head of Creativity here is the infamous Mr Dave Pop, also renowned for his kitsch songs and live appearances at various Brighton venues over the years. If you want to show him your appreciation, you can actually buy a DVD of his greatest hits or marvel at his artwork that hangs above the counter.

Cybercandy

15 Gardner Street 0845 838 0958
Mon-Thurs 12noon-5pm, Fri-Sun 11am-6pm
www.cybercandy.co.uk

This must surely be the only shop to have seven-year-old kids and 40 year olds standing side by side, drooling over the items on display. Sweetie lovers, you'll think you've died and gone to heaven when you come here. With everything from retro classics such as Pez and Texan bars (yes, they've been 're-issued'!) to special imports like almond M&Ms, banana Kit-Kats and peanut butter Twix, you'll be predicting an extra filling or two before you even get to the till. Check out the far wall, where they've got more than 50 types of jelly bean, including Bertie Bott's vomit flavour!

If esoteric sweets are more your bag, you won't be disappointed with their Swedish candy Plopp and Kack, while lovers of the downright bizarre can tuck into snake-venom lollies, vodka-flavoured ants and amber-toffee scorpions! And to think I spent my childhood chewing on Fruit Salads and Blackjacks.

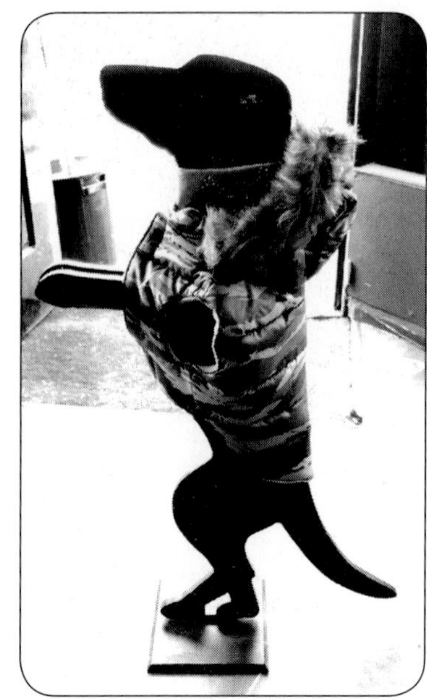

Doggy Fashion

1 Grafton Street, Kemp Town
(01273) 695631
23 George Street, Hove (01273) 777555
Tues-Fri 8.30am-5pm, Sat 8.30am-4pm
Hove Tues-Sat 10am-5pm
www.doggyfashion.co.uk

Offering everything from home-knitted Spanish jumpers and beaded collars made by the Kenyan Masai tribe to diamante collars from Vegas, Doggy Fashion is nothing less than Harrods for dogs. Half an hour in this place and your furry chum could be walking out in style in a bespoke coat, sunhat, diamante collar and bow tie. After an hour he could even be sporting a mohican, as they also offer a one-hour pooch-pampering service.

Thoughtfully placed in Kemp Town and George Street to cater for both the gay crowd and the old ladies of Hove, Doggy Fashion has been a huge success since opening nearly ten years ago, and has featured in fashion magazines and celebrity dog shows.

Pet owners take note though: they only do ***dogs***! The people who brought their rabbit in to be shaved and their budgerigar to have its toenails clipped had to be turned away. Saying that, they're cool with kinky gentlemen who pop in occasionally to purchase collars and leads for their partners!

Go on, take your pooch to Doggy Fashion and spoil it.

Taylors (tobacconist)

19 Bond Street (01273) 606110
Mon-Sat 10am-6pm, Sun 11am-5pm

A THANK YOU FOR SMOKING sign welcomes you as you enter and the wide range of flavoured hand-rolling tobaccos (including chocolate), lighters and Cuban cigars reminds me why it took ten years to kick such a pleasurable habit. Go on, have a fag.

MUSICAL INSTRUMENTS

Adaptatrap

26 Trafalgar Street (01273) 672722
Mon-Sat 10am-6pm
www.adaptatrap.co.uk

Brighton's own world music and drum emporium is still as exotic and atmospheric as ever. Of course, with the advent of the smoking ban owner Les is no longer able to restring a sitar and, at the same time, smoke an entire roll-up without taking it out of his mouth; he can still, however, offer advice on a myriad of melodic and percussive requirements while simultaneously putting the world to rights. Other than their excellent range of selected hand drums from everywhere imaginable, you'll find balafons, berimbaus, gongs and cutting-edge koras (made by the man himself); singing bowls, harmonicas, wood-block frogs and thumb pianos; and for those hard-core loved ones who truly have everything, why not plump for a wooden nose whistle? You can try it all, and the quirky but open-hearted Adaptatrap crew are always available to offer their expertise and counsel. Plenty of info about gigs, workshops and shamanic weekends, as well as teachers for those newly acquired instruments.

Brighton Guitars

24a Sydney Street (above To Be Worn Again) (01273) 628444
www.brightonguitars.co.uk

A proper old-fashioned music shop, housing the all-essential looking-for-a-bassist/drummer/ocarina player noticeboard. Owner Andrew is a keen supporter of the local music scene, often finding instrumentalists for particular events, as well as knowing his Gretsch from his Gibson,

so there's a selection of vintage guitars fine enough to satisfy the snobbiest guitar purist – 60s Silvertones, Les Pauls and even a red Mosrite in case you find £5,000 down the back of the sofa. While they specialise in second-hand stuff, there're a fair number of new guitars too, particularly Tanglewood acoustics and ukuleles (everyone's buying 'em now that George Formby is hip again), and they also offer trade-ins on your old gear.

The Guitar, Amp and Keyboard Centre

79-80 North Road (01273) 672977
Mon-Sat 9.30am-5.30pm, Sun 11am-4pm
www.gak.co.uk

Created from the barrow-boy charm of its haggle-friendly owner Gary, who turned up in Brighton ten years ago with just a broken banjo and the gift of the gab. Since then he has built himself an empire which seems to dominate half of North Road, with separate shops for every imaginable instrument. There's the Drum Cavern, Bass Basement, Didge Depot and Bongo Boutique to name but a few. True, GAK has become a victim of its own success, growing so large that the intimacy between customer and seller has been lost, but, despite that, still seems to have kept some of Gary's "*sod it, call it a tenner, mate*" approach to life. Will accept body parts as down payment.

FLEA / MARKETS

Saturday in North Laine

Upper Gardner Street
Saturdays only, 10am-4pm

This small weekly outdoor market in North Laine has been going for aeons. I must admit I've never found a bargain here but I know friends who swear by it. But then I think this world can be divided into those that come away from a jumble sale with a mint-condition original Moog synthesiser for £3 and those who end up just buying a pot plant. I know which category I fit into. But I digress, get here early and you might pick up a cool pair of jeans, an old typewriter or a good book for a few quid. Arrive after noon and it'll be you and a hundred other people all huddled round a broken cine camera that's going for £60. But, quality aside, it's pleasant to wander down and peruse the junk, and a good alternative to being squashed in Kensington Gardens on a hot, busy Saturday afternoon.

Snoopers Paradise

7-8 Kensington Gardens (01273) 602558
Mon-Sat 10am-6pm, Sun 11am-4pm

Brighton's largest indoor flea market, with two floors of stock covering everything from 70s plastic furniture to toys you'd forgotten you once owned. Snoopers really is a cherished Brighton institution; somewhere to while away an afternoon marvelling at the sheer size of it all and perusing such marvels as Victorian ephemera and second-hand undies. And for lovers of antique and retro clothes there are some good rails to be found in the back on the right. However, if you have a heart condition or are my mother, you might wish to keep away as you could find yourself taking the lord's name in vain while uttering things like, *"Sixty quid… for* ***that****?!"* or, *"I threw one of those away last year and they're selling it here for £200! Aaaaargggghhh!!!"*

Then take a deep breath and thank the lord that Snoopers hasn't yet been turned into a café bar or luxury housing. Amen.

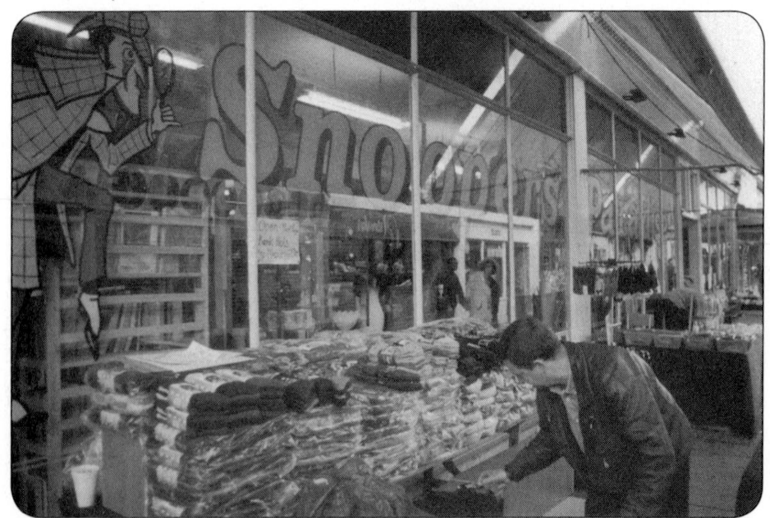

Putting the pun back in Shoppun

Brighton has a high concentration of ridiculously named shops and cafés, which is, of course, in no way related to the high concentration of drug use in the city. Here are *Jonny Young's* top eleven:

Burger Off (Brunswick Street West, Hove)
Brighton Wok (New England Road)
Wai Kika Moo Kau (Kensington Gardens)
The Codfather (Islingword Road)
Pulp Kitchen (Bond Street)
Belchers Café (Montpelier Road)
Right Hair, Right Now (Old Shoreham Road, Hove)
Bright n' Bleach (George Street)
Barber Blacksheep (St George's Road, Kemp Town)
Deja Shoes (Kensington Gardens)
Paws fur Thought (St James's Street)

The West Pier Market

Weekends during daylight hours, rain permitting

If you slept through the alarm at 11am for the station car boot sale, don't fret. A leisurely stroll down to the charred remains of the West Pier after lunch will more than compensate. Here you will find an eclectic array of stalls and friendly stallholders, flogging everything from clothes, books and hats to sunglasses and even painted eggs.

Despite council grumblings, the West Pier market reflects much more of the personality of Brighton seafront than many of the other things built here. Any old seaside resort can have cafés and clubs on its seafront, but only in Brighton will you find chancers doing head massages, magic tricks and tarot readings, writing on grains of rice (no, really) and selling bloody sea monkeys. And long may they reign. Take them away and Brighton would turn into Skegness overnight.

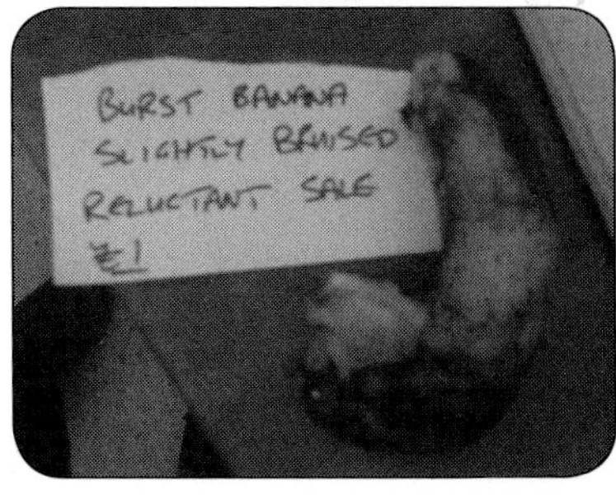

Kemp Town Flea Market

31a Upper St James's Street
(01273) 328665
Mon-Sat 10am-5.30pm, Sun 10.30am-5pm

Keep going up St James's Street and you'll find this bright pink, two-storey building just after the road bends. Compared with Snoopers it's slim pickings: there's little in the way of clothes, way too many shelves of old video cassettes and a paucity of good furniture. But unlike Snoopers, you're more likely to find a bargain or two here: prices are much more realistic and those who relish quirky old ornaments can pick up a pair of eyeless carved gazelles. Someone here clearly has a sense of humour; it's almost worth visiting just for the signs and the occasionally hilarious window display. Is it worth the trek from the city centre though? I really don't know. If only the alligator lamp was for sale…

North Laine Antique Flea Market

Upper Gardner Street (01273) 600894
Mon-Sat 10am-5.30pm, Sun 10am-4pm

Just off the beaten track in North Laine, this place has the odd absurdly priced item but in general the mark-ups are less eye watering than you grow to expect in Brighton. Clamber up to the roof space and there's a rather nifty corner of musical instruments, including a bunch of 80s keyboards for around a tenner each, perfect for recreating that Peugeot advert where the car's engine tuning was so bad it kept setting fire to fields of wheat. They've got a bit of most things except clothing, though for ancient crumbling furniture you'll find better bargains directly opposite at Brighton Antiques, a vast ancient crumbling shed full of the stuff.

STUFF THAT LEGENDS ARE MADE OF

Tony Young Autographs

138 Edward Street (01273) 732418
Opening times akin to Major Major Major Major's office in *Catch 22*. In theory they're Mon-Fri 10am-12noon and 1pm-3pm, Sat 10am-12.30pm

This tumbledown shop rescued from the 1950s has a surreal and curling collection of autographed photos and bizarre oddities. Where else could you get a copy of the homicide report of the JFK assassination *and* a broken banjo? Worth a visit for curiosity alone but treat the owner with respect, he's an old man and dislikes rowdy people in the shop. In fact, I think he dislikes having ***anyone*** in the shop.

BRIGHTON PEERS

by Cool CHEESE

ITALIAN WAITER

LIVES: TINY FLAT IN PRESTON STREET WITH FOUR OTHER WAITERS

SPOTTED: IN OCEANA'S EVERY NIGHT OF THE WEEK

FLIRTS WITH YOUR DATE WHILST HE'S SERVING YOU

WHITE SHIRT THAT'S BEEN THROUGH THE WASH SO MANY TIMES IT'S GONE **SEE-THROUGH**

TALKS JUST LIKE YOU BUT ADDS AN 'A' AT THE END OF EVERY WORD

OKAY-A?

OLD DISHCLOTH FROM THE KITCHEN

HOLD ON! WHY WOULD YOU WANT PEPPER ON A **CHICKEN MADRAS?** THIS IS A **CURRY HOUSE**!!

PEPPERMILL THAT'S **HALF THE LENGTH OF THE RESTAURANT**

HIPS THAT **GRIND** IN TIME TO THE PEPPERMILL

Cafés & Café-Bars

KEY TO CAFÉ LOCATIONS

C	- City centre
H	- Hove
HA	- Hanover
K	- Kemp Town
NL	- North Laine
OL	- Old Lanes
PC	- Preston Circus
S	- Seafront
SD	- Seven Dials
SW	- Brighton Sewers

Bill's @ The Depot (NL)

100 North Street (01273) 692894
Mon-Sat 8am-10pm, Sun 9.30am-4pm
www.billsproducestore.co.uk

A surprising but welcome export from the nearby *Wicker Man* island of Lewes, Bill's is a vision of the future for cafés the world over, overshadowing much that once seemed fresh and innovative in Brighton. Visit for the first time and it's like stumbling onto the set of an old Peter Greenaway or Jeunet et Caro film, such is the vast array of colours, sights and smells that greets you, not to mention the sheer scale of the place. Bill's is a café, delicatessen, epicerie, takeaway and greengrocer all rolled into one. There is food simply ***everywhere,*** from stacked squashes and dangling chillies to pickles, sauces, oils and biscuits adorning the walls at the back;

from fancy cakes like Ascot hats to the pies and pastries behind the counter.

In the centre of it all lies the café space: a jigsaw of wooden tables that can accommodate anything from two to twenty people, lending something of a canteen feel where you might well make some new friends.

As well as the more obvious salads, pizzas, quiches, soups and tartlets on the menu (which may sound ordinary but actually ***look*** as delicious as food can without makeup and a new haircut), Bill's also does a nice line in comfort food: try the fishfinger sandwiches, Welsh rarebit, pancakes or the eclectic array of breakfasts. Or how about the rhubarb crumble smoothie – a pudding in a drink?

Despite being located in Brighton's draughty old bus depot (hence the huge ceiling), Bill's thrives in winter and, should you feel a bit of a gust round your gusset, you'll find the staff whizzing around handing out hot-water bottles on especially cold days – another nice touch.

Unsurprisingly, this place is rather popular (particularly with Brighton mums) and space can be at a premium. Standing at the back waiting for a table during busy times can be a bit of a drag and you might find yourself in the way of those perusing the shelves or trying to get past to the loos, but you can do a little browsing of your own: marvel at the Dorset Knobs, Bill's own range of sauces or drool over the specials on the daily board.

A feast for the eyes as well as the belly and heartily recommended.

Choccywoccydoodah Bar du Chocolat (OL)

27 Middle Street (01273) 732232
Mon-Sat 11am-6.30pm, Sun 11am-5.30pm
Hot chocolate £3.49, chocolate cake £3.95

Like the Monty Python spam sketch, there's only one thing on the menu here and it's not luncheon meat. Unique, sensual and camp as Christmas, this is the café you'd expect to find in heaven, where it's perfectly

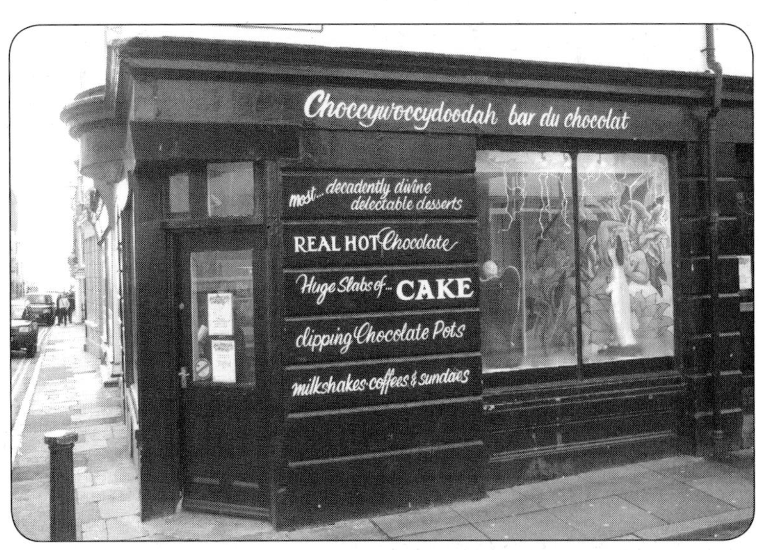

ok to have hot chocolate for starters, truffles for main course and chocolate cake for dessert, and no one gives a fig about their waistband. And it is, of course, exceptionally good; the hot chocolate is made from just pure melted Belgian chocolate and milk and is so thick you could float an egg on the top. How the staff avoid turning all bloated from OD-ing on chocolate is anyone's guess.

Located on the site of the old Choccywoccydoodahdogband shop, you'd have to be colour blind not to be dazzled by the elegance of the place. The windows are full of chocolate figurines and objets d'art while the interior, decorated by chief chocolate sculptor Dave Pop, is full of sumptuous scenes of buxom bathing beauties, scantily-clad muscled gents, strawberries, cherubs and the odd Scottie dog. There's even a private boudoir that can be hired for events, most frequently hen parties pigging out on chocolate before heading out to strike fear into young single men on the seafront.

An orgy of chocolate, friendly service and a discreet trouser-widening service round the back.

Top tip: Ladies, check out their pre-menstrual Monday menu – all you can eat for a tenner, free hankies and repeats of *Sex and the City* on the box.

The Cowley Club (PC)

12 London Road
Weekdays 12noon-4pm (I think)
www.cowleyclub.org.uk

"Is it OK to take a photo? I'm doing a review for The Cheeky Guide to Brighton."

"I dunno mate, probably have to take it to the committee. I can let you know next Friday."

Welcome to the Cowley Club, a co-operatively run anarchist café/bookshop which takes its name from Harry Cowley, a local working-class agitator who campaigned tirelessly to improve the lives of fellow workers until his death in 1971. The interior has a friendly handcrafted feel to it, with comfy mismatched chairs and panelled walls. Here you can buy zines, anarchist classics, books on anti-technology and feminism, pick up a copy of *Schnews*, have a tinkle on the piano or get your head stuck into such weighty tomes as *1983 Gender Issues in Patagonia*.

The café is open to all during the day and offers very cheap veggie food. Cuisine can be something of a mixed affair, depending on who has volunteered to cook – a friend once ordered a platter of roast veg and was a tad nonplussed when a bowl of warm tinned spaghetti turned up. But usually it's good wholesome fare.

In the evening the bar opens. It ***can*** be lairy at weekends but during the week is a great spot for occasional live-music events: its homemade authentic atmosphere is ideal for intimate gigs. The only problem is, to come here in the evening you will need to be a member, and to be a member you'll need to have your name put forward by a current member. And thus the paradox of ordered anarchy doth prevail. The Cowley Club: a tyrannical and elite political organisation dedicated to ridding the world of tyrannical and elite political organisations.

With this is mind it has to be said that, for *some*, this place will be hell on earth: the joyless food, the worthy atmosphere and the abundance of conspiracy theorists and angry anarchists who, if they ever did succeed in overthrowing the tyrants of the world, would lose their cause and probably sink into alcoholism.

And while those views are not necessarily my own, it has to be said that the policy of making available the names, addresses and mobile numbers of political party members with whose policies they disagree (along with encouragements to call them up for an argument) shows such an intolerance for others' beliefs and freedom of speech that there are elements of this place that really leave a bad taste in the mouth...

Ethel ponders the consequences of her bourgeois existence before nipping off to Poundstretcher to stock up on hairnets

The Dorset Street Bar (NL)

28 North Road (01273) 605423
Mon-Sat 10am-11pm, Sun 10am-8pm

A visit to Brighton is not complete without eggs benedict, a coffee and a pose outside the Dorset. As well as offering a range of good beers, warm drinks and Frenchified food – ranging from hot meat baguettes to mussels and a delicious seafood chowder – the Dorset has an enviable location on the corner of North Road and Gardner Street where, on warm summer afternoons, you can sit outside and marvel at the style gurus parading through North Laine. If you're local it's unlikely you'll pass an afternoon without spotting a host of familiar faces passing by to have a natter with (unless you've got no mates, that is) or even have a chance encounter with the bloke who always carries a ghetto blaster and plastic bag full of CDs and takes requests (last time he nobbled me I asked for ELO's *Mr Blue Sky* and he had it!).

Mr Cyclops enjoys a nice cuppa at the Dorset

Dumb Waiter (NL)

28 Sydney Street (01273) 602526
Mon-Sun 9am-6pm

Despite being decorated like the set of a mid-90s sitcom, this laid-back family-run café actually makes a refreshing change from the transient and overly trendy nature of North Laine. True, it still seems to attract a fair number of Brighton's dying breed of dreadlocked, roll-up-smoking new-age community but don't let their bongo playing put you off your food as this is still one of the cheapest places in town for grub and does a cracking breakfast for veggies and carnivores alike – ideal for that Sunday morning hangover cure. The rest of the menu is straightforward nosh: baked potatoes, soup, sausage sarnies and some good puddings (including treacle tart and custard). There's also seating upstairs, a couple of plastic tables outside by the loos and a noticeboard for cello tutors, eco-friendly plumbers and lonely-hearts ads for non-smoking vegetarian cats.

Guarana Bar (NL)

36 Sydney Street (01273) 621406
Mon-Sat 10am-6pm, Sun 12noon-5pm
www.guaranaco.com

Guarana is not, as many mistakenly assume when they see the sign on this odd café-cum-shop, the product of seabirds' bottoms, but rather a South American plant that makes a 'super-charged' natural energy drink, said to put a skip in your step and hairs on your chest. And very refreshing it is too, provided you like the taste of wet grass. It is, however, just one of the many unusual and natural stimulating drinks and herbs on offer here. The closest comparisons I can think of for this place are the smart bars of Amsterdam as, alongside wheatgrass, coffees and other freshly-made brews, they stock an incredible range of smoking paraphernalia (grinders, pipes, scales etc), American Spirit cigarettes, herbal and pharmaceutical highs (Head Candy, Summer Daze), nutritional supplements and aphrodisiacs. Ideal for those in search of a healthy pick-me-up or a mind-expanding experience without the risk of buying a mixture of strychnine and toffee from a hoodie on the seafront. There's also a 30-seater café space upstairs. And before you ask, yes, it does attract more than the odd nutter.

Infinity Café (NL)

50 Gardner Street (01273) 670743
Mon-Fri 10.30am-5pm, Sat 1pm-5pm, Sun 12noon-4pm

This veggie/vegan café in the heart of North Laine was born out of Infinity Foods' incredible success and has the food to match. The menu is 95% organic, the coffee is fair trade, they offer a takeaway option, and there's thorough information on which items support your current intolerance, be it dairy, wheat, gluten or myxomatosis. Expect queuing at lunchtime, though you should always be able to find a seat upstairs and, besides, those salads are well worth waiting for – you can almost feel your body quiver with gratitude as you shovel them down.

Inside Out Café (NL)

95 Gloucester Road (01273) 692912
Mon-Sat 8am-6pm, Sun 9am-5pm
www.insideoutcafe.co.uk

Formerly Jack Horner's (yes, it's on a corner), Inside Out is one of the most convivial cafés in North Laine, boasting a good chef, an interesting range of healthy well-cooked grub and the strangest toilet in Brighton. Open from

eight o'clock every morning, this is the perfect spot to start the day with a good continental breakfast, muesli and yoghurt, or more traditional treats like bubble-and-squeak cake or a lip-smacking kedgeree. They even do eggy bread if you're having one of those regression-to-toddlerdom days. At lunch you might be battling over the seats but it's worth it for their extensive array of panini, ciabatta and other sandwichey things, while their grilled halloumi salad is so good I usually moan orgasmically throughout its consumption. Particularly impressive are their kids' menu (tiger toast is a winner with the ankle-biters), proper lemon pressé, chai latte and the delicious-looking cakes that sit in the cabinet by the door begging to be sampled.

While the décor here gives a nod to the Spanish artist César Manrique's love of cacti and mosaics, and the sculpted white seating is ***definitely*** Gaudi, the two-way mirror in the toilet was the inspiration of owner James and is rather disconcertingly placed to give a full view of the café to anyone sitting down on the job. With that in mind, the obvious fun to be had here is to plonk yourself at the table closest to the mirror for the afternoon and whenever anyone goes to the loo, stare at where you think they're sat, look horrified and mouth the words, "*we can see you having a poo*". If they're new to the café they'll come out with a face like a beetroot sandwich. I know, I know, I have a childish sense of humour.

Top tip: Get here early for lunch on a sunny day and bag a seat on the lovely outside terrace for prime North Laine people-watching space.

Iydea (NL)

17 Kensington Gardens (01273) 667992

(See veggie section in Specialist Food *chapter)*

Jack and Linda's (S)

197 Kings Road Arches
Fri-Sun 10am-5pm and weekdays throughout the warmer months

Located just to the left of the Fishing Museum, this is *the* place to stop for a seafood snack on Brighton seafront. Ex-fisherman and fisherwoman Jack and Linda have been here for more than five years now, dishing out their mouth-wateringly delicious takeaway fish soup, smoked mackerel and potted crab, all at giveaway prices. The soup alone ranks among my top-ten favourite things about Brighton! Sit and slurp it in one of the upturned boats by the boardwalk and pretend you're in *The Poseidon Adventure.*

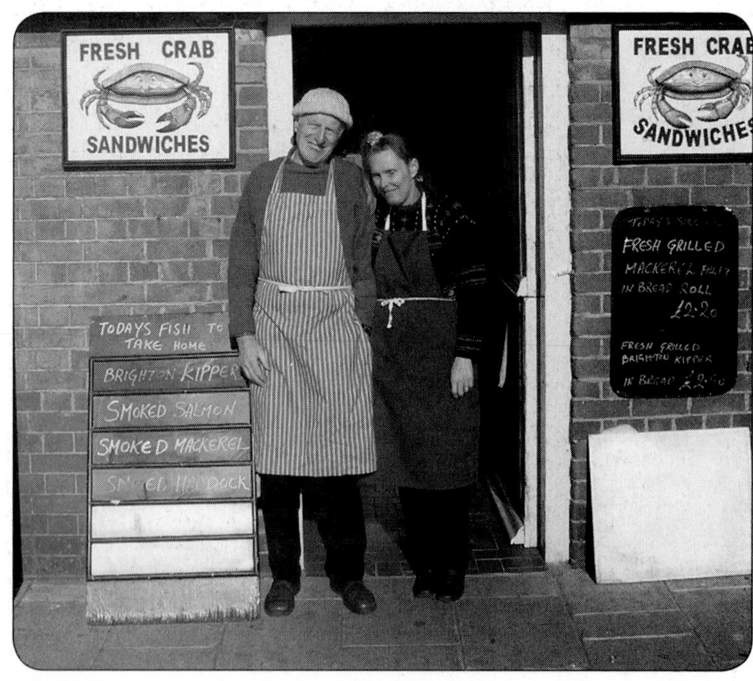

Lady Blackman's Coffee Corner

Until recently, England was in the coffee dark ages. Often was the time I'd order a 'filter coffee' thinking it was shorthand for 'a good one' only to find some tepid brown watery substance from a receptacle that had been sitting for… well, minutes!!! Things have improved but, being a coffee snob from Oz, I still only trust places that have their own baristas. For those who don't know, these guys are highly trained coffee professionals. They went to coffee school. And even did a coffee apprenticeship with a senior barista to learn their trade.

If, like me, you have a passion for good coffee, here are some failproof local delights that will land you in very capable hands.

Gold: Taylor St Baristas

Queens Road 7.30am-5.30pm
www.taylor-st.com

Offering the very best coffee in town, Taylor St Baristas began as an innocuous sideline within the confines of the Travel Bag store on Queens Road. It is the passion project of a family team from New Zealand who have been quietly changing the way we consume coffee, one creamy Bon-Soy latte at a time. They offer many usually-seen-Down-Under menu items such as flat whites, lattes in glasses, banana bread and Bircher muesli. They also are the only store in Brighton to offer Bon-Soy, the best and tastiest soymilk on the market. The name, incidentally, harks back to the roots of its owners, a reminder of the Sydney café life that they left behind upon settling this side of the world. For an entertaining read go to their website; the combination of purists' dedication, stylish aesthetic and dry antipodean wit is a winner. Coffee porn, anyone?

Silver: Coffee@33

Trafalgar Street Mon-Fri 7.30am-6pm, Sat 9am-6pm, Sun 10am-6pm

Excellent quality coffee served by friendly people who know their craft. Owners Amerigo Fusi and Taras and the team use a very fine Monmouth espresso blend, which is a well-chosen combination of Brazilian, Colombian and Guatemalan beans. As well as a full arsenal of exquisite coffees, 33 offers fresh juices, gourmet sandwiches and delicate fresh pastries, all laid out in elegant French patisserie/market style. They also feature homemade focaccia made to a secret Tuscan recipe and the town's only bespoke cookie service, whereby customers can choose their own ingredients for bake-your-own-cookie dough!

Bronze: Red Roaster

This article wouldn't be complete without mentioning that staple procurer of fine local coffee, Red Roaster in Kemp Town. The only shop to roast its own beans and by far the most excellent deluxe Spanish-style hot chocolate in town. *See later in this chapter for a full report.*

Mad Hatter (C)

35 Montpelier Road (01273) 722279
Mon-Sat 8am-8pm, Sun 10am-6pm
(alternate Sundays 11pm)
www.themadhattercafe.co.uk

Something of a welcome anomaly on Western Road, this is a spacious, colourful independent café with slight new-age leanings (judging from its hippy/boho crowd and ads on the walls for tai chi classes and wheat-free crystal unicorn therapy). The grub is a fair selection of healthy salads, toasted ciabatta, pizza, cheesecakes and various teas and cold drinks but with the *Alice in Wonderland* theme you might cringe when having to order a Tweedledum or Tweedledee from the menu.

Highlights include the outside seating area, where you can sit and soak up the sun in summer, spy the sea at the bottom of Montpelier Road and, if you're a resident, wait for the inevitable familiar face to come dashing out of Waitrose opposite clutching a small cauliflower and a bag of rice and cursing the fact it cost them £18.

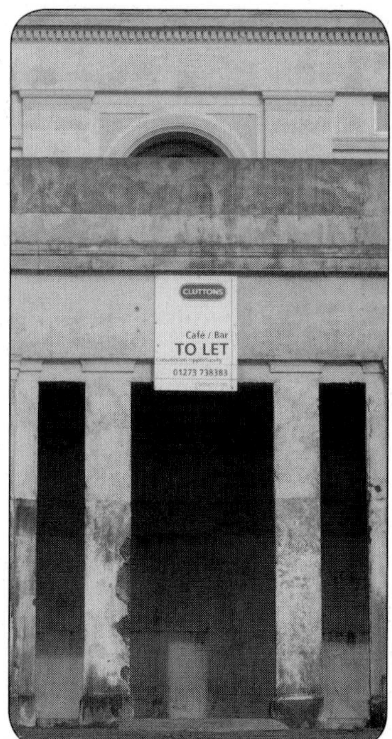

Irresistible investment. Just needs running water, walls, electricity, dead tramp fumigation, and rich playboy with cash to burn

The Meeting Place (S)

Hove Sea Wall, Kingsway, right on the seafront! (01273) 206417
7am to sunset all year round (weather permitting)

Set up as a temporary kiosk in 1935, the council characteristically dragged its heels in allowing planning permission for this seafront café as a more permanent structure and the thumbs-up only came through in 2002! Not one to miss an opportunity, its owner soon had the place rebuilt... five metres to the left, thus craftily relocating from Hove to Brighton. (Well who wouldn't, given the choice?) For me, the Meeting Place ranks amongst the ten best reasons for living in Brighton: it's literally a stone's throw from the sea, the views are terrific, it's far enough away from the piers to avoid the weekend crowds and, on a warm summer morning, is the perfect spot to have breakfast, read the paper in your pants, get a suntan and throw yourself in the sea. Heroically it stays open throughout the bleakest of winters but, as it's a Brighton tradition to make a pilgrimage here on Christmas morning for a coffee, you'll even see queues then. The food is classic caff grub – jacket potatoes, toasties and chips, milkshakes, cakes, cakes and more cakes. ***The*** café to come to if you want the traditional Brighton experience rather than the designer one.

Metrodeco Tea Salon (K)

38 Upper St James's Street 07956 978 115

Sharing space with an art deco furniture shop, this new venture has marked out its own territory (well, drinking too much tea does make you want to go) with a range of no fewer than 17 speciality teas. Green, white, black, red, a rose-coloured one called Pink Pride in honour of their Kemp Town gay-epicentre location and, my favourite, the burnt umber with yellow polka dots. Owners Helen and Maggie haven't stinted on the decor either, achieving a 30s Parisian hangout atmosphere that Toulouse-Lautrec might well have painted while he was waiting for the absinthe to kick in.

Pop in here next time you're feeling a sense of ennui with coffee shops and what Larry David referred to as *"those vanilla bullshit latte things"* and slip into a different, more elegant era.

The Mock Turtle (OL)

4 Pool Valley (01273) 327380
Tues-Sat 9.30am-6pm, lunch served 11.30am-2.30pm

When owners Gordon and Birthe Chater – the lovely couple who set this place up more than 30 years ago – threw in their aprons early in 2006, Brighton's teahouse aficionados were gnawing their nails over the future of the Mock Turtle. Imagine our delight then, when the new owners kept their word in preserving this traditional old teashop. An act which will, I believe, guarantee them a place in heaven next to Mr Kipling.

The Mock Turtle is, of course, something of an anachronism in Brighton. With its paper doilies, tablecloths, brass-dolphin door knocker, jugs and plates on the walls, it clearly revels in being utterly unhip, though for many these elements are precisely what makes it so endearing. And it really has nothing to fear from modernisation. Cherished for its dazzling selection of traditional cakes, omelettes, Welsh rarebits, pork

sausages, homemade jams, its own range of teas and some legendary doughnuts, it's no surprise *The Times* included it in its top 50 teashops of Britain while the late Ivor Cutler declared it his favourite teashop in the UK. My friend Paul loves it so much he was inspired to write a poem about it, which he's learned off by heart and will happily recite to you should you spot him in here (look for a man with a dreamy look in his eyes, covered in crumbs).

For those of a competitive nature, to eat a whole one of their cannonball-sized doughnuts is challenge enough, but if you manage it without getting sugar all over your nose and chin you deserve to be rewarded with a large slice of their lemon cake.

Top tip: In keeping with its disdain for all things modern, the Mock Turtle doesn't take cards so make sure your pockets are stuffed with shillings, guineas and florins before you turn up; you won't be able to resist those lovely cakes...

Café One Ten (SD)

109c Dyke Road (01273) 737310

Just up the hill from the station, the area by the death trap of a roundabout known as the Seven Dials (whose name derives from its Scandinavian creator Sven Dyalls) is also a popular neighbourhood with an appealing mix of upmarket and down-to-earth boutiques and eateries. Café One Ten is one such place, a reincarnation of public conveniences (hence the glass blocks) tucked away next to the bookmakers, where you can get an excellent English breakfast and a continental lunch. There are books, a high chair and sofa, and real chocolate chips on your inevitable cappuccino. Just ignore the baffling net of fairy lights in the window, and all will be well.

Pavilion Gardens Café (NL)

Off New Road behind a hedge
March-October 9am-5pm *"when it's nice weather"*
www.paviliongardenscafe.co.uk

The only café in the centre of Brighton where you can enjoy a cuppa accompanied by the gentle rustling of trees (though you may have to toe-punt the odd nosy pigeon), this Brighton institution commands a splendid view of the Royal Pavilion from its position at the edge of the gardens and is a perfect escape from the traffic and shopping hordes just yards away. Run by the same family since the kiosk was built in 1950 and still baking their famous rock cakes on the premises – if you want to receive a firm dressing down ask why they haven't got currants in – practically the only things that have changed in 60 years are the plastic furniture and the fact that you no longer need to be wearing a hat to get served. The café and surrounding gardens also have the rare distinction of being a space shared equally by that threatened species the Brighton bongo player and crusty old colonels in cravats and straw boaters, making it a special place for people watching as well as slobbing out with a Ribena and nut slice. Essential.

Red Roaster (K)

1d St James's Street (01273) 686668
Mon-Sun 8am-7pm

While the removal of the brown sofa by the counter in 2009 is still lamented by Brighton's hardcore coffee aficionados and loafers, this independent coffeehouse at the bottom of St James's Street remains king in a town saturated with unwanted Starbucks and other substandard coffee chains. Red Roaster is the only place in Brighton currently in possession of its own roaster (yes, it's red); their claims for providing

the freshest and best coffee in town should be taken seriously.

As well as offering the chance to get high on coffee – in myriad flavours and cup sizes – Red Roaster sell yogi teas (herbal drinks that actually have flavour!), steamed milk, breakfast patisserie and baguettes, sarnies, ciabatta and salads for lunch.

This is also a great place to come and mix with a genuine cross-section of the Brighton community. You'll find students, foreign visitors, poseurs, gay men, mums meeting for baby chat, an inordinately large percentage of pretty girls and always one dishevelled, disturbing-looking guy staring vacantly into space (but this is St James's Street, after all). There's even a piano in here which, sadly, doesn't get played, unless a drunk tramp happens to wander in (or was that Nick Cave?).

Come on a busy day and the queue can be a touch slow but you could while away your time admiring the owner's collection of coffee pots high up on the shelf around the back wall, checking out the clientele to see if there's anyone suitable for flirting with, or getting someone to bag the sofa by the window for you.

Top tip: Avoid sitting near the till – the sound of the coffee machine can be intrusive during busy times, especially if you're trying to have a conversation.

Rock-Ola Coffee Bar (NL)

29 Tidy Street (01273) 673744
Tues-Sat 10.30am-4pm, Sun 11am-3pm

Operating as an adjunct to The Wax Factor record shop round the corner on Trafalgar Street and run by Alan Wax's missus, the Rock-Ola takes a hefty stab at recreating the feeling that Tommy Steele (ask your dad) might be about to wander in off the street and strum a few chords while playing bongos with his quiff. The chromed-up furniture and imported US sparkly plastic seating, the novelty cruet sets, and the posters and memorabilia (did ***you*** know Marilyn Monroe used to wash her hair in Lustre-Creme shampoo?) all goose up the 50s/early-60s feel, while much of the food echoes a simpler gastronomic era with dishes such as corned-beef hash, shepherd's pie and apple-and-blackberry crumble. Even the menu's in pre-decimal currency, though your dad might have balked at paying nineteen shillings for a flapjack. Best of all, there's the ancient jukebox from which of the place takes its name, stacked with period 45s and totally free – ideal for playing Crispian St Peters' *The Pied Piper* eighteen times in succession (though the staff ***will*** lob a Betty Boop salt shaker at your noggin if you do).

Tic Toc Café (OL)

53 Meeting House Lane (01273) 770115

I've been waiting years for a decent café to open in the Lanes, with about as much optimism as a Brighton property developer with plans for a skating rink tucked in his back pocket. Now the area finally gets a whiff of North Laine bohemia with the opening of this wee down-the-rabbit-hole cafe. Splashes of primary colour are everywhere, from the giant numbers on the walls to the 50s-style vinyl seating in an odd corner, via clockwork toys and strange framed pictures. With the menus chalked on blackboard-painted doors, it's all rather redolent of a child's playroom from an episode of *The Prisoner*. All that's missing is a seesaw with a grumpy midget sat on one end.

Food is sandwiches, salads and the odd homespun comfort dish; I strongly suggest you try the Belgian chocolate on a stick which comes with a glass of hot milk to dunk it in – like eating a warm lolly.

Despite the unimpressive cubic capacity there's a wealth of different seating aspects to choose from, whether you want to be tucked into a cubby hole or perched on a stool in the window where you can watch people emerging from the alleyway wearing the traditional lost and bewildered where-the-hell-am-I Lanes visitor expression.

Should they pause here for refreshment, the Tic Toc is perfectly placed to keep that expression intact for a little while longer.

The Tea Cosy Tea Rooms (K)

3 George Street (01273) 677055
Wed-Sun 11am-6pm
www.theteacosy.co.uk

"David and James would like to welcome you to the Tea Cosy Rooms. To avoid embarrassment we ask you to take notice of the tearoom etiquette." A reminder that Brighton does eccentricity better than anywhere else in the UK, this royalty-obsessed teahouse harps back to the days of sugar tongs, china teacups, standing up for the National anthem on a Sunday and lifting the pinkie when slurping your tea. The whole place is decked out magnificently with Charles and Di memorabilia, flags, signed photos of Dot Cotton, a pianola with a mind of its own, paintings of the royal family and a bizarre cabinet of knitted creatures. You could easily spend an afternoon here on your own, letting your gaze wander from the Cliff Richard plate clock to pictures of Bet Lynch and the Charles Spencer quote on the side of the pianola.

If you do decide to stay for tea (which we highly recommend) owners David and James will expect your very best table manners, as I discovered on my first visit.

"I've switched my mobile off," I assured David once sat down.

"Good job too; I carry a hammer..." he replied.

But it's good-natured fun, and not to be taken *too* seriously, though they did manage to upset one customer by flying the Queen's flag, the Royal Standard. *"I am the Queen. In residence,"* David cheekily told her. And while it briefly made the local papers, their rules on good etiquette has been a news story the world over.

As for the food, you can choose from the likes of Queen Elizabeth

Coronation High Tea – a superb selection of scones, rarebit, crumpet, caviar, cream cheese, olives, cakes and biscuits, or you could be brave and opt for what they claim is the lengthiest-titled meal in the world. If you do, you'll be expected to read out the whole name: *Lady Diana Spencer, Princes of Wales, Queen of Hearts, 10 Year Anniversary, Your Death Has Torn Our Lives Apart, Farewell Dear Princess Queen of Hearts, Forever in Our Thoughts, Memorial Afternoon Tea!*

Kitsch, entertaining and camp as Christmas, this is a place to be cherished.

Tearoom etiquette (according to the good folk of the Tea Cosy)

The unsavoury habit of dunking biscuits is strictly prohibited and will result in you being asked to leave.

There is a correct way to hold your cup and saucer. Pick them up together – holding the saucer in one hand and the cup in the other. Hold the saucer under your cup while you sip your tea (lest you should spill or dribble).

When stirring your tea, kindly refrain from clinking the sides of your cup. Gently swish the liquid back and forth being careful not to touch the sides of your cup if possible. Please ensure you introduce a little milk or cold water to your cup before pouring your tea to prevent cracking of the china.

Guests are invited to adopt correct posture and avoid resting elbows on our tables.

Conversation should never be louder than two tones above the chink of a teacup and good table manners are expected at all times.

As a display of respect, guests in residence at the stroke of 4pm on Sundays are required to rise for The National Anthem, followed by three cheers for Her Majesty Queen Elizabeth. Un-cooperative guests will be promptly issued with their bill and escorted from the premises (disabled and infirm exempt).

A HEARTFELT DEFENCE OF GREASY SPOONS

by lard-lover Brian Mitchell

For nearly ten years now on these pages I have been extolling the virtues of Brighton's greasy spoons, only to see their numbers sadly dwindle. I have felt rather like a latter-day Canute, trying to resist the tide of coffee chains, gastro pubs and juice bars that has swept across the town. It has been dispiriting to watch the place I once adored for its character come perilously close to resembling every other city you might mention (excepting, of course, in its still unique and characterful lack of facilities). Now Divall's, The Brunswick Breakfast Bar, Becky's and a host of others have joined the Clock Tower Café, Jack Horner's and The Egremont in the ranks of the dear-departed. Towards the end of last year, for a few happy moments, I fondly imagined that the credit crunch would change everything, would tear down the false idols of Starbucks and Costa and restore sanity to the town. But it was not to be. Fortunately, there are still, for those prepared to explore the nooks, crannies, out-of-the-way places and outskirts of the town, some very fine independent eateries where one can still buy a tea for under a quid and they don't just bung a bag in a mug and expect you to fish it out yourself. Here is my (wholly subjective) list of the very best of them.

Mac's Café

30 Arundel Road (01273) 692621

My friends and I make trips to this place as some people take jaunts in the country. When I remember its existence and that, with only a little effort, I can actually go there, I am cheered up in a way mere Nature could never accomplish. Admittedly, it does look a tad soulless with its plastic seating and spartan interior, but don't let that fool you: I have achieved the heights of ecstasy eating their homemade steak pie and seen the Godhead in their bubble and squeak – Mac's truly puts the transport in 'Transport Café'. Also, as it is situated conveniently opposite Lidl, you can, after a hangover-cure fry-up, simply scoot across to stock up on more cheap booze for your next massive bender – like holy water from Lourdes. Make your pilgrimage today.

The Corner Café

Coleridge Street, Hove

Having spent the past twenty years roundly disparaging Hove and all her works in every conceivable medium, I now find myself in the somewhat invidious and (for me) unique position of having to admit that I was wrong. Hove, as I have only lately grown aware, has considerable charms, not least of which is this truly great (and I use the term advisedly) greasy spoon. The city long ago declared war on character and eccentricity, so it comes as a surprise that this place remains unmolested. On entry you will discover a bog-standard caff with small plastic tables and chairs – nothing to turn your head. But go through to the extra-seating area and you will find yourself in someone's living room circa 1983. To use the toilet you must make your way deeper into the private, more lived-in regions of the house. You would be forgiven for, Goldilocks-like, trying out some of their beds for a postprandial snooze. Outside is a small backyard with a couple of picnic tables that feels similarly private and is a lovely place to sit in the summer. The staff are friendly and service is prompt. Best of all, the food is terrific and extremely good value. I particularly recommend the homemade bacon pudding, which once moved my colleague David Mounfield to tears and has certainly brought me close to the condition known as Stendahl syndrome.

Dave's Diner

Lewes Road

One of the best breakfasts in town is available at this pleasant, if slightly worn at the edges, spacious café. The incongruity of mock-Tudor styling and prints of old street scenes alongside a metal picture window and polystyrene ceiling tiles only adds to the charm. The steak and chips is a snip at just under a fiver.

Marion's

Beaconsfield Villas

Once Pam's Diner, these charming, airy premises were acquired by the couple who had previously run the Top Ten Café in Kemp Town. A very high standard is maintained throughout the menu. Worthy of special mention are the roast dinners and the jam roly-poly – possibly the best in town. Staff are also surprisingly amiable.

Belcher's

Montpelier Road

I find I have done a gross injustice to this café by hitherto excluding it from this article. I am not sure why I should have neglected it so shamefully. It has long done sterling service to the hungover of Brighton, and I cannot fault it. I did once have a bit of a run-in with the proprietor for referring to him in another article as a "surly Irishman", but he soon realised, after I grovelled my apology, that the term was meant affectionately. Anyway, whatever the reason, it is high time I made reparation: this is an authentic greasy spoon and the breakfasts are great. Do not, as I have done, take it for granted.

The Kitchen Café

Trafalgar Street (at the bottom)

The food here is invariably well prepared, and of an unarguably high quality. The roast dinners are satisfying and affordable and their homemade sausage-and-onion pie is a particular favourite. I am stunned this place is still in business, surrounded as it is by trendy eateries catering to every taste but mine, but, fortunately, it soldiers on, quaint 50s décor intact. It is, I regret to report, probably the only top greasy spoon extant in the city centre. And thus the whirligig of Time brings in his revenges!

Specialist & Veggie Food

SPECIALIST FOOD STORES

Archer's

128 Islingword Road (01273) 603234

A halfway-decent butcher's is as easy to find as a Churchill Square pigeon with both feet intact these days, but Archer's also has the distinction of being the only organic one in Brighton. As well as a range of extremely fine meats, the odd bit of game and some organic groceries to save you the schlep to Infinity, they produce a sausage so mesmerisingly good it will spoil other sausages for you forever. Be sure to ask for theirs as they also bus some other types in from Chichester. The other reason to go is for the pleasure of being served by Brian Archer: a bewhiskered gentleman in a stripy apron and one of a vanishing breed of Brighton shopkeepers who will berate you for calling a cut of meat by the wrong name one minute and then tell you a blue joke the next.

Bona Foodie

21 St James's Street (01273) 698007.

Just to clear up any confusion, Bona Foodie is a titular pun – a test, if you will, of the clientele's dedication to Radio 4 and all things homo: bona means good in Polari, the language of gay slang, and is pronounced "*bone-ah*" (not "*bonn-ah*"), as in "*that chicken is giving me a boner*".

Pronunciation lessons aside, Bona Foodie is one of Brighton's best delis, with a great selection of cheeses, olives, anchovies and a few delicious experimentations of their own. For under a fiver they'll knock you up the best sandwich you've ever tasted and, for slightly over, they'll let you sit down among their prettily packaged food and eat it. They also do a good line in desserts which should be dubbed Really Big Cakes – meringues, brownies, flapjacks and the like in monster portions.

The Butlers Wine Cellar

247 Queen's Park Road (01273) 698724
Tues-Sat 11am-7pm
www.butlers-winecellar.co.uk

Run by the ever-genial Henry Butler and his mum, this is a proper wine shop that really knows its stuff and tends to favour smaller producers, so you won't find any Hardys or Lindemans generic brands here. You can however pick up something eminently drinkable for around £7, or if you feel like raiding your Swiss bank account they often have the odd bottle of twenty-year-old Château Margaux, and even some wines dating back to the 1920s! Henry also runs supremely entertaining winetasting events (details from the shop) that usually involve some good-natured barracking as well as informative and amusing tasting notes. I recommend booking the following day off work though since Henry insists on every bottle being finished once it's opened.

The Real Eating Company

86 Western Road, Hove (01273) 221444

Though previous editions of the guide have taken this place to task, there can be no more moaning about overpriced muesli since all they sell here now is cheese (and the occasional biscuit). But what cheese! There's a particular focus on Sussex cheeses, which means that they stock the impossibly hard to find Lord of the Hundreds, possibly the finest sheep's cheese ever manufactured in an old egg factory (while I'm bleating on about cheese, there's usually a tiny stall at the Upper Gardner Street Saturday market that has just three or four varieties each week at knock-up prices, but of a quality you won't find in Sainsbury's).

The café downstairs is pretty nifty as well and does a sterling breakfast – and, being far from the madding crowd (ie in Hove), it's often quite easy to get a table.

Brian & Carol Archer with a slab of the "special stuff"

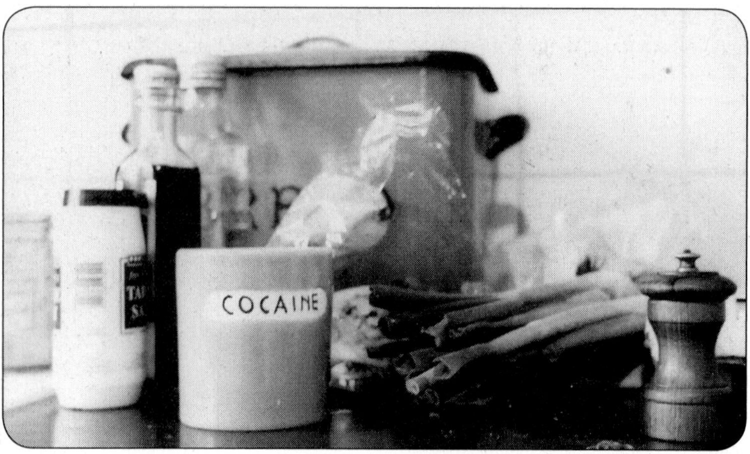

Real Patisserie

43 Trafalgar Street (01273) 570719,
25 Western Road, Hove (01273) 711110
www.realpatisserie.co.uk

These bakers of traditional French breads, cakes and tarts seem to be mounting a takeover of flour-based production in Brighton, with a second shop appearing in Hove, and their bread – including the superlative chewy brown – now stocked by a number of small outlets around town. Their counter is sensibly surrounded by plastic to deflect your dribble as you drool over their glossy fruit tarts, and they make some spectacular customised cakes to order that can even be decorated with real flowers. They're not too keen on chrysanthemums though.

Yum Yums

22 Sydney Street
Mon-Sat 10am-6pm, Sun 12noon-5.30pm

A rarity in Sydney Street (in that it's been there for more than five years), Yum Yums is a traditional Chinese supermarket packed to the hilt with a fine selection of Asian goodies in bulk sizes. The freezers at the back store dim sum, pancakes and a host of other mysterious items requiring Chinese translation for identification. It's a little pricey but, as rents in Sydney Street are astronomical, who can blame them? For the very brave they also stock ice cream flavoured with durian, a fruit whose odour has been likened to custard in a sewer.

WHERE EXPATS STOCK UP ON GROCERIES

Magdusia (Polish)
20-21 Chatham Place, Seven Dials
(01273) 203920

Polskie Smaki (Polish)
36 St James's Street (01273) 606522

Tastes From Home (South African)
28 Blatchington Road, Hove
(01273) 233330

Thai Siam (Thai, amazingly)
Open Market, London Road
07974 204 023

Unithai (Asian)
10 Church Road, Hove
(01273) 733246

VEGETARIAN BRIGHTON

By Joseph Nixon

A typical vegetarian

If you're a vegetarian, a vegan or even a fruitarian, one of the best things about Brighton is that it's possible to live an animal-product-free existence with great ease. Unlike certain towns in this country, which will remain nameless (although Mansfield comes pretty close), you won't be met with a look of blank incomprehension if you request a veggie sausage in a café nor burnt at the stake for witchcraft, effeminacy and general oddness if you enquire about the possibility of a nut roast in your local *("Aye, we'll be having a nut roast tonight alright. Fetch the flaming torches, Bert")*. **So** veggie-friendly is Brighton that I've seen clueless meat-eaters who request roast beef being turned away from vegetarian pubs with a cry of *"sorry mate, we don't do that sort of thing in here"*.

To anyone who, like me, spent his or her teenage years subsisting on a diet of burger-bar 'vegetarian specials' (a roll and salad, without the burger) or the ubiquitous restaurant veggie dish of the day (always, ***always*** bloody lasagne or some bland pasta dish), this city is a godsend. It's great living in a place with so many veggie-only eateries, where for once you'll be free of the paranoia (which secretly affects all vegetarians) that you'll accidentally be served a meat dish which you'll consume with relish while saying, "*bloody hell, these sausages are good. Almost like the real thing*".

The best thing about Brighton veggie grub is that the eateries don't conform to the 'vegetarian food must be worthy, earnest, bland, look like a beige cowpat and taste like the contents of a lawnmower' rule. Some of the stuff on offer in Brighton looks and tastes so good that even your hardened carnivore mates might be tempted.

VEGGIE SHOPS

Infinity Foods

25 North Road (01273) 603563
Mon-Sat 9.30am-6pm, Sun 11am-5pm
www.infinityfoods.co.uk

Brighton's much-loved healthfood shop stocks everything your (healthy) heart desires. Yogi teas, organic turnips, grains, nuts, seeds and tofu burgers all under one roof, and organic bread baked on the premises. Whether you're a veggie, a vegan or allergic to yak hair, you'll find something here to suit your palate. Twice the size it used to be having taken over the premises next door, it's also handy for its notice board (if you're looking to share a room with a cat-owning, non-smoking vegetarian or need a lift to Belgium) and is a co-op too, so you can even feel saintly about shopping here.

Vegetarian Shoes

12 Gardner Street (01273) 685685
Mon-Sat 10am-6pm
www.vegetarian-shoes.co.uk

Yes, very funny, I know you don't eat shoes (unless you're Charlie Chaplin). This shop sells leather-free shoes in various styles, from Doc Martens to Birkenstocks. They've also got trainers made from hemp, so I guess you could smoke 'em if you were desperate.

Typical vegetarian on his mobile

VEGGIE PUBS & CAFES

The George

5 Trafalgar Street (01273) 681055
Food served Mon-Sat 12noon-9pm, Sun 12noon *"till we run out and then there's light snacks"*

Brighton's most notable veggie and vegan boozer offers good food in light, airy surroundings. The extensive menu includes such old favourites as sausages 'n' mash, Thai fishless cakes, nachos, fajitas, burgers (including the Elvis Special in case you're feeling a bit *too* healthy) and (a rarity) tasty vegan puddings, including ice cream. Vegetarian beers and wines are also available, as are a selection of soya-milk coffees. The downside of this place is that when it's crowded (and sometimes, bafflingly, when it's not), it can take upwards of an hour for your nosh to arrive. So don't wander in for a bite to eat twenty minutes before an important meeting/appearing in court/getting married, etc. More encouragingly, they've given the entire place a thorough sanding down so your plate no longer remains stuck to the table when the staff try to take it away.

Iydea

17 Kensington Gardens (01273) 667992
12noon-4.30pm
www.iydea.co.uk

Fast food for vegetarians who abhor chips and ketchup, this cosy caff has quality main courses such as casseroles, enchiladas and their slightly alarming brie-stuffed veggie balls, over which you get to throw as many salads and cooked veg as you can carry. For a refreshing change the prices (£5ish to less than £7) actually reflect the cost of vegetables and the food is tasty

Typical vegetarian family on holiday

enough to get even your carnivorous mates smacking their lips. The place inadvertently functions as a kind of veggie dating agency as it's not uncommon to end up sharing a table with strangers, so brush your teeth before you come.

The Sanctuary

51-55 Brunswick Street East
(01273) 770002
Mon-Sun 9am-11pm
www.sanctuarycafe.co.uk

This well-established and chilled-out vegetarian café has been one of Hove's best assets for many years now; it's spacious, offers tasty comestibles and has an intimate basement venue. There's a good range of salads, quiches, pies, pastas, soups and hot dishes of the day to choose from, and it's all homemade using local or fairtrade produce wherever possible. Those with a sweet tooth and large disposable income will enjoy the excellent range of vegan and non-vegan cakes, and those who just like to get quietly pissed will enjoy the organic wines and beers. Incidentally, breastfeeding is positively encouraged, so you're well in if you're currently milky, or a pervy voyeur.
The downstairs Cella is still host to many evenings of poetry, music and comedy where real actual jokes about breastfeeding can also be experienced. My friend Denise swears she once saw an act here called Fish and Chip Strip, where a girl did a striptease and proceeded to smear herself with… yes, you guessed it. But this is Brighton after all. Sorry, Hove actually.

Wai Kika Moo Kau

11a Kensington Gardens (01273) 671117
Mon-Fri 9am-5pm, Sat 9am-6pm

This successful and popular veggie café (pronounced "*why kick a moo cow*") now has only this single outlet left in Brighton. A second one in the Lanes decided to start serving meat, prompted by too many diners looking at the menu and going, "*eurgh, broccoli*"; it ended up with too many vegetarians going, "*eurgh, dead animals*", and promptly closed. Meanwhile, it's business as usual back at the North Laine branch albeit with a somewhat reduced selection on the menu these days – burgers, wraps, pastas, and breakfasts, as well as a constantly refreshed variety of rather scrummy cakes.

It's also useful to know that this is one of the few North Laine cafés to open ***really*** early. If you're partial to an early dip at the Prince Regent (as I am, occasionally), this, along with Inside Out, is one of the best places for miles around for a hearty post-swim breakfast.

(For veggie/vegan restaurants, see special section at the back of Restaurants*)*

BRIGHTON'S BEST CHIPPIES

Brighton has many advantages as a town, but really good fish-and-chip shops is not one of them. Perhaps it's the embarrassment of other, more exotic eateries on offer that has served to marginalise our humble national dish; or maybe the bank-holiday crowds allow poor-quality outlets to flourish. Whatever the case, to help you avoid a bad case of the runs after sampling fish and chips from some of the more dubious outlets on the seafront, detailed below are (in my opinion) the two best chippies in Brighton. And yes, I ***am*** aware that we have a Harry Ramsden's...

Bankers

116a Western Road (01273) 328267
Mon-Sun 11.30am-10pm
www.bankersrestaurant.com

An excellent takeaway and sit-down chippy on the high street, Bankers' fish and chips are near-perfect, they offer decent portions for the price and the fish can even be cooked in Matzo meal (a Jewish alternative to batter and definitely worth trying). If you're still feeling peckish afterwards, ***you are a glutton***, but I can recommend the cheesecake.

Bardsley's

23 Baker Street (01273) 681256
Tues-Sat 11.30am-2.30pm, 4pm-8.30pm
www.bardsleys-fishandchips.co.uk

Arguably the very best in town and well worth the long hike from the sea to the arsehole end of Brighton (off the London Road). Eat here once and never again will you be able to face the polystyrene-flavoured fish and cardboard chips they dish out on the seafront. For maximum effect it's best to eat in. True, there are no French waiters to rush over and top up your mug of tea or sprinkle yet more salt on your chips, but you can stare out of the window here and reminisce about the old hairdresser Mr Cooper who used to work opposite and do haircuts for 100p. Or you could even plan what puppy you're going to buy from the pet shop next door.

Buddies

46-48 Kings Road, Brighton seafront, just down from the Odeon (01273) 323600
www.buddies24hour.net

Open 24 hours a day every day, right on the seafront and yet weirdly civilised, even at four in the morning on a Saturday night when every pissed lunatic decides it's time for a pizza and a punch-up.

The Market Diner

19-21 Circus Street (01273) 608273
Mon-Thu 8pm-3pm, Fri 8pm-10am, Sat 8pm-6am, Sun 8pm-12midnight, Mon 6am-3pm

The Market Diner is one of the most famous landmarks of Brighton's nightlife. This is your classic greasy spoon, boasting ashtrays made from the foil of Mr Kipling's apple pies, a near-legendary gut-buster and the added bonus of being open all night. Now that the fruit market has closed, all pretence of staying open to serve truck drivers delivering in the small hours has evaporated and the clientele exclusively comprises drunks, deranged lunatics, deranged lunatic drunks and incapacitated clubbers. It is, however, a must for that post-club hunger and ***the*** place to meet and socialise with dangerous people. And hats off to the staff here – they're like experts in linguistics. Not matter how off your head you are, they can ***always*** tell what you want.

The Brighton Bystander

1 Terminus Road, Brighton (01273) 329364
Mon-Sun 8am-12midnight

Opposite the station, this greasy-spoon café will deliver the goods if your tastebuds are none too discerning. Quite a chilled atmosphere if you get a table but don't let them rope you into giving a hand behind the till, as I've witnessed here on at least two occasions. It's also a good place for picking up magazines and flyers for local events, and a perfect opportunity to amuse the staff with the joke *"Waiter, waiter there's a flyer in my soup"*.

Restaurants

There are more than 400 restaurants in Brighton, with cuisine ranging from African, Mexican, Asian, soul food, Japanese and Lebanese to Cajun, French, Italian… even English. But as the restaurants in this town vary wildly in quality (not to mention quantity), this chapter offers up the most characterful places, combined with a range of styles and prices to suit everyone's pockets. So, after all this hard work, not to mention putting on 200lbs in the process, I'll be very annoyed if you end up in McDonald's.

BELGIAN ECCENTRIC

Bom-Bane's

24 George Street, Kemp Town
(01273) 606400
Tues-Wed 5pm-11.30pm, Thurs-Sun 12.30pm-11.30pm (10pm Sun)
www.bom-banes.co.uk
Stoemp and sausage £10

Nothing short of magical, Bom-Bane's is one of the best things to have happened to Brighton in the last ten years. If you're only in town for a day or a weekend, this should be top of your list for both food *and* entertainment.

Set up and run by eccentric performer Jane Bom-Bane (with plenty of help from her equally-talented partner and musician, Nick Pynn), this is a two-storey restaurant offering modestly-priced quality food, much of it Flemish influenced, with a superb selection of sausages and a range of Belgian beers to match.

If you drop by during the day, chances are you'll eat upstairs and have a chance to marvel at Jane's unusual furnishings that include Aesop's Tables, Tablerone, TurnTable and the Twenty-

Seven Chimes Table. All Jane's creations (though the spirit of Wilf Lunn and Willy Wonka are in there somewhere too), some contain beautiful models of Brighton, some seem to move of their own accord, while others set off eerie chime bars when you… well, I'll leave you to discover that for yourself.

But excellent food and quirky tables are only the beginning of your adventures here. Both Jane and Nick are hugely-entertaining performers, Nick for his world-class fiddle playing and performances with the likes of Lost and Found Orchestra; Jane for her eccentric hats, harmonium-soaked sing-along songs ("*There's a Goldfish Bowl on my Head*"), poems and gentle charm. No surprise then that Bom-Bane's has also evolved into one of the smallest but best venues in town, serving up weekly cabaret, film and food nights. It even has its own musical performed twice monthly, a unique combination of a three-course set meal interspersed with original songs, tunes and surprises all performed by the staff, using anything and everything as musical instruments from bass mandolins to kettles and cheesegraters. What other restaurant could demand "*the ability to sing well*" as a pre-requisite to working there or boast that your spoons will have been played before you eat your pudding?

Come here for the musical, a classic movie or a surreal performance night with the likes of Foster and Gilvann, drink too many bottles of Belgian beer and you'll wake the next morning convinced you dreamed the entire night out. If Ivor Cutler and The Bonzo Dog Band had set up a restaurant together it still wouldn't have been as good as this. I can't recommend the place enough.

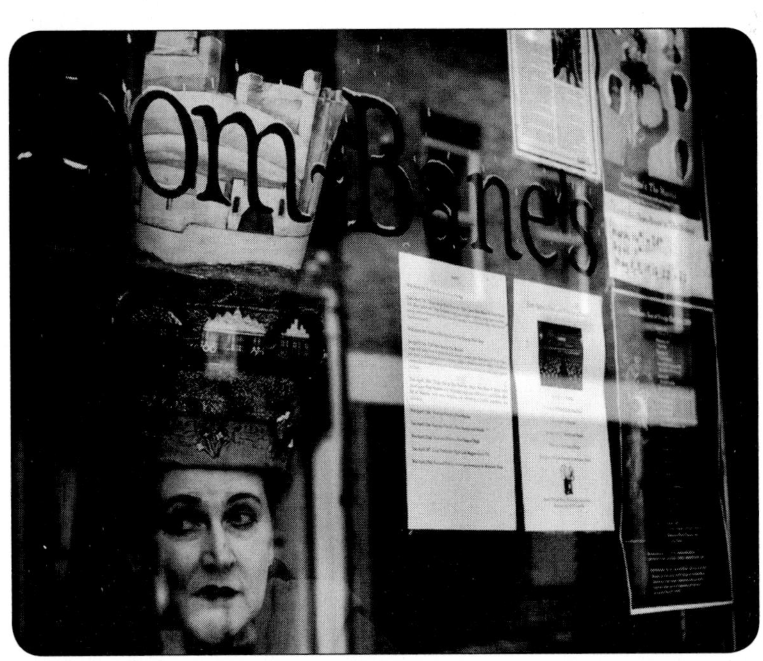

CHINESE

Brighton Pagoda

Brighton Marina, West Jetty, opposite the Seattle Hotel (01273) 819053
Daily 12noon-2pm and 6pm-10.30pm
www.brightonpagoda.co.uk
Set three-course menu £18-£28 per head

This can claim, without fear of contradiction, to be Brighton's ***only*** floating restaurant. There is no point in living if you don't experience the odd sensation of slurping good Chinese food as the waves rock you to and fro (unless, of course, you're the kind of landlubber who only has to ***look*** at a boat to start re-enacting the mushy-pea puking scene from *The Exorcist*, in which case this really isn't the place for you).

There are no quirks to the menu but the fare is surprisingly above average, given how cheap it is – you might expect to pay double for the ambience alone. The waiting staff can be incredibly pushy on a Saturday evening but be firm and they'll let you go at your own pace. A wonderful place to surprise somebody with – the lower deck is especially romantic for newfound loves. If you want to impress without breaking the bank, this exotic little one-off can be just the ticket.

China Garden

88 Preston Street (01273) 325124
Daily 12noon-11.30pm
www.chinagarden.name
Main course around £10

While the decor leaves a lot to be desired, the food here is such high quality, and the service so good, that to avoid this place for the sake of a few tacky features would be a real shame. Having eaten at China Garden several times with large groups, I can vouch that everyone has savoured every morsel, from the hors d'oeuvres platter right through to the toffee banana at the end, with the food receiving nothing but glowing praise from all concerned. A far cry from the typical stodgy Chinese takeaways we've grown accustomed to. And, as far as I know, this is the only Chinese in Brighton offering dim sum, which means you get to sample a plethora of delights and try out strange new dishes. And who could resist ordering "Pig's Skin, Fish Balls and Turnip in Soup" just to see what shows up?

Top tips: Try and get yourself a sea view, as the restaurant overlooks the charred remains of the West Pier. And if you're a veggie you'll need to ask for the special vegetarian option, as it's not on the menu.

ENGLISH & PROUD

Harry's

41 Church Road, Hove (01273) 727410
Mon-Sun 9am-5pm, evenings Fri-Sat only
www.harrysrestaurant.co.uk
Breakfast £6-9, main course £10

Remember how in *The Beano* every week one of the characters would foil a couple of burglars (dressed in black striped shirts and carrying a bag of swag), to then be rewarded with a nosh-up of bangers and mash? Dennis the Menace would be happy here, where they serve hearty, meat-heavy, traditional English dishes that range from liver and bacon to beefsteak pie. Desserts are equally robust and include such classics as sherry trifle and jam rolypoly (but unlike the ones you had at school, the custard isn't lumpy and Simon Timmins won't have flicked one of his bogies in it when you weren't looking).

Of course, there will be some among you who might scoff at the notion of traditional British grub, recalling the *Goodness Gracious Me* sketch where they all go out for an 'English' and try to order the blandest meal on the menu. "*Surely,*" you say, rising to your feet, "*running a restaurant that boasts a purely English menu is madness, on a par with opening a German comedy club or an Italian war museum?*" Well, not Harry's. In fact, those among us who privately assert that apple crumble is a superior dessert to pannacotta, and that roast beef and horseradish sauce can never be supplanted in our affections by Mai Ped Pad, hold Harry's to our breast and whisper: "*Cry Harry for England and Saint George!*"

Generous portions, locally sourced and fresh ingredients (the fish is from Shoreham, the sausages from George Street), reasonable prices and beautiful simply cooked meals (the Sussex smokies and the liver and bacon are justly famous): truly, there is a little corner of Hove that is forever England.

Boss Randall tucks into a seagull trifle at Harry's

Top tip: Breakfast is superb and served until 4pm! In fact it's worth noting that with the menu being **so** breakfast heavy, and the restaurant only opening in the evenings at weekends, Harry's might now be considered more a top quality English breakfast bar than restaurant.

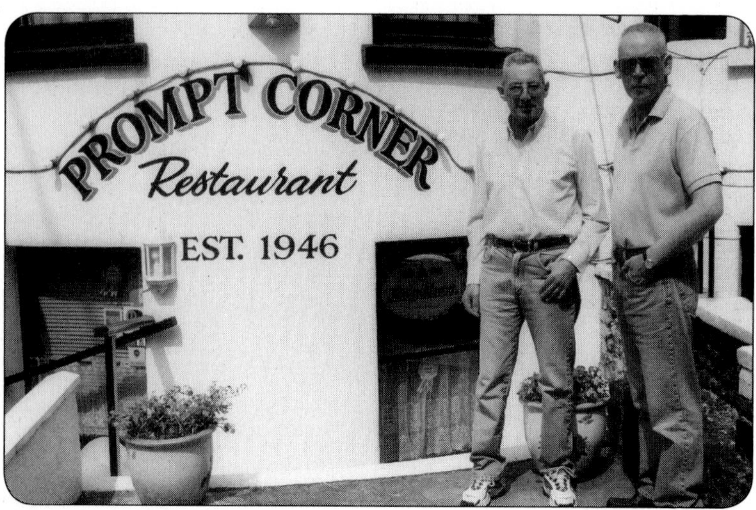

Prompt Corner

36 Montpelier Road (01273) 737624
Dinner served from 6pm,
Sunday lunch 1pm-4pm
www.promptcorner.com
Sunday lunch £10, main course around £10

Since its grand opening in 1946 by actor Bob Dean, Prompt Corner has continued to uphold and cherish its theatrical theme. When current owners Ken and Alan took over in 1979, they decorated the place with hundreds of photos of stars from the 30s to the 60s. Sure, there's a picture of Tom Cruise in here somewhere but, as one customer grumbled, "*he just doesn't* ***belong*** *here*".

And I know what he means. For it is the style and relaxed pace of this golden era of the movies that are evoked by the ambience of this restaurant. From the moment you step in and Ken greets you, takes your coat and sits you at the bar for an aperitif, you can actually feel time slowing down a pace and putting its feet up. Almost nothing has changed here since Alan and Ken took over. In a town of transience and ever-changing fashion, Prompt Corner is a rare and almost surreal delight, reflecting a bygone era when style meant Lauren Bacall, not some floozy from *Big Brother*.

The cuisine is classically English (with a few French numbers thrown in for good measure) – plenty of steaks, fish and seafood dishes to choose from and the likes of chocolate pud and ice cream for afters.

Unsurprisingly, Prompt Corner has had more than its fair share of celebrity customers over the years, from Joan Collins, Frankie Howerd and John Inman to Cynthia Payne. "*She gave me one of her* ***luncheon vouchers***," commented Ken, "*but I never used it*".

In fact, Alan and Ken have great tales to tell about some of their famous customers (make sure to ask Ken about the time David Blunkett popped in) and the two of them together make a great double act, Ken acting as foil for Alan's wry but good-natured quips. Ken has a wonderful way of floating around the restaurant – adjusting a napkin here, picking up an empty glass there – and there's a distinct air of the Peter Sellers about him.

Like all good places with a theatrical connection, Prompt Corner has its own resident ghost. The mistress of a Jewish landlord, she is said to have hung herself at number 37 (now the bar area) and while no-one has seen her directly, Ken said: "*Sometimes I'll think I see a shadow over someone's shoulder and presume a customer's gone off to the toilet, but when I look... there's no-one there!*"

For those who love Brighton as much for places like the Mock Turtle, the Colonnade Bar and the Pavilion as for its trendier brethren, this restaurant will not disappoint.

FISH & SEAFOOD

English's

29-31 East Street (01273) 327980
Mon-Sat 12noon-10.15pm,
Sun 12.30pm-9.30pm
www.englishs.co.uk
Set menu £15-£30, luxury seafood platter £35 per person

English's has, for countless years, enjoyed a reputation not only as ***the*** seafood restaurant in Brighton but, for many, as ***the*** restaurant in Brighton. Unchanged since it opened in 1946, and housed in three old fishermen's cottages in the Lanes, English's is both an eat-at-the-counter oyster bar (which still has the original marble counter-top) and a high-calibre seafood restaurant.

You ***can*** do English's for a modest price but chances are you'll get carried away and opt for the deluxe seafood platter, which will have you delirious with joy when you spot it being wheeled to your table like a mad mobile sculpture.

This restaurant has many appealing qualities quite apart from the food: the Edwardian decor, red velvet furnishings and the journey up two flights to the ladies for terrific views of Brighton for starters. There are some nice touches to the service too – I love the fact that the waiters present the desserts on a silver tray to help you select your choice. And speaking of service, the formal appearance of the outside belies a distinctly friendly interior. Sure, you'll probably watch your manners if you're sat inside rather than out, but it really isn't the stuffy "*Certainly sir, whatever sir requires, sir*", type of establishment that some imagine. The service manages to be effortlessly regal without being uptight. And the clientele ranges from young couples and seafood fanatics to flirty gay men trying to chat up the waiter with a French phrasebook (despite his obvious Italian accent) and groups of old duffers sitting around puffing on cigars and swapping anecdotes about going to school with Denis Compton.

Incidentally, should you end up

Happy oysters just itching to be eaten

seated downstairs near the window in the Red Room, have a good look at the mural closest to you. The original owner, Clifford Lee Jones, is the guy pictured holding a glass of wine. Look carefully at the other characters, however, and you'll notice they all look strangely similar. Apparently the artist could only afford one model, hence the eerie *Boys from Brazil* experience.

Fashions come and go in Brighton but sitting by the window of English's, slurping on a bowl of lobster bisque, eavesdropping on three old queens at the table behind and watching the plebs eating pizza at the restaurant next door, has to rank in the top five quintessential Brighton experiences.

The Regency

131 Kings Road (01273) 325014
Mon-Sat 9am-12midnight, Sun 9am-10pm
www.theregencyrestaurant.co.uk
Main courses £5-15

Yet another essential Brighton experience – sitting outside the Regency fish restaurant with a good plate of haddock, chips and mushy peas. Particularly recommended are their seafood platters: they're excellent value and the calamari can be chewed without having to take out dental insurance. From £5 for the basic haddock and chips to £15 for the Dover sole, if you're after an inexpensive sit-down fish-and-chip dinner with plenty of choice and a sea view, forget Harry Ramsden's and come here instead.

Curiously, the restaurant next door, the Melrose, has similar prices, menu and style, and I've never been able to figure out why the Regency is always much, much busier. Some friends reckon the food is better in the Regency but, having eaten at the Melrose on many occasions, I have nothing but praise for the place. Added to the fact that the Regency lost some of its charm after a refurbishment several years ago, ***and*** that their eccentric waiter (the one who wears thousands of badges on his waistcoat) defected next door, I'm beginning to ***prefer*** the Melrose. But then, being British, I'll always champion the underdog.

FRENCH

Arrogant Frog Brasserie

64 Kings Road (01273) 721488
Mon-Sun 11am-11pm
www.thearrogantfrog.com

I'm surely not the only one to have felt an initial twinge of disappointment at the transformation of this place from a top-notch French restaurant in darkest Hove to a seafront brasserie in 2009, with burgers, pasta and pizza on the menu. But times have been hard for restaurants in Brighton in recent years and I guess these guys saw an opportunity and ran with it. And to be fair, as seafront eateries go you'd be hard pushed to find better quality for the price in this touristy stretch along Kings Road. The staff here are still as welcoming and respectful (take note, Alfresco) and actively encourage feedback on the food and service. The cuisine, while unremarkable in its range, stands head and shoulders above the usual offerings on the seafront, though making head chef Thomas knock up burgers instead of rich sauces and garlic trifle does seem a bit like making Jacques Brel sing Oasis. But with its prime location and well-priced fare, the Arrogant Frog now makes a good place for families, visitors or anyone down on the seafront looking for more than doughnuts and chips to curb their hunger.

Top tip: The Special of the Day is a welcome reminder of the French cuisine they used to excel in!

The Gingerman

21a Norfolk Square (01273) 326688
www.gingermanrestaurants.com
Three courses £30

Having engineered a dignified retreat from Drake's Hotel, the Gingerman

empire has expanded in other directions in the last couple of years, converting The Ginger Fox and The Ginger Pig pubs to their modern foodie focus. So far though, The Ginger Gull in Hangleton has refused their attempts at takeover and remains steadfastly independent. Meanwhile, back at the original restaurant the dining is as fine as ever, their way with a sauce just as beguiling, the dessert assiette of different crumbles and fondants a wonder, and the homemade bread ruddy marvellous. You really can't go wrong with anything on the menu, and I don't say that lightly because I'm a fussy eater who still wishes his mum was there to cut up his sausages for him.

If you do book a table, please don't follow the example of an impecunious acquaintance of mine who offered a young lady a slap-up meal here then, having wound through every possible course including liqueurs, said to her *"ah, you haven't got any cash have you? I'm skint"*.

In Vino Veritas

103 North Road (01273) 622522
Sun-Fri 12noon-10pm, Sat 12noon-11pm
www.in-vino-veritas.co.uk

Often missed by passersby due to their discreet sign, but ooh la la this place is good. Its two French masterminds Fabian and Steve have managed to provide a warm and cosy place to nibble and slurp your way through their impressive wine (they stock more than 200!) and food menu. On the ground floor you can sample a variety of exquisite French flavours from their tapas menu or upstairs choose a three-course menu involving dishes such as crispy pork belly and pan-fried lemon sole. In fact so good is their cuisine that if you're after a quick bit of grub I'd recommend you go elsewhere; this food deserves savouring over a decent glass of wine. The name incidentally comes from Latin, meaning "*in wine there is truth*". Not to be confused with "In Lidl El Cheapo Vino".

INDIAN

Bombay Aloo/Bombay Mix

39 Ship Street (01273) 776038 &
119 St James's Street
Mon-Thurs 12noon-11pm,
Fri-Sun 12noon-12midnight
www.bombay-aloo.co.uk

Worth knowing about if you fancy a sit-down meal and are poor (ie. a student/ musician/actor/web designer). This all-you-can-eat vegetarian Indian buffet includes bhajis, salads, dips, curries and rice for under a fiver. The food is standard fare and there's plenty of variety of flavours to keep the palate sated. Make sure to ask for the comments book at the end: there are some corkers including, my favourite, "*I luv your grub; had a fat poo afterwards*"!

They've also got a sister shop in Kemp Town (Bombay Mix) for meat-eaters, with meat and veg all-you-can-eat for £6.95. Mid-afternoon they're both even cheaper. Starve yourself for three days and clear them out.

Top tip: The St James's Street branch is far more convivial and quieter. Worth the extra five-minute walk if you want to escape the town centre or simply enjoy watching the St James's Street freakshow parade.

Chilli Pickle

42 Meeting House Lane (01273) 323824
Mon and Wed-Sat 11.30am-4pm,
6.30pm-10.30pm, Sun 11.30am-4.30pm
www.thechillipicklebistro.co.uk
Main courses £8-£15, street food around £3.50 each

There're a lot of posh Indian restaurants around these days (I blame the overpriced Red Fort in London's Soho, where I once saw Jeremy Beadle having a red-faced argument with Janet Street Porter over who could eat the hottest poppadoms) but the

Chilli Pickle serves it up in a decidedly more relaxed environment akin to the streets slightly left of Paris's Left Bank. The pink and turquoise decor and industrial metal lamps lend the place a cared-for canteen feel and the service is attentive and exceedingly friendly, though try not to get too relaxed and start plucking at the sitar in the window – it induces palpable rage in the other diners, particularly if your technique is as untutored as mine.

The casual setting belies the ferocity of imagination at work in the kitchen, which covers a multitude of Indian cooking disciplines by corralling staff from Kerala, Kathmandu and Nepal. Their oxtail madras is rightly celebrated by all carnivores who believe you should start at the back end of the cow and work your way forwards, and there are some sublime vegetable dishes for those who find either end of the beast alarming. The real star of the show here though is the lunchtime street food menu, a kind of sub-continental Woolworth's (RIP) savoury pic'n'mix where you can stuff your face with a stupendous variety of flavours, be it the minty marinade of the tandoori salmon or the toasted ajwan in the feta dumplings. It seems criminal that only a meagre selection of these dishes is available in the evenings.

And finally let's not forget the beverages: a good range of beers (tasting notes up on a blackboard for the beer fetishists) including the only true Indian pale ale still brewed, courtesy of the Meantime Brewery – a whopping 7.5% alcohol content designed to survive the long ocean journey to the former colonies, though your own journey may end somewhat abruptly if you don't share these champagne bottle-sized beers with a friend.

Authentic home made, Indian food
made by authentic home made Indians
VEGETARIAN

Indian Summer

69 East Street (01273) 711001
Tues-Sun 12noon-3.30pm, 6pm-10.30pm, Mon 6pm-10pm
www.indian-summer.org.uk
Three courses £25

High ceilings, wall-mounted candles, the gentle strum of sitars on the stereo… these guys know how to create a seductive ambience; perfect for starry-eyed young lovers. But wait, won't all those bright-red tikkas and make-your-nose-sweat vindaloos have our starry-eyed lovers reaching for the tissues a bit ***too*** early in the evening's proceedings? Fear not. The menu here forgoes the bog-standard Indian fare many punters might expect in favour of subtler, more ornate, European-influenced creations combined with traditional southern Indian cuisine. Customers anticipating the usual fiery rumblings in their nether regions after a night out on the curry will be pleasantly surprised by dishes that include stuffed colocasia leaves, handmade dumplings, salmon steaks, almond marinades and tomato-encrusted mashed-potato crusts, and the service is top notch. "*Our menu is designed with the more delicate European palate in mind,*" the waiter politely explained as he brought the hors d'oeuvres. Of course those with delicate European wallets be forewarned – an evening out at Indian Summer is a good deal pricier that your average curry house, but worth every extra penny.

Planet India

4 Richmond Parade (01273) 818149
Tues-Sun 6pm-10pm

Despite the existence of 200 million vegetarians in India, precious few have been inclined to nip over to Brighton to open a restaurant; it's taken a man from Luton to redress that balance a mite with a meatless menu and inexpensive curries like black chickpea or spinach-and-potato that'll barely set you back a fiver. Well, £6.64 for two of them with rice, to be precise, since this place has the oddest random pricing you've ever seen. It fair gladdens the heart to see underused figures such as 67p and £1.51 getting their moment in the sun. To wash down your meal, may I suggest a bottle of the encouragingly named Thumbs Up, the Paul McCartney-endorsed fizzy pop made by Coca-Cola for the Indian market. While delicious, the main courses do tend to lack a firmness of consistency but there are some fascinating and unusual starters to balance things out, like ketcheris (a sort of pea-and-coconut cannonball) and a couple of takes on bhel puri street food that have a wonderful fresh clean flavour.

Now that it's moved from the old Preston Street premises the ambience is rather less redolent of a laundromat but it's still got a bohemian feel in both decor and clientele, and with the owner always padding about in shorts and bare feet you'll never feel underdressed, even if you've come straight from your job at the Pussycat lapdancing club. Recommended.

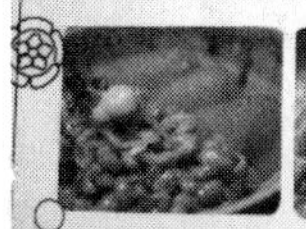

mourn the absence of the bento boxes there are still sushi and sashimi sets on stylised chopping boards (featuring Cornish catches of the day from tame sustainable fishermen), things with tofu, and a variety of hot meat dishes including that weird one with deep fried breaded pork in curry sauce that seems like it should be on a menu in Amsterdam. Desserts are a surprisingly entertaining option too – try the green tea brulée. They do take an awful lot of trouble to explain the menu to you here, which is a nice touch – it's just a shame I never listen properly. Despite previous reviews' guardedness about the level of excellence of the cuisine, I have still to find another Japanese eaterie, in Brighton or elsewhere, that is actually better, while there are many that are significantly worse. To put it bluntly, the acid test is the effect on your digestive tract, and Moshi leaves no sign of an erupting Vesuvius.

And of course the belt makes for top entertainment: you can send notes to people you like the look of or, if you get your partner drunk enough on sake, put on your best Bruce Forsyth voice, stick a cuddly toy and a set of steak knives on the belt and you should be able to convince them they're on *The Generation Game*.

LEBANESE

Kambi's

107 Western Road (01273) 327934
www.kambis.co.uk
Mixed grill £11, chicken shawarma £8.50

A favourite haunt for many years, Kambi's is the perfect size for bringing a group of friends to take the place over and share endless platters of dishes from the meat grills, falafels or side dishes like batata harra (sautéed potatoes with coriander, garlic and lemon), although rounding it off with a drag on the old hookah pipe is a pleasure you'll have to forego these days unless you can prove you're a Member of Parliament and the restaurant is actually a de facto House of Commons bar.

Incidentally, a few years ago there used to be a band of musicians who occasionally dropped into Kambi's to play eastern European folk music. Knowing they did requests, my friend handed over a couple of quid for them to come over and embarrass me with a short serenade while I ate. Instead, bizarrely, they played *Happy Birthday* to **her**, and everyone in the restaurant joined in. She now has two birthdays a year, like the Queen.

MODERN CONTINENTAL

Due South

139 Kings Road Arches (01273) 821218
12noon-4pm, 6pm-10pm
www.duesouth.co.uk
Main course £13-20

As the truism goes, simple ideas are often the best. And what could be a more straightforward key to success in Brighton than to set up a high-quality restaurant overlooking the sea with an emphasis on organic, fairtrade, free-range, seasonal menus and locally grown produce? A staggering 80% of the food cooked here comes from within a radius of twenty miles around Brighton, with much of the veg grown on the bio-dynamic farms of Forest Row. Even their wine list includes a number of English varieties, including one from Sussex which is surprisingly palatable. And they do love their meat and seafood dishes here – you'll find everything from wild-rabbit kebabs, pheasant and lamb to sea bass and specialist seafood dishes, all cooked to perfection (my favourites include the seafood ravioli with lobster bisque, raw fish platter and their Horlicks ice cream).

Carla toasts the devastating good looks of the *Cheeky Guide* authors

While restaurants of comparable quality can feel a little uptight, Due South strikes a good balance between smart and laid back. The candle-lit setting in the seafront arches is rather magnificent (the window seats are the ones to bagsy if you can) and the cuisine faultless, yet the staff aren't afraid to join in a bit of silliness or debate. Last time I ate here, the waitress, Carla, indulged us in our stupid conversation about why you can't buy turkey eggs by sneaking off and going online to find out a few genuine facts (and probably to help shut me up).

To cap it all, Due South even filter and bottle their own water, 'Life', the proceeds of which all go to charity. Can these people do no wrong? Top marks all round.

Hotel du Vin Bistro

Ship Street (sea end) (01273) 718588
www.hotelduvin.com/brighton/bistro
Three courses £40

While the start of my most recent meal here was delayed as I waited for my friend Jason (he'd just nipped into the gents, decided his just-got-out-of-bed barnet needed a spruce up, and foolhardily employed the expensive liquid soap on offer – fifteen minutes of struggling with a hilarious gigantic foam afro ensued) I had the opportunity to survey the murals of saucy semi-naked ladies splashed around the dining room. The contrast with the cool serenity of the elegant furnishings and crisply laundered quietly efficient waiting staff is pleasantly marked, and nicely parallels the range of punters that frequent the bistro. Tweedy moustachioed old buffers inhabit some corners, family groups get the occasional look in, and cool young Brighton couples make up the numbers.

The food is still well up to scratch here if a little more expensive than average, comprising French standbys such as pork rillettes and chicken liver parfait along with more straightforward fish and meat courses, and the occasional surprise like wood pigeon. And of course the wine selection is peerless – even the house red is several cuts above what you end up with at many restaurants when you try to look classy by avoiding the two cheapest bottles on the list. They even have a dessert beer. In the evenings the bar is a good place to meet well-heeled singles (or "*an upmarket pickup joint*" as Jason insisted on phrasing it), but wherever you're lounging, one of the beauties of this place is that the service fails to conform to the French stereotype of sniffy superiority. Or maybe all the staff are faking those accents.

NORTH AFRICAN

Blue Man

11 Little East Street (01273) 325529
Mon-Sun 6pm onwards
www.bluemanrestaurant.co.uk
Kemias £15, Blue Man banquet £20 a head

Relocated to the site of the old Momma Cherri's and originally set up nearly ten years ago by Majid and Georgie, this authentic North African restaurant is a real gem. Taking its name from the Tuareg (a tribe of Saharan nomads who, being supporters of Valencia United, only ever wear indigo), Blue Man serves a plethora of tasty dishes ranging from goat and turmeric

or lamb with chickpeas and prunes to Moroccan omelettes. Particularly recommended is the £20 banquet – perfect if you're with a large group and want a wide selection of dishes to sample. The meat dishes are superb, the Merguez sausages and goat stew being personal favourites. Veggies don't despair: there's grilled halloumi, bountiful salads, fine couscous, cumin houmus, sferica (olive and herb bread) and plenty of tasty hot vegetable dishes. And there are still further pleasures, in the shape of homemade baklava, espresso with cardamom and shisha pipes.

As well as excellent cuisine, Majid and Georgie have got the atmosphere spot-on too. Rather than fill the place with stuffed camels, the Blue Man feels authentic and characterful without being tacky. Little touches like the original desert artwork on the walls and the coloured lanterns mean you can really leave Brighton behind in here – not an easy thing to do in this town.

Top tip: Even though they now have an alcohol licence you can still bring your own booze Monday to Thursday.

SCANDINAVIAN

Northern Lights

6 Little East Street (01273) 747096
12noon-late, happy hour Fri 4pm-7pm
www.northernlightsbrighton.co.uk
Mains £7-£10

Set up by Finnish couple Manu and Paliina in the wake of The Strand going under, Northern Lights is a hugely welcoming and entertaining eaterie, not least for Manu's enthusiasm for the twenty-odd flavours of vodka behind the bar. By the end of the night you'll be the one providing the entertainment, dancing on the tables with your pants on your head. This is a dangerous man to befriend.

The food here is good hearty fare: meatballs in strange brown spicy sauce, open rye sandwiches and pyttipanna (fried potatoes, ham and eggs) all for under £10. The reindeer* remains the star attraction on the menu; sweet, delicious meat served traditionally with mashed potatoes.

Manu gets another customer all horny

And speaking of tradition, it's expected of all newcomers to don the Viking helmet from behind the bar when munching on Rudolph, as is trying every flavour of vodka. There's everything from blueberry to salty liquorice and once you've found your flavour (courtesy of Manu's zeal), you'll be hooked. Fisherman's Friend seems to be the current favourite with regulars, and of course with a name like that it brings new life to the old joke about "sucking on a Fisherman's Friend". Now you can say you swallowed too.

Lovers of the supernatural will be delighted to know the upstairs room here is haunted by the ghost of a friendly fisherman who can occasionally be heard whispering on the stairs and fiddling with his herring. The room also plays host to fancy dress parties, film clubs and a group dedicated to helping Brighton newcomers find their feet and make new friends. This, combined with Manu and Paliina's passion for hosting such events as an Annual Wife-Carrying

**For the record, their reindeer is free-range and comes from a family-bred herd in Lapland*

Competition and Big Lebowski Day seems to be at the heart of Northern Lights' success. This is not just somewhere to eat a nice meal and talk about your new patio; it's a place to hang out, socialise, eat, drink vodka, share some tall tales with strangers and, if you arrive at the right time of the year, get a stitch from running down the street with your partner slung over your shoulder and a belly full of reindeer.

THAI/ORIENTAL FUSION

Sukhothai Palace

62 Middle Street (01273) 748448
Mon-Sat 11.30am-11pm, Sun 11.30am-10pm
www.spalace.co.uk
Main course around £8

"*I've had, the Thai of my life, yes, I've never felt this way before...*" as the hideous song nearly went. And they so easily could have been singing about this little charmer of a restaurant. The proprietess, a lady called Oy (I think that's how it's spelled), seems committed to the freshness and quality of her ingredients, which at the end of the day is what lifts Sukhothai up over the heads of most of the competition. (That and the ever-smiling, petite, gorgeous Thai waitresses, he said, receiving a nasty clonk round the head with a saucepan from his girlfriend standing over him as he writes this.) And while a cosy, homely atmosphere pervades, it always seems busy here, even at lunchtimes – which is the best advert a restaurant in this over-provided city can have and due in part to their amazingly good-value two-course set lunch for a staggering £4.95!

The ideal spot for a sneaky midweek date, followed by a couple of pints at the excellent Hop Poles or downstairs in the snug of the Globe, all just a few yards away. And where else can you shout to the proprietor, "*Oy! What's for dessert?*" and get away with it?

Sawadee

87 St James's Street (01273) 624233
Daily 12noon–3pm, 5pm–11.30pm
www.sawadeethai.co.uk
Main courses £6-12

Authentic, reasonably-priced and newly refurbished Thai restaurant in the heart of Kemp Town with consistently good service and quality of food. Seafood is their speciality; try the crab's claws or steamed mussels, though all the curries, noodles and stir fries are equally delicious. The name means "how are you?" in Thai by the way, which leads me to wonder if they have English restaurants in Thailand called "All Right Me Old Mucker?'

The plates still taste great at Bodega

SPANISH

Bodega D Tapa & Solera D Tapa

111 Church Street (01273) 674116,
42 Sydney Street (01273) 673966
Mon-Sat 12noon-11pm
www.d-tapa.com
£3.50-£4 per tapa

Originally opened purely as a shop with a product-tasting area showcasing the brilliant wines and vinegars of parent Andalusian company Cala & Arrobas, the eating and drinking side of the business became so popular that the focus shifted to that, and Bodega rapidly became the most authentic tapas experience in Brighton. Nowadays you can sit at one of the four tiny tables surrounded by shelves full of much of the stuff you're stuffing in your face. While the quality of the cold dishes has remained startlingly high, the black pig ham in particular being a mouthwatering delight, the hot ones such as the fabada and paella have become a tad unreliable, and you may find yourself picking through them searching for traces of the fabled sausage and seafood that they are supposed to contain. Genial host Genaro has also gone missing, so without his flesh-pressing mingling there's a smidgeon less conviviality around than before. Nevertheless, your proximity to the other diners still engenders a bit of banter (or do I just like interrupting other people's conversations?) and there are even open-air smoking tables in the backyard these days.

Solera D Tapa is the more recent offshoot that serves up similar style in similar surroundings, only with a bit more elbow room and more of an accent on main course dishes. In fact, smiley manager Javier is shaping up to be the new Genaro, so I reckon that's the better location to immerse yourself in Iberian charm and practise getting the gender of Spanish nouns wrong ready for your next beach holiday.

Bombay Aloo *(see Indian restaurants)*

Food for Friends

17-18 Prince Albert Street (01273) 202310
www.foodforfriends.com
Main course around £10-14

Long gone are the canteen service, cheap stir fries, quiches that always made me fart and the down-at-heel hippiness that made the name so apt. Nowadays Food for Friends is all about neutral decor and fancy food. And while I'm not alone in missing what's long gone, it can't be denied that the food here is infinitely better. Like Terre à Terre, the meals are mini works of art and (with the exception of the curry I had here last time) extremely flavoursome. Expect the likes of three tahini dips, stuffed Portabello mushrooms, tempura maki, wok-fried veg and roasted organic almonds, and even posh bangers and mash. And with vegan, gluten-free, macrobiotic and low-fat options on the menu too, no matter how 'Brighton' your diet is, Food for Friends can rustle up something tasty for your delicate palate. And speaking of unique Brighton diets, they even do coffee with Tuaca!

If there's one thing the place could do with a bit more of, it's atmosphere. The bland neutrality of the decor and art combined with Mick Hucknall warbling away in the background might have been a winning formula twenty years ago but now seems a bit lacking.

What is entertaining however, is sitting by the big windows on a Friday night when you're guaranteed to have hen parties dressed as *Wonder Woman* and mulletted weirdos gawping at you as you wolf down your Japanese bar snacks. As my vegan companion said, on our last visit, it's Terre à Terre for bigger groups and mates, Food for Friends for romantic meals for two. Think Food for Dates rather than Food for Friends and you won't be disappointed.

Top tip: Don't eat your wasabi tofu square all at once or you'll have steam coming out of your ears.

Terre à Terre

71 East Street (01273) 729051
Tues-Sun 12noon-10.30pm,
Mon 6pm-10.30pm
www.terreaterre.co.uk
Main course around £16

With a deserved reputation as one of the best restaurants in the UK, Terre à Terre has as much in common with standard veggie cuisine as Nick Cave does with George Clinton. The dishes here are totally unique, change seasonally, and are presented as works of art (many curiously reminiscent of Gehry's old design for the King Alfred Centre). The food is so well cooked that you really ***can*** taste all the delicate flavours of the meal you ordered; there are flavours here that will genuinely take you by surprise. Of course some might find the menu a trifle confusing – try the Chana Chaat or just plain ridiculous dish names such as Wotzyuzu Ithai Gnocchi, or Hellraiser and Cranberry Kraut – but this is merely Terre à Terre's way of showing they have a sense of humour (something often lacking in a restaurant of this calibre), and staff are eager to explain and help you out with your pronunciation.

For newcomers, their tapas are a perfect way to sample the variety of dishes on offer; they even do dessert tapas (highly recommended) that come with the warning: "*Do not approach alone and don't forget to share*". Otherwise, you can expect the likes of wasabi cashews or pickled quail's eggs for appetisers, Truly Truffly Risotto for starters and halloumi dipped in chip-shop batter with vodka-spiked tomatoes. It's hard to find fault with this place, as demonstrated by its endless accolades and awards; we used to gently rib them about the rotten decor but then they went and had a tasteful refurbishment. And if their Boozy Rum Truffles are anything to go by, their ever-expanding range of produce could be bestsellers in a few years' time too. A much-loved and cherished institution.

Dave 'Gordon Blue' Mounfield's Restaurant-to-Toilet Proportionally Representative Inverse-Vortex Manifestation Theory

The quality of a restaurant's toilet facilities is directly proportional to the quality of its food. A flashy but annoying and not very well cleaned or maintained toilet is, therefore, the worst of all worlds. That means your food will be expensive AND bad. On this basis alone I often make it my duty to visit a restaurant's toilet before even sitting down. If I do not like what I see, I may leave. I have seldom been proved wrong in this respect. The inverse of this rule comes into play, however, with respect to greasy spoons: the worse the toilet, the better the fry-up. True. I swear to God.

Photo by kind permission of Walkabout Backpackers hostel

MOBILE RESTAURANTS

Posh Nosh

Sutherland Road
Mon-Fri 8.30am-2pm (not licensed)

Situated in a small van parked at the bottom of Sutherland Road in Kemp Town, Posh Nosh (previously known as "Fanny's Rest Stop") supplies breakfasts, snacks and refreshments to a uniformly excellent standard. Among the usual suspects of egg and bacon butties and cheeseburgers, there are standouts like their scrumptious pork and stuffing rolls, while the quality of their tea and coffee rivals the best local cafés. Other firm favourites are the Specials Of The Day, which can be anything from the nutritious (smoky chicken curry with a chunk of French farmhouse bread) to the exotic (spicy green Thai cuisine on a bed of smouldering rice or, if the rice runs out, a perfectly respectable jacket potato) served with a winning smile and a cheeky quip to keep the customer satisfied.

While you probably won't be lingering on their al fresco plastic chairs on a crisp January morning, if you're looking for incredible value carry-out you could do worse than take a stroll down Sutherland Road to see Lisa & Shelley (and sometimes their friend Lisa II) for some of the most wholesome food in the whole of Kemp Town.

PRESTON STREET

Despite the glut of restaurants in Brighton, if it's Saturday night, you're in town, hungry and have forgotten to book somewhere to eat, you could be in trouble. One of your best bets therefore is to head for Preston Street (which runs from Western Road to the seafront): it contains more restaurants per square inch than anywhere else on the face of the earth. They are of varying quality (so please don't blame me if your steak tastes like an old pair of Campers) but you do have an incredible choice of Chinese, steak houses, Italians, Japanese, Indians and countless others. And if you don't like food at all, there's always Alfresco on the seafront.

Watering Holes

Chances are that during your time in Brighton you might be tempted to pop for a swift half somewhere, so you'll be pleased to know that we have enough pubs and bars in the city to satisfy even the thirstiest of Glaswegians: from the tiniest (Queensbury Arms) and the tackiest (anywhere on West Street), to the campest and most flamboyant (Regency Tavern).

This chapter contains a carefully chosen selection of pubs and bars that not only cater for all you fresh-faced hipsters but are also welcoming to the merely young at heart. Cheers.

Or "Bottoms up", as they say in Kemp Town.

KEY TO PUB LOCATIONS

OL - Old Lanes
C - City centre
NL - North Laine
HA - Hanover
K - Kemp Town
H - Hove
S - Seafront
PS - Preston Circus
SD - Seven Dials
A - Aberystwyth

WHERE TO SAMPLE A BIT OF LOCAL COLOUR

The Charles Napier (HA)

Halfway up Southover Street
(01273) 601413

With maps of the British Empire on the walls, a collection of golf balls in a glass case, Spandau Ballet quietly playing in the background and a good pint of HSB on tap, the Napier remains a safe haven for the 30-plus crowd in Hanover who still carry their own personalised tobacco tins and do a good line in facial hairiness. Only the jarring presence of a TV and video game give any indication of a nod to modernity in this cherished time warp of a pub.

For warm afternoons and evenings they've got a sweet little beer garden round the back with its very own red postbox, which you can use to send letters back in time to 1966.

Top tip: If you're out with a friend, make for the yard of ale hanging above the doorway by the ladies, grab the two armchairs and you'll be immovable until chucking out time.

The Colonnade (NL)

10 New Road (01273) 328728
www.goldenliongroup.co.uk/ the-Colonnade-Bar.html

This is the bar for the Theatre Royal next door and is bizarre at the best of times; the atmosphere ranges from that of a morgue to a Simon Callow party, with everyone throwing their arms around each other, shouting

The Napier – still a popular pre-club haunt

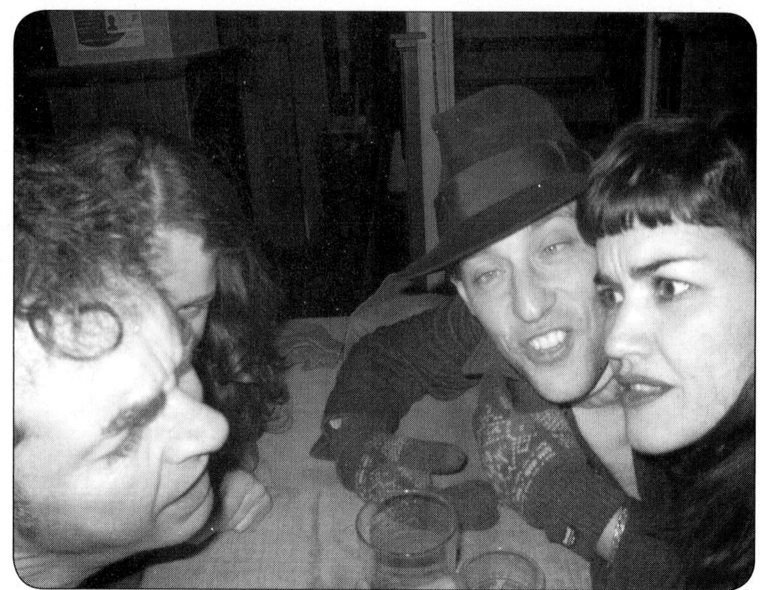

– *"Darling, I thought you were simply wonderful!"* The walls are decorated with signed photos of cheesy celebs (Roy Kinnear, Jeffrey Archer etc) which inevitably steer conversation around to trying to work out who they all are, and if anyone can remember the name of the bloke who played Eddie Shoestring.

While not to everyone's tastes, the Colonnade ***will*** appeal to anyone who doesn't mind sharing their pub with a barmaid singing along to the *War of the Worlds* album, a load of hammy actors arguing over whose round it is, Su Pollard trying to coerce a shag out of the assistant manager, and an elderly gentleman in a three-piece suit who, completely unnoticed by all, passed away several hours ago.

And if none of ***that*** appeals, at least it's one of the few places in the centre of Brighton where you can pretty much guarantee a seat on a Friday night.

The Evening Star (C)

55/56 Surrey Street (01273) 328931
www.eveningstarbrighton.co.uk

One of only two independent breweries in Brighton, the Evening Star is the place to come if you're passionate about your beer. As well as offering such heavenly brews as the award-winning Hop Head, Old Cocky and American Pale Ale, their choice of bottled Belgian beer is unrivalled in Brighton, as are their ***ten*** hand pumps (seven for the real ales, two for cider and one for Horlicks).

True, this pub does have its fair share of real-ale types (those who smack their lips a lot and have a leather tankard hanging from their belt) and it's a rarity to see large groups of ladies in here, but if you're looking for somewhere to sample some genuinely excellent ales and true Brightonian hospitality, this place will not disappoint. The Evening Star is hugely popular at weekends when it adopts a kind of village-pub feel against a conversational background noise so loud you'll end up having to shout to be heard.

Dress code: Bad 'tache, mullet and beer belly for the guys, crew cut for the ladies.

Cheeky Fact *Back in 1908 the landlady here gave birth to conjoined twins, Daisy and Violet Hilton. They became the highest paid perfomers in travelling shows in the US, earning up to $5,000 a week, and later became famous through the Hollywood film Freaks. They were even both married for a short time, which does make the mind boggle about how they all dealt with bedroom etiquette!*

The Greys (HA)

105 Southover Street (01273) 680734
Food served Tues-Thurs 6pm-9pm,
Sat 12noon-3pm & 6pm-9pm,
Sun 12noon-4.30pm
www.greyspub.com

This tiny but celebrated pub has been an institution in Brighton for as long as I can remember and is in almost every posh guide you can think of, including Egon Ronay's. Spats the chef may be gone but his ample footwear has been filled by Roz, who turns out modernised versions of the sensational food for which the Greys is rightly hailed. Expect such delights as pig's ear goujons (!), potted game, goose cassoulet, pancakes and handmade peanut-butter ice cream.

Despite its diminutive size, the Greys also puts on some excellent live events with a slant towards such blues and folk heroes as Bridget St John and Martin Carthy, and some quality storytelling and comedy. Check out the poster-lined stairwell for past illustrious performers, then see if you can guess where the stage normally goes – you're probably sitting on it. Combine this with some select Belgian beers and a conviviality that'll find you talking to strangers for hours on end and you have a pub that really has no need of lava lamps and designer furniture to create personality. The Greys attracts a hardcore following of Hanoverians of all ages, most of whom seem to be on first-name terms with each other.

Speaking of which, apologies are due to landlord Clarence – the previous edition of this guide got his name wrong and he subsequently endured six months of cheeky locals deliberately referring to him as 'Mike'. And a bit of eavesdropping at the bar never goes amiss, like the time I heard an old guy saying to his mate: *"...so she's embarked on this four-year aromatherapy course... two years for each nostril".*

Highly recommended.

The Hand in Hand (K)

33 Upper St James's Street (01273) 602521

The place for lovers of real ale, the Hand in Hand is the last pub in Brighton where the beer is actually brewed locally. Instead of spending £3.50 on a pint of gassy rubbish, treat yourself to a creamy pint of Black Moggy or try the Olde Trout ("*named after the landlady,*" according to the landlord). They also do a good line in German beers and hard-boiled eggs.

A one-room bar, the Hand in Hand is decorated with newspaper stories (Kennedy's assassination's up there somewhere), has a working one-armed bandit by the door, naked Victorian ladies on the ceiling (pictures, not real ones), a piano that actually gets used, a rather pointless collection of ties and nearly always a friendly dog or two loping around.

Worth noting however, is that this is a very small pub. Most of the week you'll have no difficulty finding a seat as there'll just be:

a) You
b) A table of students
c) A couple who look like extras from *Last of the Summer Wine*
d) An old Irishman called James who'll show you his scars from when he was shot and stabbed (whether you want to see them or not)
e) A pissed bloke at the bar boring the barmaid.

At weekends however, it can get busy, so prepare to be standing. It's not so bad though, chances are you'll fall into conversation with someone. And if they start to show you their scars, you'll know who...

Top tip: Check out the landlord's funny blackboard messages outside.

The Heart and Hand (NL)

75 North Road (01273) 624799

The marmite of Brighton pubs, you'll either find this antiquated North Laine pub unfriendly, cliquey and cramped or you'll worship the place. If you play in a guitar band it's more likely to be the latter as this remains ***the*** hangout for Brighton musos. The reason for this is simple – the pub's famous jukebox, which features the likes of Love, The Electric Prunes, Scott Walker and Tim Buckley. Weekends in here you can play "spot the bassist from..." as denim-clad blokes with interesting hair spill Guinness down your back while they stand around arguing loudly about the Beach Boys. Juxtaposed with the muso crowd you'll find North Laine traders, old-school antiques dealers, spivs and wrinkly old soaks. Or was that Peter and the Test Tube Babies?

ANYONE FOUND LIFTING THE LID OR
ADJUSTING THE VOLUME
ON THE JUKE BOX WILL BE SEVERELY
BEATEN BY BERT
YOU HAVE BEEN WARNED!!!!!!
PLAYS
ROCK-OLA 477
RESET
SCOTT WALKER
SMALL FACES

And if you use the toilet without buying a drink, the Heart and Hand's affable landlord Bert will force-feed you your own faeces

One Hove Place (H)

43 First Avenue (01273) 738266

Imagine for a moment that, through no fault of your own, you find yourself in Darkest Hove and desperately in need of a drink. This could be the answer to your fervent prayer. Let's be clear though – under no circumstances should you glance at the carpet in the main bar lest it induce an acid flashback or at least mild nausea. This odd little basement bar does have a few more welcome tricks up its sleeve though, not least in the form of the grand oak-panelled room immediately at the foot of the entrance steps, where you can sit and toy with your frilly cuffs as if awaiting Sir Philip Sydney's pleasure in his vestibule. Outdoors there are two oases of calm: choose from the rear "Italian" garden for a good nose at the well-heeled neighbours' horticultural misadventures, or the front terrace where you can get a view of the sea without having your hair ruffled by Brighton's mistral.

Punter-wise this place still attracts a contingent of heavy gold jewellery-bestrewn blokes discussing the best way to tarmac a flat roof but it's generally a mixed crowd with a far more congenial atmosphere than you'll find in most pubs in the area. This is Hove, remember, where shouting at yourself in public is the norm.

The Quadrant (C)

12-13 North Street 0871 917 0007

Bang in the centre of town, the Quadrant has survived years of closure thanks to nearby building work, and a facelift that (mercifully) didn't deprive it of its charm. While upstairs has been gentrified somewhat (flock wallpaper and tasteful Georgian scenes on the wall) it now feels like a homely old gentlemen's club, perfect for the spoken-word nights that are occasionally held here. The windy staircase that leads up here must still vie for steepest and longest in Brighton; the journey from the top bar to the gents in the basement is a pretty mammoth expedition – if you suffer from a weak bladder I'd stick to shorts or hide an empty milk bottle down your trousers.

Downstairs remains the same, like some miniature old-school London boozer but with the all-important sepia prints of a bygone Brighton, that beautiful glass, and after-hours office workers sinking pints and gossiping about the latest fumblings in the photocopying room. At weekends, the presence of a security guard may be too sobering a reminder that you're only a stone's throw from the ghastly West Street, otherwise this is the perfect city-centre pub for an early evening or cheeky afternoon pint.

A Cheeky Tale

Years ago they used to have a bar upstairs at the Quadrant. My friend Gerard – a comedian – used to work there at weekends and regularly help himself to drinks. One evening, blind drunk, he staggered home with his girlfriend, who happened to mention that she liked the handbag in the shop they were passing.

"I'll get it for you," said Gerard, and put his elbow through the window before she could stop him.

Realising his folly, Gerard ran home and hid in a cupboard above the kitchen door.

A few minutes later the police arrived, following a tip-off. Let in by Gerard's girlfriend, they searched the house to no avail, but just as they were about to leave, they heard a noise from the cupboard. One policeman asked if anyone was in there.

Unable to resist the comic opportunity of a lifetime, Gerard cried out *"No!"*

After several hours of questioning, the police decided to let him off with a caution, putting the incident down to 'high jinks', combined with the pity they felt after Gerard's heart-wrenching and shamefaced confession that he was a closet transvestite.

The Ranelagh Arms (K)

2 High Street, on corner of St James's Street (01273) 681634

So I walk in here one Easter Sunday to meet friends, and I'm confronted by two guys doing the Hokey Cokey to the orchestral break in the Beatles' *Day in the Life* (?!), while at one of the tables near the bar, a guy is shouting, *"I've taken more acid then every fucker in here. And anyone who says not is a fucking liar!"* Welcome to another St James's Street anomaly. Sandwiched between gay bars and posh restaurants lies the Ranelagh, the last bastion (in Kemp Town at least) of the professional beer belly, blues aficionados and musicians with corrugated faces. Come and meet an array of characters, from friendly middle-aged blokes with ponytails and leather waistcoats to the kind of person one might simply describe as potentially violent.

The music-themed decor ranges from the quaint to the naff, with albums stuck to the ceiling, pennies glued on the bar, banjos, guitars and accordions everywhere and a few dodgy photos and illustrations of old guitar legends on the walls. The Ranelagh does still pay homage to its theme, offering live music every Sunday, from boogie-woogie pianists to blues guitarists. And this, of course, is the time to experience the pub at its best. Otherwise, it's the perfect starting point for anyone foolish enough to take the challenge of a Tuesday night 'alternative' Kemp Town pub crawl.

The Regency Tavern (C)

32 Russell Square (01273) 325652
Food served lunchtimes and evenings, except weekends when it's only till 4pmish

A colourful local with a genuinely eclectic clientele, the Regency Tavern has gay couples, locals, grannies, students and hammy old actors all mucking in together amongst the kitsch splendour of gold-leaf palm trees, bright-green wallpaper, plastic flowers and plaster cherubs. Part of the charm of this old Victorian boozer is the utterly OTT decor, which could easily pass as a set from *The Avengers*. Even the gents is decorated with a glitterball and mirrored tiles.

Being one of Brighton's two remaining 19th-century 'beer houses' (the other is the Druids Head), when anyone could start selling beer from their front room without a licence, the Regency retains some of the atmosphere of popping round your mate's place for a drink, albeit one with distinctly flamboyant tastes who doesn't leave empty pizza boxes on the sofa. A change of management here means that birthdays are no longer celebrated by firing bubble guns in your face, more's the pity, although they are still *"contractually obliged"* to play their eccentric, operatic version of *Happy Birthday*, and rest assured that the disco mirrorball will be twirling as merrily as the batty old Brunswick landlady who will try to drag you out of your seat to do the Black Bottom. Still the campest pub in Brighton.

FASHIONABLE DRINKING DENS

The Bee's Mouth (H)

10 Western Road, Hove (01273) 770083

Inauspiciously flanked by kebab shops and often camouflaged by a dense throng of smokers, the Bee's Mouth will reward your penetrative persistence once you burrow inside as a moody twilight world awaits.

With cosy booths, trumpet candleholders and spinning heads beneath the bar, the Bee's Mouth feels more like a bohemian hangout from 60s Paris than a Brighton boozer, with only the expensive wine list on the blackboard at odds with its eccentric, down-at-heel decor.

Squeeze past the bar and you'll find a chilled-out area at the back with a curtained corner for canoodling couples, and if you're feeling brave venture into the basement performance area (Wednesday open-mic nights are pretty wild down here) where there's some truly disturbing artwork fit to rival Hancock's *Aphrodite at the Waterhole*.

My one whinge is that there're only two toilets, one of which is so miniscule you have to back into it, so form an orderly queue ladies and gents. On the other hand you will make lots of friends while you're comparing notes on gender differences in approaches to toilet hygiene, so if you're after an attractive arty crowd, enjoy the occasional slice of far-out jazz, and don't mind rubbing shoulders and probably other body parts too on busy weekends, the Bee's Mouth will deliver. Highly recommended.

The Barley Mow (K)

92 St Georges Road (01273) 682259
Food served 11am-10pm

This convivial Kemp Town local is the Michael Palin of Brighton pubs: an all-round good egg, thoroughly entertaining and prone to the odd bit of silliness. It boasts a big heated beer garden to keep the smokers happy, a great range of ales, free board games, sells rolling tobacco behind the bar (often the hallmark of a good pub), does roast dinners until 10pm and has an old-school tuckshop selling the likes of Texans and flying saucers. Where else in Brighton could you have a pint of Harveys with a banana candy top? Guinness and Chomp chaser? Malibu and Kinder Surprise? Plus it's the only pub in Brighton – or the world, for that matter – to have a 'sperm table'. But you'll have to discover what that is for yourself.

Top tip: I know I've already mentioned it but it bears repeating that the Barley Mow does pub grub until 10pm!

The Eagle (NL)

125 Gloucester Road (01273) 607765
Food served 12noon-9pm most days

Probably the most critical aspect of a pub is the kind of conviviality you get from behind the bar. The place can look like a skip that's previously been set on fire for all I care as long as you get a chirpy warm welcome from the staff. And after a disagreeable experience in here a couple of years ago when a particularly obnoxious member of staff spent fifteen minutes talking to his mate on his mobile while everyone waiting at the bar got **very** pissed off, the Eagle still doesn't seem to have learned the vital art of customer care, as some friends found out recently:

Friends: "*Hello, are you serving food yet?*"
Barstaff (looking rather annoyed at having their discussion interrupted): "*No*".

The barstaff return to their discussion and my friends, realising they were not going to receive any information on when food service might start, if ever, went over the road to the Basketmakers instead.

It has to be said though, since the Eagle is owned by the same bunch as the Hop Poles the cuisine *is* worth sampling despite the belligerence of certain staff members. It's best therefore to come in the evening when they're less likely to be suffering from the previous night's come-down and taking it out on the customers...

Oi fuckheads! Who's the wanker who ordered braised auk on a bed of pureéd moss? Come and get it before I shit on it

Earth and Stars (NL)

46 Windsor Street (near the top of Church Street) (01273) 722879
Food served Mon-Sat 12noon-10pm, Sun 12noon-6pm

Brighton's most environmentally friendly pub, the Earth and Stars is carbon-balanced, has solar panels on its roof and used to pride itself on being 100% organic, from the beers, wines, soft drinks, peanuts and roast dinners to the floorboards, loo paper and staff. Ask for a pack of fags and you'll still get American Spirit, but they've been forced to cave in on the beers – alongside the Freedom organic lager are now ranked the labels of oppression, Kronenbourg and Amstel. This is still a dimly-lit, pleasantly woody and often reggae-tastic chill zone though, and seems to continue gently buzzing throughout the week, pulling in drinkers of all ages and lovers of semi-organic food. I had a rather extraordinary meal here of lamb shank crashlanded into a shepherd's pie along with the usual mince. Oh, and there was bacon on the side too in case one was dissatisfied with the extent of one's meat ration.

Smokers are catered to upstairs with a frankly bizarre erection (nothing wrong with that) involving a wooden platform nailed onto the outside of the building, surrounded by an eight-foot-high panel fence to keep you from falling off. Apparently the weight limit is 28 persons, so before entering it's customary to poke your head out, count the assembled, and then shout out the new total as you light up. Don't wittily shout "*37!*" though unless you want to be killed in the stampede for the doorway.

The Foundry (NL)

13-14 Foundry Street (01273) 697014

Staggering groggily out of the snowstorm that was the distinctly dangerous Pedestrians pub, the tiny little one bar Foundry has quickly found its feet with a simple but charming recipe; an open fire, weatherbeaten red leather sofas and chairs, wax and wick powered wall candelabra, well kept beers, and pizzas made on the bar in giant Breville-style toasters (mind your fingers if you're sitting at the bar when they're on though, or you may add an unintended extra topping of toasted human flesh). Despite its relatively recent opening, the pub seems to have already gained a faithful clientele primarily amongst a friendly 20s/early 30s crowd, proving you don't need expensive refits and silly pub names to draw the punters. And as one of Brighton 's vanishingly rare independent boozers it warrants the support.

The Globe (OL)

78 Middle Street (01273) 727114

This place has gone full circle in ten years, from being a pleasant seafront local called the Globe to a garish turquoise hellhole (the Squid & Starfish) and back again. The blood-red walls and shelves of books downstairs add a welcoming boudoir-cum-library feel to the place. Being so close to the seafront, however, the Globe's elegance does evaporate somewhat at weekends, when it packs out with the seafront clubbing crowd who can get a touch lairy and the music often way, way too loud. Like the Cricketers down the road, it's ***much*** better to experience the Globe mid-week when you can hear yourself speak, get a seat and enjoy the hard work that's gone into making this a good boozer. Better still, pop in for a cracking Sunday lunch. It's a touch on the gloomy side during the day but you can still marvel at such singular features as the mechanized colonial-style fan, the Betty Boop statuette, the mini library

Aah, lovely ladies

areas downstairs and the album-sleeve menu holders (We had *Hits of the 80s* last time I was in).

The Fortune of War (S)

157 Kings Road Arches (01273) 205065

This long-established seafront pub gets stupidly busy during the summer weekends when it is mobbed by seafront crowds. In fact, be prepared to experience such a long and frustrating wait at the bar that you'll wish you'd simply gone to the off licence and headed straight to the beach with some bottles. Come off-season, however, and you'll discover that it's actually quite a charming bar. Like the inside hull of an old wooden boat, the upstairs has plenty of charm and some good seating areas, though if they haven't fixed the wobbly pew at the far end, you might end up on your backside with a Pernod and black all down your new shirt.

Top tip: Arrive early, bag yourself the window seat with a sea view and you'll be loath to leave.

The Hop Poles (OL)

13 Middle Street
(01273) 710444/710010
Food served 12noon-9pm weekdays,
Fri-Sat 12noon-7pm, Sun 12noon-9pm

Once called the Spotted Dog, the Hop Poles thrives on a tradition of good-value quality food, sweets behind the bar and a gay-friendly attitude, while those with flexible necks can also enjoy their wacky car hubcap sculptures by the mysterious Ptolemy – seek out the reptilian one.

The pub is popular (perhaps too popular if you expect to sit anywhere other than the beer garden) with a young, fashionable, mixed gay/straight crowd and, unlike so many others in the vicinity, does not attract the weekend nutters.

The only stain on its character is the exclusion of any decent ales in favour of Greene King, the choice of masochists everywhere. And there's no shortage of ***them*** in this kinky town.

here recently and simply delivered our chipless meals with a shrug, I'd be more inclined to recommend the grub.

Om Lounge (S)

5 Steine Street
(01273) 607304
www.ombrighton.co.uk

Modern cocktail bars often seem to me to be fairly humdrum affairs where the elegance and frivolousness of the 1920s has been exchanged for a few fairy lights and a chunk of grapefruit.

Tucked away down a narrow side street a doughnut's throw from the pier though is this exotic den, offering a sensory overload of Asia-influenced decor and tropical tipples. Massive backlit murals of Hindu deities and naughty naked ladies (or were they naughty naked deities? That may have just been one of my many recurring dreams) loom over rolling hills of plump satin scatter cushions and there's enough bamboo in this place to keep a family of five pandas going for a month.

The Asian theme even seeps into the cocktails too, with ingredients such as chilli, lemongrass, coconut, basil and mangosteen, the latter reputedly much cherished by Queen Victoria, particularly following a couple of tequila slammers.

Upstairs there's a weekend club called the Spirit Loft but slide downstairs on the giant bamboo handrail to discover the unisex toilets, where you can break wind and boogie at the same time to the only water closet-based DJ in Brighton. There's even a cluster of miniature mirrorballs over the decks and a chaise longue if you want to take the weight off your latest release and soak up the lavatorial ambience. Most refreshing.

The Open House (PC)

146 Springfield Road (01273) 880102
Food served daily 12noon-9pm

One of the only decent pubs in this neck of the woods (by London Road Station) and still the best place for a post-film discussion and pint after an evening at the Duke of York's.

The Open House is decorated with colourful art , has a covered garden area (thumbs up from the smokers) and three big seating areas, including one which resembles a living room – being as it's full of sofas, paintings on the walls and the occasional pair of pants on the floor by the telly.

Most of the food here is locally sourced and organic, and if they hadn't run out of chips when I came

The Reservoir (HA)

1 Howard Road (01273) 269728

Food served Sunday only 12noon-6pm

Home to some of the nicest barstaff in town (so consistently that I suspect they have a special training programme or possibly electro-shock therapy built into the beer taps), the Reservoir is one of the top dogs of the Hanover pub scene, effortlessly blending a clean modern vibe with old-fashioned pub staples; there's constantly interesting guest ales, fantastic Sunday roasts by local culinary whizz Alexander, and their legendary Sunday quiz hosted by Coz, whose mastery of the iPod during the music round is always fodder for good-natured abuse. Well, mostly good natured; he did snap under the weight of heckling one week and loudly threatened to bring in a machine gun and mow everybody down.

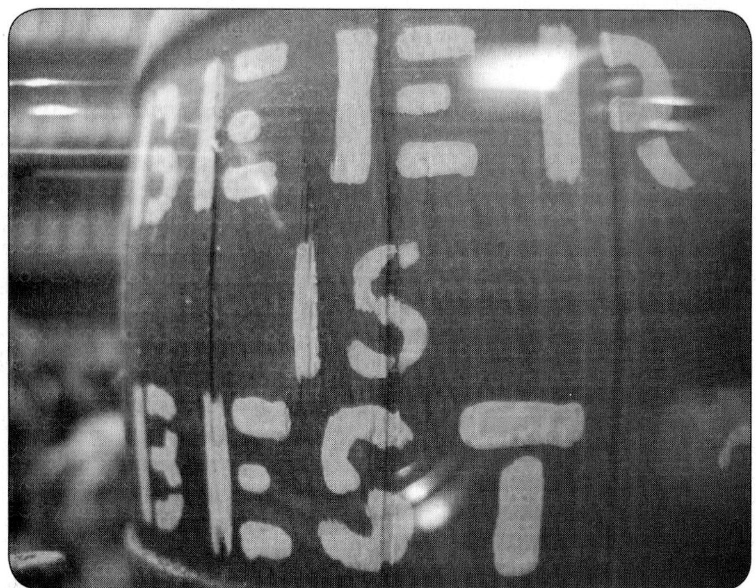

It's unfortunate that the latest redecoration job has removed seatbacks in favour of stools and contains enough black to hide a van-full of goths, but the pleasant patio out the back is a good place to top up your vitamin D if you're feeling as pasty as Robert Smith's foundation cream. In any case, such is the rapid turnover of Brighton décor the bar will probably be covered in orange astro-turf by the time you read this.

Shakespeare's Head (SD)

1 Chatham Place, on the corner of New England Road (01273) 329444
Sausages served Mon-Sat 5pm-10pm, roasts Sun 12noon-5.30pm

One of the first pubs in the city to be given a hip makeover in the slash-and-burn modernization of the 90s, the Shaky now has a nicely worn and frayed feel that might encourage you to put your feet up on the furniture. There is also a simply irresistible attraction in the form of the exclusively sausage-and-mash menu, featuring such locally made delights as merguez and mushroom-and-tarragon, a staggering seven different types of mash and four gravies. Thankfully the chicken chipolatas have now bitten the dust, which either goes to prove the incredible influence of this guide, or simply that people will only tolerate poultry in its naturally-grown nugget form. Pogo-ing bar staff are not unusual – they do like their music in here, though there's a veto on *Moon Safari* as the landlord got fed up hearing it in every other Brighton pub for years on end; should you accidentally start whistling *Sexy Boy* when you go to the bar, you may end up having a pint thrown at you. Apart from that, it's generally so laid back in here that every day is like Sunday (except that on Sunday you can't order sausages), and they've even got board games for when you've finished reading the paper.

St James Tavern (K)

16 Madeira Place (01273) 626696
www.myrumclub.com
Thai kitchen serving food 12noon-9pm

Halfway up St. James's Street lies this old-fashioned pub: a small, popular and cosy place to have a few bevvies and some tasty Thai food. Apart from during Pride in August (when the pub throws wide its doors and blasts music onto the street) it is perhaps at its best in the winter months as a welcome refuge from the cold and windy weather, offering both a roaring open fire and a chance to sample a hot rum toddy (rum with lemon, cinnamon and brown sugar mixed with hot water). And speaking of rum, herein lies the St James Tavern's USP: this pub offers 69 different types of the sugar-cane-procured spirit. The selection ranges from the cheapest light rum for under two quid to the Havana Club 12 year for a tenner. Should you attempt to imbibe all available rums in one evening just remember to watch your back for the Kemp Town pressgangs. Drink too many and you may find yourself coerced into singing *I Am Sailing* over the road at the Zone…

"Chars!"

Three and Ten (S)

10 Steine Street (just off St James's Street)
0871 917 0007

Formerly the Queen's Head (long-term residents will recall the Freddie Mercury pub-sign, now residing in a gay museum in Hull), this is a bar you're unlikely to stumble across by accident. And a good thing too. The rule in this town often seems to be the closer to the seafront, the lairier the bar. Despite being street level, The Three and Ten is so low-ceilinged and dimly lit it almost feels like stepping into a secret basement bar. And unlike so many Brighton pubs (the White Rabbit springs to mind), this place has been decorated with subtlety and care: the odd art deco lamp, old pre-war radio and bare brick walls give it character, rather than looking like a dog's dinner.

Of course we'd be lying if we said it didn't get a ***bit*** out of hand at weekends – the music levels can be a bit challenging and you will occasionally find the shirts-out brigade and groups of office girls with voices that could stun a badger at 100 metres, but when you've got Brighton's best entertainment venue just upstairs (run by Other Place Productions) you can't fail to have a certain charm. Most evenings you'll find curly-haired Nicky, Tom or Robyn from the venue having a fag outside, running the box office or loafing around with a pint. Other nights you might find yourself sharing a table with comedians like Robin Ince, spot Bob Mortimer who's popped down to check out a cracking new comedian, or nattering with a group of burlesque dancers between rehearsals. If only they served food and provided sleeping bags, I could happily while away an entire weekend here.

WHERE TO GO FOR A GOOD NATTER

The Basketmakers Arms (NL)

12 Gloucester Road (01273) 689006
Food served most of the time

Cherished by long-term residents, the Basketmakers is simply a damned good local with no frills, no pumping music, no trendy lagers, no vile artwork on the wall and plenty of decent pub grub. And, hidden away in the backstreets of North Laine, it's a place that weekend revellers rarely stumble across.

Part of the Basketmakers' unique charm lies in the thousands of old tins that cover the walls from top to toe, in which you can leave messages or look for any that have been left. I hid one in the Huntley & Palmers dundee-cake tin (though I can't guarantee it'll still be there now) and found another with the message "*Simon Amphlett cooks smelly kippers all the time. And liver. PIG'S LIVER. I do not approve*" in a puncture-repair kit tin. Other finds over the year include the message "*Ruth Hutt licked my face*" (?). Or how about the photo of this woman with the message on the back: "*Please help us find this woman*".

If you visit the pub it is your sworn duty to continue this fine tradition, particularly if taken with the urge to write fruity comments about other customers, such as this discovery: "*The man in the black dress coat needs to ring Kate or have sex with her and then leave*". Lately I've been coming across some peculiar but rather fetching drawings (below) and even found a seven-inch single crammed into a container up near the ceiling. Now, I must nip off to the dry cleaner's and pick up my black dress coat.

CALL ME FOR A POLITE CONVERSATION
07981591761
OR
07733317027
Please Leave Here

The Battle Of Trafalgar (C)

34 Guildford Road (01273) 882276
Food served weekdays 12noon-2.30pm, weekends 12noon-5pm

Once the hangout for Brighton's theatrical types (possibly due to its close proximity to the original Nightingale Theatre at the bottom of the road), the Trafalgar is a relaxed, spacious local with plenty of seats, a suntrap beer garden and lots of lovely old theatre and comedy posters from days gone by.

The clientele and staff here have always been a friendly and mellow bunch; the chance of witnessing a fight in this place is about as likely as Elton John's hair growing back of its own accord. The bar billiards table has long since gone (the manager told me it was broken but a cheeky local chipped in that it was due to 'cost-cutting'!) but if you like your bar snacks decidedly old-fashioned, as good locals go it's one of Brighton's finest.

The Cricketers (OL)

15 Black Lion Street (01273) 329472
Food served weekdays 12noon-3pm, weekends 12noon-5pm

One of Brighton's oldest pubs, the Cricketers was once a whorehouse and is suitably decorated with red Edwardian-style furnishings, old gramophones, ornate table lamps, stags' heads and wallpaper that'd make your granny blush.

For literary fans and historians a trip upstairs is a must (if it's closed off, ask the barstaff nicely and they should let you take a peek). The Greene Room contains letters and articles from Graham Greene (it was his favourite Brighton boozer and earns a mention in *Brighton Rock*) while the Jack the Ripper Room is like a mini museum

After four pints she's anyone's

with newspaper articles and photos about a certain Robert Donston Stephenson, one of many nefarious characters believed to have been the Ripper, who once stayed here. One article about him lists his hobbies as magic, prostitution and murder, though I somehow doubt this was taken from his work CV.

This pub is best avoided at weekends when it's stuffy and uncomfortably busy, although you would get the opportunity to spot the forlorn character who stands on his own at the bar with a champagne bucket and a single glass. On a quiet winter weekday however, the Cricketers transforms back to an eccentric aunt's front room where you can bag the window seats by the trophy cabinet, or sit at the back by the fire and admire the chamber pots and gaudy furnishings and quietly pen a murder mystery.

WHERE TO HAVE A CRAFTY FAG

The ban on smoking has meant getting into pubs can now often mean fighting your way past a gaggle of desperate puffers standing around in the cold unforgiving rain. Smokers of a more leisurely bent may wish to investigate the following places that allow you to sit under cover, usually whilst basking in the fiery glow of an outdoor heater:

North Laine: Lord Nelson (rear), George (rear), Fountain Head (side), Dorset (front), Colonnade (front)

Old Lanes: Victory (rear), Hop Poles (rear)

The Level: Caroline of Brunswick (rear), Park Crescent (rear)

Preston Park: Open House (rear)

Hanover: Dover Castle (rear), Hanover (side), Walmer (front)

Kemp Town: Barley Mow (rear), Sidewinder (side, of course)

Hove: Lion and Lobster (upstairs)

The Great Eastern (NL)

103 Trafalgar Street (01273) 685681
Food served Mon-Sat 12noon-11pm, Sun 12noon-10.30pm

Another unspoiled Brighton pub with old wooden tables, shelves of books at the back, newspapers, friendly barstaff and a genuine mix of clientele from students to beardy old men (I even saw a vicar in here one Sunday necking a pint of Guinness).

If you're coming for the night it often pays to arrive early as seating is limited; the tables facing the bar can get a bit cramped if it's busy, while the big tables at the far end of the pub are perfect if you're bringing a crowd. The Eastern is also popular for its pub grub and does one of the best (and cheapest) Sunday roasts in Brighton. Recommended.

The Iron Duke (H)

Waterloo Street
Free pool Mon-Thurs
Room £40-£100

Where to begin with a Brighton pub that still has friends who've lived here for 20 years asking "*where?*", "*the iron what?*" and "*remind me where Waterloo Street is again…?*"

And yet the more I get to know the Iron Duke, the more I've come to appreciate what a gem it is, being the official venue for the annual World Sparks Convention, home to the legendary "I Predict a Pop Quiz" and Collage Club hosted by Miss (Sarah) Pain, three real ales on tap (including Harveys), a piano that actually gets played, a cracking Sunday lunch and two landlords, Pete and Gez, who remember your name and always make you feel welcome on your return.

What's more, this is a Hove local (well, it's bang on the border) that covers every angle from soporific afternoons where there're just a few fellas doing the crossword to mid-week gaggles of skinny-legged indie alternatives talking band politics and full-on messy Saturday nights where you have to stage dive to get to the bar and don't get home before three.

But it doesn't stop there: it's the official bar for St Andrew's Church over the road (which rivals the Spiegeltent during May for quality shows), there are nine guest rooms ("*handy for guests who can't quite make it home*") and while some Brighton ghost experts will tell you the city's 'most haunted' is the Druids Head or the Regency Tavern, the amount of TV coverage, strange occurrences and apparitions here suggest that those interested in the paranormal would

be best served with a pint of Harvey's before stumbling off into the cellar to look for the 'angry man', the woman and baby in Room 2 or the ginger cat often seen around the place. In fact you can even buy a DVD made by the Paranormal Investigation Group or PIGs (and yes, they really are a bunch of ex-coppers!) revealing spooky goings on.

My one and only genuinely spooky encounter was down here in 1999 when I saw a vodka bottle fly horizontally across the room and drop to the floor by my feet. While I stood speechless the old landlady looked up from her book, rolled her eyes, tutted and said, "*uh, bloody ghosts*", and went back to reading.

Like many of the best albums, this place reveals itself by degrees. A true Brighton boozer.

HARVEY'S BEER

Forget fish and chips and sticks of rock, if you want to be a real local, head to the nearest pub and order a pint of Harvey's. Still a traditional family business, Harvey's have been brewing in nearby Lewes for more than 200 years; for those who like a drink or two, a pint of their Best can be synonymous with Sussex, the rolling Downs and lost weekends in Brighton.

Aside from the regular Best there are also many occasional beers. In fact, there's a beer for all seasons: Harvey's Kiss in February, South Down Harvest in September, Bonfire Boy in November (brewed to coincide with Lewes's legendary bonfire celebrations) and Mother-in-Law for winter. The darker (and stronger!) Christmas Ale was recently listed among the world's top 50 beers.

To sample the more interesting brews you need to frequent tied houses such The Lord Nelson, near Brighton station (they even use it in their steak-and-ale pie), or the Mitre Tavern, home to octogenarian landlady Pauline Bickell, Brighton's longest serving publican, who still remembers back in the 30s when you could buy a house in Brighton for as little as £150,000. Let's drink to that.

The Lion and Lobster (H)

Sillwood Street, Brighton (almost Hove)
(01273) 327299
Food served 12noon-9pm, and they don't scrimp on the portions either

As many pubs in the city fall victim to the modernisation process, the Lion and Lobster remains a true traditional seaside boozer with psychedelic beer-stained carpets, seafaring tales from salty old dogs, burned-out clubbers in their late 30s, and an ocean of paunches. Escape from the roar of the pub's Sky screens is now possible thanks to a gutting of the old first-floor bedrooms, creating a labyrinthine network of galleries, a bar, some quite posh dining rooms and a shiver-free enclosed multi-level smoking terrace that would probably receive some kind of award if the world didn't openly hate all smokers and wish they'd hurry up and die a bit quicker. It's entertainingly easy to get lost up here, with interconnecting rooms and assorted stairways heavily lined with framed posters, but you can always take a breather by flopping out on the crimson chaise longue outside the bar area. Oh, and the gents is a hoot too, a multiplicity of mirrors making it possible to see parts of you that you, ahem, may not have seen before.

Top tip: Find the unmarked side door that leads directly upstairs and save yourself the hassle of shouldering past the barflies that pack the main entrance.

The Lord Nelson (NL)

36 Trafalgar Street (01273) 695872
Food served Mon-Sat 12noon-2.30pm, Sun 12.30pm-3.30pm

Halfway down Trafalgar Street the Nelson is often overlooked, even by long-term residents, which is a pity as – together with the Great Eastern, the Trafalgar and the Basketmakers – this really is one of the best locals in North Laine. With tobacco-stained walls, *Sooty* collection box, pork scratchings, food "*like granny makes it*", a mismatched collection of stools in the main bar and an unspoken policy of conversation taking priority over music, the Nelson has been spared the makeover treatment and remains a cherished old-school drinking establishment.

It also has a terrific reputation for its food, which is really top notch. Sunday roast is a lavish serving of roast and veg (and they do a tasty nut roast for veggies) with crumbles and the likes of spotted dick and custard – of heroic portions – for pudding fans afterwards. It's also popular with the Brighton & Hove Albion football crowd. Come here of a wet afternoon, sit down with a pint of Harveys Armada, bangers and mash and a copy of *The Argus* and, within a few hours, you'll be shouting "*Come on you Seagulls!*" in a genuine Brighton accent.

Curiously, for years now a *Dungeons & Dragons* group has been coming to the Nelson every Monday night dressed up as wizards and goblins and losing themselves in their Tolkienesque fantasy world, though how welcome they are is another matter. An innocent enquiry to the barman – "*Do you still have the Dungeons & Dragons here on a Monday?*" prompted him to roll his eyes, throw his arms in the air and say, "*look mate, it's got nothing to do with us all right? They just keep* ***bloody*** *turning up*".

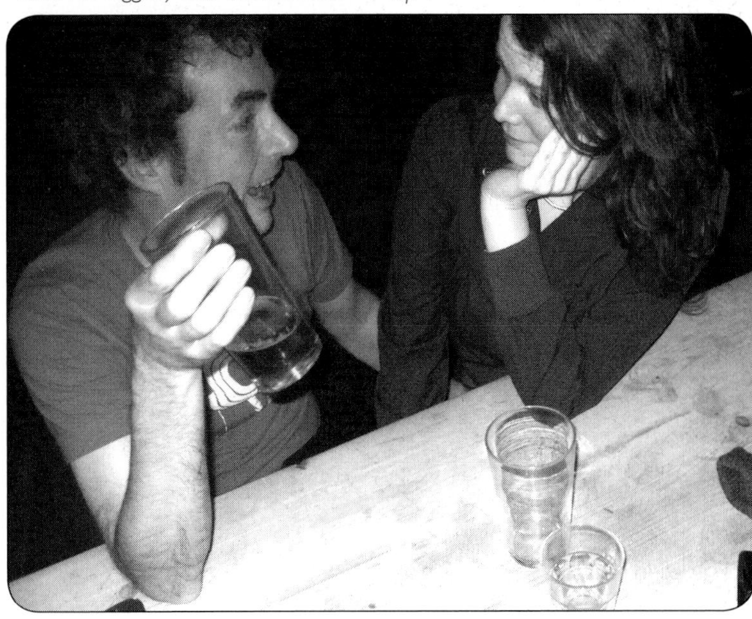

"So that's where you hid my keys!"

Pub Du Vin (OL)

7 Ship Street (01273) 718588

Right next door to the Hotel Du Vin, this new venture is a revamped version of the old Sussex Arts Club, minus the live entertainment and media whores. For the most part it's like an old gentlemen's club with leather chairs and lots of elegant and thoughtful touches like the proper tankards for beer and the volume adjustments for music in the snug room. Whoever thought having faux half-plastered walls and fake brickwork in the bar was a good idea however, ought to have their gonads squeezed. And despite the elegance, it has to be said over-all it's a deeply confusing concept: on the one hand there's the name, the accent on local ales, and the ill-advised references to "traditional pub fayre", and then I turn up another evening only to be refused entry on the grounds that they have a "non-vertical licence" and all the non-vertical spaces are taken. I volunteered to lie on the floor but for some reason this cut no ice.

FOR A CRACKING SUNDAY LUNCH

Seven Dials: ***Prestonville Arms/Shakespeare's Head***

North Laine: ***Lord Nelson/ Earth and Stars/The Eagle/ The Basketmakers***

Kemp Town: ***Barley Mow***

City centre: ***Regency Tavern/ Sussex Yeoman***

Hanover area: ***Hartington/ Reservoir/Dover Castle/The Hanover/Greys***

Hove area: ***Coopers Cask***

Old Lanes: ***Hop Poles/Globe***

Preston Park: ***Open House***

DOG-FRIENDLY PUBS

Those of you who own a canine are probably used to being told to bugger off by pub staff, but here's a short checklist of places that appreciate the hound pound:

The Barley Mow

The Great Eastern

The Hand in Hand

The Park View

The Greys

The Charles Napier

MY BRIGHTON & HOVE

Name: DAVE 'The Wedge' WEDGE bus driver

1. Western Road between Montpelier and Waterloo Street I bloody love this stretch because it offers the chance to burn off cyclists at the traffic lights and leave them for dead behind some parked vehicles, followed by a beautiful open 200 yards where you can pick up a bit of speed and overtake another bus or two, before slamming on the anchors and making one or two passengers stumble drunkenly about and drop their shopping if they've been silly enough to get out of their seats before we reach the stop.

2. Union Road, top of The Level A classic pair of 90 degree turns, first a right hander off the Lewes Road, taken at speed so the passengers on one side of the bus have their faces squashed against the windows, then a rapid sprint to the next lights for a sudden left hander and no worries if the lights suddenly change against you, there's a three second lag on this junction so you can jump the red. When this happens I usually make a little cowboy-style whooping sound.

3. East Street Not really an official bus route I know, but it makes a handy short cut when the Old Steine's all clogged up with taxis. Why they let them use the bus lanes I'll never understand. The going gets a bit rough on East Street when you reach the cobbled bit but it's worth it to see all the surprised pedestrians and fortune tellers jumping out of your way. I like to put my head out the window and shout "*didn't see this coming did yer?!*"

DISCOTHEQUES

Home to the Ocean Rooms, Audio, the Honeyclub, Catskills Records and Skint, Brighton's club/DJ scene boasts everything from cool underground jazz and retro to dubstep and electro nights, as well as hosting the biggest gay club on the south coast. Combine this with regular visits from big-name DJs, plus our own Norman Cook, and it's not surprising that Brighton's clubs are packed every night of the week. What other town can boast more than twenty clubs within walking distance of each other, and most a stone's throw from the beach?

One of the very special things about Brighton's nightlife is that, unlike so many other UK cities, the clubs here do not merely represent weekend escapism from drudgery and boredom. If anything, some of the best nights here are mid-week, and most venues are refurbished so often that by the time you turn up again on a Saturday the seats will be a completely different colour and the toilets moved to the DJ booth. Clubbing in Brighton seems nothing less than a shameless celebration of living in a party town, which is probably why upbeat and carnival-type music like Latin jazz and Afro-bhangra are particularly popular here. And with long running club nights like Da Doo Ron Ron, Wild Fruit and Born Bad, the scene has a glitz, glamour and kinkiness that Manchester, even in its heyday, could never have provided.

Audio

10 Marine Parade (01273) 606906
www.audiobrighton.com

While quintessentially Brighton in that it virtually insists you wear trainers and a T-shirt, Audio's clammy grip on the best of everything has slipped a little recently. In Supercharged they still have a sublime Wednesday breaks event, but you can no longer just turn up on any night of the week and expect to find something great – bad news for people who are too lazy to check the listings then. When they re-opened in 2004, kicking off the apparently endless Brighton obsession with club refurbs and name changes, they divided the old Escape Club into two

separate venues, with Above Audio as a separate, less hectic bar experience; you can still move between them but you have to go back outside to do it, which I'm sure is purely to ensure unhealthy clubbers get an occasional dose of sea air to restart their vital organs. Not as consistently hip as it once was, but still a member of Brighton club royalty nevertheless.

A CHEEKY TALE

If you look above Audio you'll see a flat which has a commanding view of the beach and, in particular, the phone box in front of the club. Two guys, Mark and Bruce, used to live up there and some nights after the club had almost cleared out, they'd ring up the phone box, wait for some inebriated clubber to answer, take a note of how he was dressed and then play these weird 50s adverts down the line. It would start with some cheesy music and then go –

"Hi, and welcome to the world of Lux soap, a new powder that'll get your clothes whiter than white"

– and then a different voice would say –

"You are wearing a red shirt, jeans and a blue hat."

Click

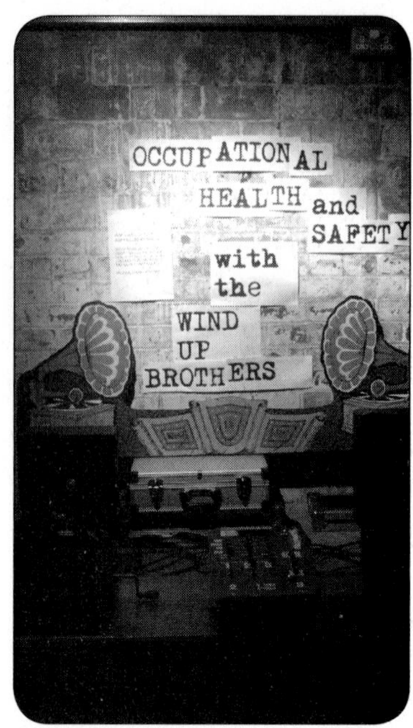

Babylon Lounge

Kingsway, Hove (01273) 207100

No club adjoining Hove's bowling greens and lagoon will ever be cool, particularly when it closely resembles a school gymnasium. That said, Babylon Lounge doesn't even try, offering twice-weekly salsa lessons and hen-friendly male strippers every Saturday (see Adonis Cabaret review in **Sex** chapter). The only other distinguishing feature is that it's the first nightclub in the country where you can officially marry, offering the bride the opportunity to go straight from her hen night to the wedding ceremony, pausing only to remove the stripper's thong from her head. Unless you live in darkest Hove, you'll need to get a cab here. I'd recommend paying the driver an extra quid to wait around for a couple of minutes as, after a quick nose around inside, you ***may*** choose to make a sharp exit.

Casablanca

3 Middle Street (01273) 321817
www.casablancajazzclub.com

This club specialises in Latin jazz and jazz funk, and is refreshing in that it has live bands and not just DJs. With such a strong DJ culture here, you forget sometimes what a pleasure it is to experience danceable live music, especially when the bands really know how to let rip. True, you might turn up, look at the outside, and think, "*oh God, no*", and yes, it is cheap and cheerful, but you will have a good time despite yourself.

Although the club has two floors I'd recommend sticking to the downstairs bit where you can dance in front of a real live car provided you don't mind the presence of an office party making beep-beep noises.

If the funky music and those horns ***don't*** move you to boogie, you're in the wrong city.

Dress code: Flares, corduroy cap, goatee.

Coalition

171-181 Kings Road Arches
(01273) 772842
www.drinkinbrighton.co.uk/brightoncoalition/

Now billing itself as an 'arts and entertainment venue', in its glory days as The Beach this place hosted Fatboy's Big Beat Boutique and Digweed's Bedrock. You won't find many big names here these days, although Brighton's own Prok & Fitch are doing their best to conjure up an aura of celebrity. Other than that, the architectural wonders of the brick arches and pillars tend to be more interesting than the mish mash of trance, funky house, indie, live bands, comedy and hula hooping policewomen.

Concorde 2

Miles from anywhere, Madeira Drive
(01273) 673311
www.concorde2.co.uk

Built out of the ashes of the Water Rats (a one-time greasy bikers' hang-out), the Concorde 2 took over where the original Concorde left off by specialising in live music, cracking club nights (from reggae and punk, house to hip-hop and dirty acid techno) and odd one-offs such as the UK Air Guitar Championships. While the Concorde works far better for live music than club nights it's always fantastically relaxed, reasonably roomy, and you never have trouble getting a drink at the bar. A special ***Cheeky Guide*** prize though, a bag of extra sour lemon sherbets, awaits anyone who can extract a smile from the bar staff.

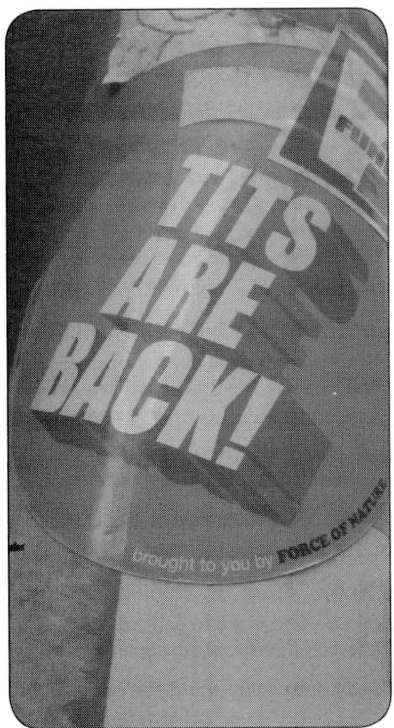

Digital/Micro

187-193 Kings Road Arches
(01273) 227767
www.yourfutureisdigital.com/brighton

After a lot of twitching and moaning the poor old Zap Club finally lay down and turned up its toes two years ago, and the premises were swiftly grabbed by the Newcastle firm Digital. They've done wonders with the sound rig, although the doormen aren't so happy with having to wear cap-sleeve shirts all winter. The entertainment itself is a tad schizophrenic, veering from great live bands and some of the best major new and established DJ talent you'll find anywhere, to nights where the music seems less important than the fact that you have to wear either a hat or a pair of shades to get in (I predict moustache nights will be the next big thing, you mark my words), and that old standby the indie disco (do I really have to hear sodding Blue Monday again? *"Yes I'm afraid you do, it is the law"*). On the right night though, this is one of the best clubs in town and a welcome shot of adrenaline in the heart of the seafront arches scene.

Micro is the old tiny Zap back room given its own personal front door, and hosts special events of its own. It's a bit like the secret disco at Bestival, only easier to find and lacking that heady aromatic blend of body odour and bean burps.

The Engine Room

5 Preston Street (01273) 728999
www.engineroomclub.com

Confusing as the concept of live death metal may be, that's one of the delights on offer in this hardcore rock/punk/glam/goth den. It's a sticky little basement with lots of odd corners and anterooms to hide in, red gothic-arched seatbacks and huddles of fetishistically adorned groovers, who may accidentally poke you in the eye with an exocet-shaped piercing but will apologise unreservedly and offer to mop up any blood afterwards. On some nights there's so much PVC in here that the squeaking and rustling

almost drowns out the music, yet still there's a curiously inclusive feeling that welcomes even the most conservatively dressed. If you're lucky you might get to see a professional pole dancer using the facility in front of the stage, but if not then feel encouraged to have a go yourself – they offer prizes for the rudest gyrations. There are plans to do this place up a bit, but let's hope they don't make it ***too*** clean.

Emblematic fragrance: Wet eyeliner and Castrol GTX.

Funky Buddha Lounge

Kings Road Arches (01273) 725541

Intimacy is inevitable at this living-room-sized club, its two parallel tunnels holding the bar and dancefloor like a giant Twix. Well they've made all the other chocolate bars huge, it must be the turn of the Twix soon, surely. If you're looking to pull then you're laughing; there's a crush of lovely secretaries, and gents who feel they're not dressed without a proper shirt and shiny loafers, and the place is so small you can't help snag your signet ring on a lady's garments 'by accident' and then find a beautiful, crazy relationship unfurling before your eyes as you attempt to disentangle each other – *"You won't believe how we met, it all started when Darren suddenly found his arm trapped in my culottes"*.

Unfortunately if it's music you're after then fun could prove a little more elusive, unless of course you view Rose Royce as some sort of seminal act. Probably the best idea is to come here for the Sunday morning 3am till 8am techno session when the night/morning always finishes with a conga all the way to the end of the pier.

Emblematic fragrance: Denim.

MOST EMBARRASSING REQUESTS

1. KYLIE - The Locomotion
2. ABBA - Dancing Queen
3. DJ CASPER - Cha Cha Slide
4. SPICE GIRLS - Wannabe
5. CHRISTINA AGUILERA - Dirty
6. GUNS & ROSES - Paradise City
7. LEO SAYER - You make me feel like dancing
8. BAYWATCH - Theme from Baywatch
9. S CLUB 7 - Reach
10. OPERATION BLADE - Bass in the place London

Funky Fish Club

19-23 Marine Parade, underneath the Madeira Hotel
(01273) 698331

Like a cow standing alone in a field of sheep, the Fish barely seems to be a club at all in Brighton terms. Insisting on a strict diet of 60s and 70s soul and 'classic' rock, it has no truck with name DJs and attracts a wide-ranging crowd who come to have fun rather than pose. Strict rules have now been imposed on hen parties though, banning matching outfits, bunny ears and *"inflatables of any nature"*.

Admittedly, it does have the strong flavour of a wedding reception with its state-of-the-ark lighting, white tablecloths and occasional pensioner, but there's a friendly vibe about the place, even if they will still insist on testing the theory that you can dance to *Sweet Home Alabama.*

Ladies, expect to be chatted up by visiting insurance salesmen staying in the hotel above, who will attempt to make conversation with opening gambits like, *"Oh, yes, I've always been a big fan of Diana Ross and the Pips"*.

The Honeyclub

214 Kings Road Arches (01273) 202807
www.thehoneyclub.co.uk

Now expanded into something like 86 rooms the Honey is suddenly among the biggest clubs in town, though given that the company includes places like Oceana, that isn't necessarily a positive. If mainstream hard house, techno and trance are your bag and you still think glowsticks and Ministry of Sound compilations are pretty cool you'll find satisfaction here, though once you've paid the often stiff weekend door tax you'll need some smelling salts too. What the sound system seriously lacks in fidelity it makes up for in denture-rattling volume and this is where many of the pretty people come out to play, so if you're after a bit of deaf eye candy this'll suit. And be nice to the gentleman who runs the concession table in the loos and he'll give you a special squirt of cologne *"down there"*.

Komedia

(See review in *Music* chapter)

New Hero (formerly the Church, Club New York, the Shrine-tastic, Poppa Belly's GoodTimey Hoedown Barn)

11 Dyke Road

Possessing even more of a chequered past than the rest of the city's clubs, New Hero is shaping up to be the favourite haunt of sharp young things who've realised that indie was old hat even before Oasis came along and ruined it. As well as providing a platform for acts like Hot Chip and Little Boots in their upstairs live room, New Hero's rather lovely curator Henron also pushes up-and-coming electro sounds downstairs, on top of which Boogaloo Stu (of much-missed Brighton clubbing institution Dynamite Boogaloo), does his new Pop Kraft night here. You won't get the acres of chrome and zinc that many of Brighton's clubs offer these days but what you actually get are weird junk shop paintings of tigers and a little girl holding a kitten, which I think is an improvement. True, they still have the odd dodgy 80s night, but overall this is one of the most interesting and forward-thinking clubs in town. Give it a go.

Dress code: Geeky glasses and tweed thigh boots.

Oceana

West Street 0845 296 8590

"Like going clubbing in Disneyland" as my friend Rick recently described this £6 million refit of the old Event II, albeit a theme park where Big Brother seems to be watching your every move to ensure that you only 'enjoy' yourself in the prescribed manner. There are security staff round every corner of this massive venue and comforting screens that tell you exactly how many bodies are in each room at any given

moment, and there're a ***lot*** of rooms. With a whopping five bars featuring such themes as ski lodge, Parisian boudoir, and Tahiti, erm, bar, as well as two dancefloors, the glossy white Reykjavik icehouse and a New York 70s-style disco, it's easy to get lost and you regularly will. Luckily the wafting fumes of the hotdog stand at the top of the main staircase will help to relocate you in such an eventuality. Or perhaps you've been to one of the fifteen other identical Oceanas across the country, in which case you'll know what to expect and have brought a map.

Tinnitus-inducing volume aside, the music doesn't really merit much of a mention so I won't bother. Suffice it to say that at weekends wearing trainers won't get you through the door but a wet-look-gel hairdo and a nice pair of slip-ons will.

The Ocean Rooms

1 Morley Street (01273) 699069
www.oceanrooms.co.uk

A tip of the brim first to the sound system downstairs, which has experienced possibly the greatest sonic upgrade of any Brighton club (bar Digital) in recent times. In fact they can't leave this place alone as the decor, inside and out, changes so often you'll think you've come to the wrong club if you've been here within the previous fortnight. There're three floors here, each with their own bar: the main basement room is spacious and lovely, the ground-floor one is now a sofa-strewn lounge (I kind of miss the old bedstead though) and the VIP room on the top floor changes colour more often than my Auntie Eileen's hair, although it was pink last week.

Music-wise, it's also quite tricky to keep track of what's going on, partly because the Ocean Rooms seem to have given up on their website, and also owing to the music policy being perhaps less clear cut than it was. Nevertheless, this is still one of the top four or five clubs in town for those of taste and discernment. Fairly cool electro and drum and bass still feature, on top of which they now play host to Torture Garden, so if you can't decide what to wear for your evening out, you can come to that and wear nothing at all.

Emblematic fragrance: Chanel Allure.

Tavern Club

Castle Square (01273) 827641

This place has been a popular spot for indie music ever since Brighton's legendary Basement Club imploded after one of the DJs left a Shed 7 record playing all night by mistake. The Pav Tav, as it's usually known, is basically a big purple function room above a pub, with subdued lighting, a wide bar and a few sofas to try to make it more intimate. Friday's Kick Out The Jams indie night has been running here since about 1940, although extended pub licensing hours haven't done it any favours since the pasty-faced emo-grungers and girls who've filled up on two-for-one cider can now carry on in the pub downstairs, where the music is almost as loud, for most of the night.

Tru

78 West Street (01273) 321628

Formerly Creation, this ruddy great barn is owned by Luminar Leisure, who proudly boast *"the largest square footage of nightclub capacity in the country through our branded estate of venues" and that they "invest in coherent physical and flexible spaces"*. There're three dancefloors operating a mix of various urban music flavours, and a balcony in the main room where you can pretend to be the Queen (or just ***a*** queen if it's a Wild Fruit night) and wave regally to your subjects far below.

The natural habitat of Hassocks Man and full of weekend revellers in their late teens, this is the ideal place to get your arse groped on a Saturday night.

Dress code: Henri Lloyd shirt and thousand-yard stare.

The Volks

3 The Colonnade, Madeira Drive
(01273) 682828
www.volksclub.co.uk

Hidden away off the main clubbing drag, the Volks is a bit of a gem for its unsniffy attitude and discerning choice of sounds. I've been to some dynamite breaks nights here and there's a host of other specialist fixtures from jungle and afro to DnB, grime and psy-trance. The main room upstairs is surprisingly airy (unlike the downstairs which is about the size of a sheet of A4), packed with excessively friendly people (I left a friend on his own in here and when I came back he hissed *"people keep smiling at me")* and run by tasteful DJs who, for a change, know how to build a room up rather than throwing the entire bucket of bricks at it from minute one. If there's one carp de diem, it's that there's hardly anywhere to sit down, but then I am getting on a bit. For a taste of the original Brighton underground clubbing experience, this is the one.

Emblematic fragrance: Sweat/patchouli.

AT A GLANCE...

Chart/disco/party tunes: *Oceana/Tru/Coalition*

Drum'n'Bass: *Volks/Digital/Audio*

Easy listening/soundtrack/lounge/retro: *Hanbury/Komedia/Prince Albert*

Goth/industrial: *Engine Room*

Hip-hop: *The Loft/Jam*

Breakbeat: *Audio/Volks/Concorde 2/Digital*

House/electro: *Audio/Ocean Rooms/Honeyclub/Digital*

Indie/rock: *Tavern Club/Engine Room/Concorde 2*

Jazz/funk/salsa: *Casablanca/Komedia/Babylon Lounge*

Northern soul/Motown: *Funky Fish/Hanbury/Komedia*

Reggae: *The Jazz Place/Volks*

70s/80s: *Oceana/Tru/Funky Buddha*

Techno/trance: *Honeyclub/Volks*

Electronica/krautrock/underground pop: *Ocean Rooms/New Hero*

Legendary Brighton Club Nights

Supercharged

Audio, Wednesdays

Breakbeat supreme led by Krafty Kuts and a slew of big breaks bananas.

Born Bad

Komedia, monthly

Dirty girls in pvc and tattooed blokes with quiffs moshing to rock'n'roll in an underground supermarket stockroom.

Different venues, monthly

Play your five favourite records to an adoring crowd of your own mates, then watch everyone else have a go. Mixing is "*actively discouraged*".

Digital, monthly

Any excuse for themed dressing up from Starsky & Hutch to the Mad Hatter's tea party.

Shitsmacker

The Shed, quarterly

Elevator music made from the sound of real lifts, DJ-ed by the legendary Otis "maximum load eight persons" Croissant.

Wild Fruit

Tru, monthly

Bigger, gayer, glammer and more outrageous than the rest. So good you won't even notice it's held at Tru.

Da Doo Ron Ron

Komedia, monthly

60s girl-group sounds, lack of snobbery compulsory, beehive optional.

Snake-Eyed Mamas Club

Engine Room

Old school psychobilly and the cream of 1950s stuff for purists and tourists.

I'LL MEET YOU AT, ER, WOSSITCALLED?

The ever-changing names of Brighton clubs...

Escape → Audio
Beachcomber → Honeyclub
Passion → Funky Buddha Lounge
Cuba → Club Blue → Arc
Zenons → Core Club
Enigma → The Loft
Opium Paradise → Lidl
Catfish → Funky Fish
Top Rank Suite → Event → Event II → Oceana
The Zap → Union → The Zap → Digital
Sherry's → Pink Coconut → Paradox → Creation → Tru

Entertainment

CINEMAS

See a Hollywood blockbuster on Friday night, the latest David Lynch on the Saturday, then a documentary about Voodoo S&M on the Sunday. Here's how.

INDIE CINEMAS

Duke Of York's Picturehouse

Preston Circus 0871 704 2056
Cheaper tickets Mon-Thurs before 6pm
www.picturehouses.co.uk

Found at the end of London Road, this building is pale yellow and has a large pair of stripy legs sticking out over the balcony. It's easy to miss, however, as all the houses on the street have copied the idea and now there are hands, elbows and feet sticking out all over the place as far as the eye can see.

Celebrating its 100th birthday in September 2010, the Duke's can claim to be the oldest independent cinema outside London, and shows a fairly wide selection of cult, art house and world films. It has an intimate bar and balcony upstairs and, rather than the usual cinema junk food, offers a fine selection of cakes and hot and cold drinks. The auditorium itself looks magical, with coloured lights around the screen, and those blue velvet seats have to be the most comfortable in Brighton.

Despite its website declaring that in its past *"the cinema has suffered various indignities including punk rock concerts"*, the Duke's continues to host some magnificent music events ranging from cutting-edge bands to its annual live *Eurovision* when 300-odd gay men prove they can outdo a whole crèche of ankle biters when it comes to screaming the loudest.

Whether you're a movie enthusiast, music lover, interior designer, cake obsessive or leg fetishist, the Duke's remains one of ***the*** best reasons for living in Brighton.

Top tips: If you fancy seeing one of their late-night cult screenings at the weekend, buy your tickets in advance, they often sell out. For maximum pleasure, pay the extra couple of quid and luxuriate on the new balcony sofas upstairs.

Duke of York's trivia

The Duke's was originally built for theatrical impresarios Violette Melnotte and Frank Wyatt. Violette, always known to staff as 'Madame', was the archetypal iron fist in a velvet glove and, when one of the actors at the theatre gassed himself, she apparently instructed her solicitor to reclaim the cost of the gas from his estate.

The Duke's famous legs once belonged to a cinema in Oxford known as 'Not the Moulin Rouge' and, every Sunday at 3pm, they do the Can Can.

WHERE TO SEE THE LATEST BLOCKBUSTER

Cineworld

The Marina 0871 200 2000

Loads of screens and all the latest movies from Tinseltown. You won't find anything adventurous in their billings, and it ***is*** located below the multi-storey car park in the far-from-glamorous Marina, but serves a need if the Odeon is sold out or you fancy a drive into the middle of nowhere. At weekends you may find yourself ankle-deep in popcorn, teabags and litter. The fact that it seems to be run by surly teenagers has nothing to do with it.

The Odeon

West Street 0870 505 0007
www.odeon.co.uk

The biggest cinema in the town centre and, with Oceana next door, handy if you're seized by the urge to snog a few teenagers after the film.

ENTERTAINMENT/ THEATRE VENUES

The Basement

24 Kensington Street (01273) 699733
www.thebasement.uk.com

Deep in the vaults of the former Argus building lies this vast underground space, home to live art, performance and experimental theatre.

Dedicated to supporting local and emerging artists, such as Ragroof Theatre and comedians The Two Wrongies, the venue has four unique spaces: auditorium, large performance area, bar and study. It's easy to overlook – tell someone you're off to an event at the Basement and if they're not a performer, chances are you'll be met with a blank response. Recently however it's begun to broaden its profile, thanks in part to a regular brochure for its two seasons of art events and special club nights. Past highlights include Daniel Kitson's C90, when a complete room within a room was built out of second-hand furniture to house Kitson's show and filled with thousands of hand-customised cassettes; and a live horse that turned up for a month. Irregular club nights have featured performance art, parlour games and singsongs round the piano.

And while the lack of soft furnishings and windows might not be to everyone's taste, there's no doubt that under the gentle guidance of its creator (and former Buddhist monk) Helen Medland, the Basement plays an essential role in developing and showcasing the best of live art in Brighton.

Komedia

44-47 Gardner Street (01273) 647100
www.komedia.co.uk/brighton

Impossible to miss, owing to the fact that its outrageous red lighting turns Gardner Street into an enormous brothel every evening. That aside, god bless the Komedia; I've had many unforgettable evenings here whether it's been jazz group Polar Bear giving me a nosebleed, drunken messy dancing at Born Bad or laughing myself stupid at Count Arthur Strong's live radio show. I even met my wife here. Well, one of them. Happy memories.

Having expanded over the years (a mixed blessing) there are now two big venue spaces. Upstairs is kitted out more for comedy, theatre and cabaret (with an irritatingly cramped staircase for the loos), while downstairs you can expect to see more comedy, live music and club nights. There's also a smaller *studio* for more avant garde music events, poetry and beard stroking.

Alas it's true that the Komedia ***has*** become more commercial over the years. It doesn't seem that interested in theatre any more, makes its dosh from run-of-the-mill weekend hen- and stag-friendly comedy nights and is even prone to putting on horrible tribute bands like Status Clone, Punk Floyd and Leo Slayer (Leo Sayer songs with a metal twist). But while weekends can get a bit "Jongleurs", there's plenty of other club nights, music and cabaret to redress the balance. Nights to be championed include Voodoo Vaudeville, Born Bad, Da Doo Ron Ron, Hammer & Tongue, Short Fuse, Vive La FIP and Brighton Jazz. If you've never been to any of these events, or the Komedia for that matter, it's just possible you might be living in the wrong town.

Hanbury Ballroom

83 St Georges Road (01273) 605789

Mausoleum for the illustrious Sassoon family, council mortuary, furniture shop, decorator's, "The Bombay Bar", live music venue, private members' club; the Hanbury has had more incarnations than Jesus' little-known twin brother Jimmy, who made a habit of creeping up on people and pretending to be the resurrection.

Now back to its most comfortable state as a music and clubbing venue after a few trials and tribulations, this magnificent domed building is looking pretty posh inside with some flash wallpaper and black lampshades; it makes for a stylish night out, particularly on clubbing nights such as the long-established Margot's Parties, where people make an effort to get glammed up, wear their underwear on the outside, and flash as much thigh as they've got. And the girls look pretty good too.

It's also a great venue for more intimate live performances that lean towards Americana such as Devon Sproule and The Broken Family Band, and if you're tired of the modern tendency of people standing right next to you to rabbit away to their mates all through someone's set, then the respectful attitude of the audiences here should provide some welcome relief.

Latest Music Bar

14-17 Manchester Street (01273) 687171
www.thelatest.co.uk/musicbar

To some, this venue will always be known as the Joogleberry. And like many, I still have to correct myself every now and again when talking about it. But while "Latest Music Bar" does sound a bit corporate, at least jokes about dangleberries, fartleberries and the like can finally be buried. Having changed hands a few years ago things did look a little shaky at first but after a cabinet reshuffle in the programming department, all seems to be working out fine. What they've lost in the way of comedy and cabaret, they've gained with live music, as most evenings you'll find local bands, jazz outfits, acoustic sessions and indie bands squeaking around in tight trousers. Other than that, little has changed over the years; it's still a laid-back and welcoming café/ restaurant by day, and magical candle-lit Eastern European-style basement club by night. Just order a spot of food, park yourself at a table and marvel at the nighttime scenes of houses with real lights twinkling in the windows that line the walls. And finally, congratulations are due for the best venue website in Brighton. It's simple and informative with good, clear images. What more could you ask of a venue, except for the downstairs loos to be working...

Top tip: For those who like spoken word as a change from singer-songwriters, legendary debating/spoken-word nights the Catalyst Club and The Space can be found here (see later in the chapter).

foot-tapping finger-snapping
hip-swinging ear-ringing
jive-talking moon-walking
foot-stomping food-chomping
body-popping knicker-dropping
smooth-moving soul-grooving
eye-blinking beer-drinking
tear-jerking hard-working
death-defying satisfying
mind-blowing far-going
life-changing far-ranging
head-banging cliff-hanging
side-splitting hard-hitting
spirit-lifting god's-gifting
belly-filling heart-thrilling
free-living party-giving...

latest musicbar

thelatest.co.uk/musicbar

01273 687171

14 - 17 manchester street, brighton

only 100 metres from the pier

brighton's favourite party venue
to book your private party FREE* call now

* Terms and conditions apply

for full weekly brighton listings pick up latest 7 / latest homes

The Nightingale Theatre

29-30 Surrey Street (above Grand Central)
(01273) 702563
www.nightingaletheatre.co.uk

After many years in the wilderness, the theatre once described as "Brighton's best-loved venue" made a welcome return in 2004. Run by resident company Prodigal Theatre, they offer drama workshops, Scratch Nights (a chance for performers to try out short extracts of new work) and performances by local and international theatre groups – all in a well-kept 50-odd-capacity studio space. True, this place does evoke varying reactions from Brighton's arty types: some find the atmosphere unwelcoming ("they act like they breathe rarified air"), others think it's the bee's knees. What can't be denied is that the Nightingale continues to support and nurture some outstanding and genuinely groundbreaking work in a town where all too often "I can't be arsed" is the motto of the day.

Theatre Royal

New Road 0844 8112 121
www.theatreroyal.co.uk

For the more conservative theatregoer. The Theatre Royal may offer a predictable array of farces, thrillers and musicals starring Tom Conti, Jason Donovan and Elaine Paige but for an authentic old-style theatre experience it can't be beaten. The auditorium, with its plush red-velvet seats, is stunning – and they have private boxes for those who really want to do it in style. I once saw Barbara Windsor in the nude here, but that's another story.

Dress code: Loafers, slacks and cardie. Monocle optional.

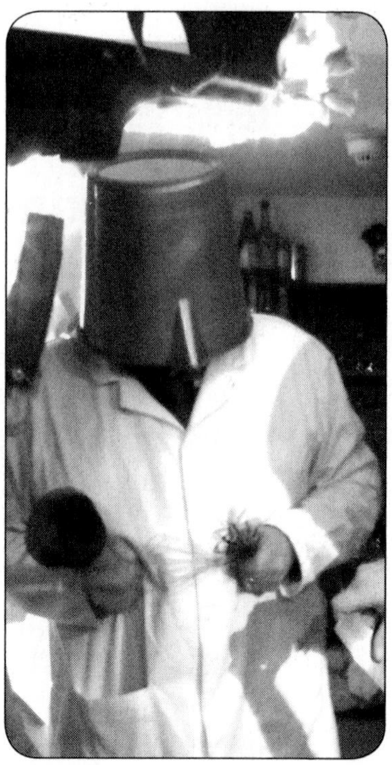

The Sallis Benney Theatre

University of Brighton, Grand Parade
(01273) 643010
www.brighton.ac.uk/gallery-theatre

Dead as a dodo for six months of the year, out of the blue, the Sallis Benney will sporadically have a sizeable world-music, theatre or dance season before sinking back into hibernation again.

It's like a drunk relative at your party who wakes up and dances their way across the living room only to collapse unconscious in the kitchen moments later.

Worth keeping an eye on during the summer term, as all the performance-art students put on free events here for a couple of weeks as the final part of their degrees, before settling down to lives of unemployment.

Upstairs At Three and Ten

10 Steine Street 0780 0983 290
www.otherplaceproductions.co.uk

Just off the bottom of St James's Street, above one of the town's best and most chilled out late-night boozers, lies a hidden gem of Brighton's arts scene: a tiny boutique theatre providing a full range of fringe events, from cult comedy and acoustic music to alternative theatre and spoken-word nights, which operates on a shoestring thanks to the dedicated efforts of its staff. Run by Otherplace Productions, a theatre company based on the principles of the A-Team (*"if you have a problem, and no-one else can help, and if you can get hold of them…"*), the venue has played host to some of the comedy world's top talents, such as Daniel Kitson, Josie Long, Robin Ince, Richard Herring, Phil Kay and Pappy's Fun Club, and is ***the*** best place to catch up-and-coming acts in Sussex. Furthermore, if you've ever wanted to see some new and original theatre, where a small budget is used to sharpen the imagination rather than soften it, then this is the place to go. You also get a chance to mingle with the acts and staff in the bar afterwards, although half of them will probably be out on the pavement having a fag.

Top tip: Now one of the main venues in the Brighton Festival Fringe, Upstairs at Three and Ten also hosts previews for some of the main Edinburgh shows in June and July. They're always on the lookout for new staff and volunteers too, and have good links with other arts organisations, so if you want to get involved in Brighton's arts scene, this is a good place to start.

Brian Gittins and Angelos at the Three and Ten, next in line for the comedy throne (hopefully)

COMEDY & CABARET

The Krater Comedy Club

Weekly at the Komedia (01273) 647100

Running weekends at the Komedia, the Krater follows the tried-and-tested Jongleurs format of compère and three acts. Regularly hosted by local comedian Stephen Grant, known for his speedy delivery, the Krater is unquestionably popular but does demonstrate the frightening lack of original material from most of the comedians currently crawling the national circuit. Attracting stag and hen parties in their droves (an established Brighton epidemic), this is hardly a discerning audience but at least they don't seem to mind listening to desperate single men and women in their mid-30s drone on about masturbation. With moronic heckling and mobile phones going off every ten minutes, this is my idea of hell.

Voodoo Vaudeville

www.voodoo-vaudeville.com

"*Think of a nurse in a short PVC outfit. Give her a syringe, put a monkey mask on her and get her to inject a three-piece-suit-wearing gorilla to make it do a striptease.*"

That – according to creator and host Chris Cresswell – is Voodoo Vaudeville.

A kinky Victorian freak show for lovers of real pantomime, cabaret, comedy and dance, this is Pontin's cabaret seen through the eyes of Lewis Carroll; where giant rabbits abound, ghostly puppets give acerbic advice to the audience, glamorous girls do teasing (and often hilarious) dances, dominatrixes wander through the audience meting out punishments

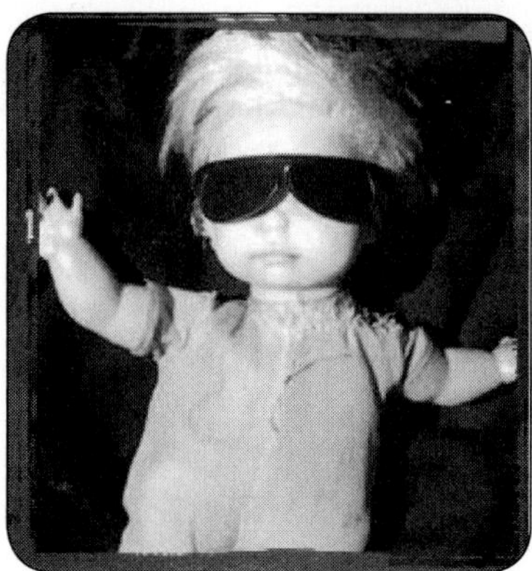

Voodoo Vaudeville's Baby Warhol

and Chris and the team ham it up on stage and generally have a ball.

Ever-evolving, Voodoo Vaudeville has performed around the globe in recent years, but its spiritual home is still the Komedia, where it appears every few months or so in various guises. Regulars will be heartened to know that Baby Warhol is still around to give advice to the needy, there's a disco at the end and, yes, you can all still join in the snake dance. Recommended.

Dress code: Victorian Gothic with a kinky twist.

Rabbit in the Headlights

Last Fri of every month, Three and Ten pub on Steine Street
www.otherplaceproductions.co.uk
www.katyschutte.com

A stand-up comedy night for new acts and new material that runs the gamut from glorious success to ignoble embarrassment. Since the night was started in 2005 by Katy Schutte and Tony Harris there have been successes such as Sean Walsh, Brian Gittins and Paul McCaffrey (if you haven't heard of them yet, you will) and, erm, quite a few failures. Each act is nominally granted a five-ten minute stand-up slot, though the stage lighting does have to be flashed at any determined ego-mongers who try to remain glued to the stage boards – one truly dire act once managed to stay on for 25 minutes, prefacing every trite remark with 'seriously'. There has also been some most unseemly blubbing on occasion. See some great comedy, witness some life-affirming deaths and most of all, be happy that you aren't up there.

Comedy Profile No. 3*
THE TWO WRONGIES

Proving that women really can be far filthier than men when it comes to sex, The Two Wrongies serve up the kind of outrageous comedy which, if ever performed at a *Daily Mail* dinner would kill off half of those present before the hors d'oeuvres got the chance to. Often performing naked (except for the occasional swimming caps and leg warmers), the girls offer everything from synchronised swimming routines to 'air sex' which, with a bit of audience participation, can get hilariously out of hand. About as far away from Corbett and Barker as is humanly possible yet still very funny, catch them around the country or locally at the Basement Arts.

**(You'll have to buy previous editions for the first two profiles, but it'd be well worth it to have the set)*

SPOKEN WORD & DEBATE

The Catalyst Club

Latest Music Bar
Second Thurs of every month,
8pm-late
www.catalystclub.co.uk

Set up and hosted by the notorious Dr Bramwell, the Catalyst Club is a night for those who enjoy a bit of debate and learning with their glass of wine or beer, as each month the Catalyst plays host to three different guests who speak for fifteen minutes on something they're passionate about.

Talks range from anecdotal stand-up, such as the gentleman whose brilliant and funny talk on *The Persuaders* was really about his 70s childhood, to the challenging ("*Why we should all go to church*" and "*Debunking Quantum Physics*" raised an eyebrow or two) and the fascinating and bizarre – zombies, giant squid, occultism, Tin Tin, naturism and tinned meat have all got a look in.

There's usually a Q&A session at the end of each talk where the audience, and sometimes the bar staff too, chip in with their comments. And if that's not enough, there's often a short film or a specific musical theme with free CDs given out by guest DJs. But rather than blow my own trumpet too much, I'll leave you in the capable hands of satisfied punter Tom Sheriff:

"The Catalyst Club? It's the only night out in Brighton, or perhaps anywhere in the UK, where you can get thoroughly pissed, get free stuff and go home knowing more than you ever thought you could or would need to about such unlikely topics as the history of the martini, the life of Herman Goering and why toast always falls butter side down."

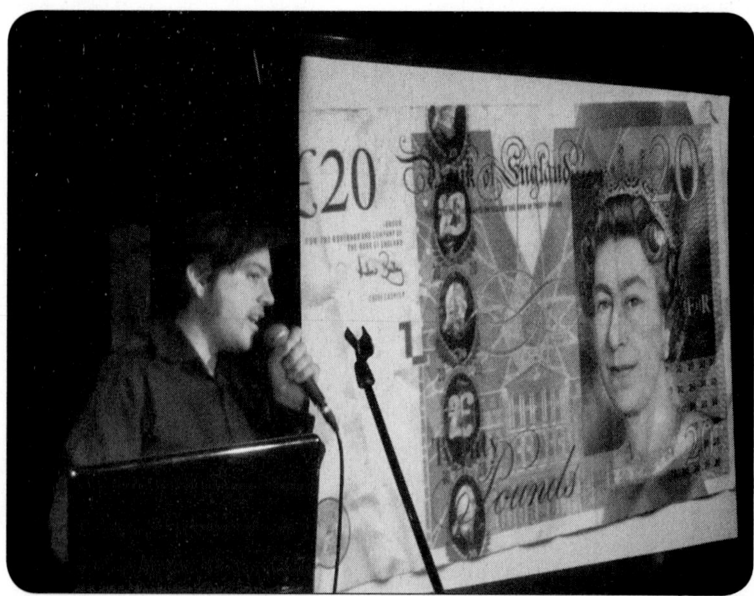

Pete 'Pop Quiz' Fijalkowski reveals his passion for unusual wallpaper at The Catalyst Club

THURSDAY
10TH FEBRUARY
10TH MARCH
14TH APRIL
THE
CATALYST
CLUB
A MONTHLY COCKTAIL OF LECTURES
SLIDE SHOWS
QUIET MUSIC, DEBATE AND
CONVERSATION.
IF YOU COULD SPEAK
ENTHUSIASTICALLY
ON ANY SUBJECT FOR
15 MINUTES, WHAT
WOULD YOU
CHOOSE?

Café Scientifique

www.cafe-scientifique-brighton.org.uk

Long-established science debating club which meets monthly at the Quadrant (or did at time of going to print) and features a talk from a guest scientist, usually clutching his/her latest tome, followed by a one-hour Q&A and a whip-round to pay for some new corduroy. The whole event is very relaxed and informal and can – at times – spark some fascinating debate. Check website for details.

Short Fuse

Komedia

submissions@shortfusestories.co.uk

This vibrant monthly live literature night is entirely devoted to the short story and provides the perfect platform for writers to read their short fiction to an audience. Celebrated local authors share the stage with newcomers, and music and a bar between readings offer the audience a chance to socialise. Run and hosted by local writer Tara Gould, this is a popular event ideal for the modern attention span. Stories are selected from submissions on merit alone, and are chosen for their craftsmanship and innovation - if you want to give it a go you can email your stuff to the address above, but keep it to less than 3,000 words; they have lives too you know.

The Space

First Tues of every month,
Latest Music Bar
www.myspace.com/thespaceuk

A shining example of what you can accomplish through sheer hard graft, The Space is a monthly media and arts event which invites famous creative types to come and talk about their work and ideas. The creation of Wayne Imms (whose phone bill must be astronomical), The Space's list of interviewees so far is incredibly impressive, from Factory Records artist Peter Saville to Barry Cryer, Jeff Wayne and William Orbit. Not only that, it's a good place to socialise and brush up against the guests, the raffle prizes are often sensational and the door price extremely modest.

GAMBLING

Brighton Mint

6-8 Preston Street (01273) 725101
2pm-6am daily (4am Sat), bar until 5.30am daily (12am Sun), Texas Hold'em poker nights Tues, Thurs and Sun
Free membership with ID
www.stanleycasinos.com

Taking itself more seriously than the Grosvenor round the corner, as you step in and hear the lilting tones of Phil Collins and Philip Bailey singing *Easy Lover* you'll realise that this place means business. Like the Grosvenor, the decor reeks of the 80s, with mirrored walls, fake wood panelling and a clientele to match – for whom the mullet is still not a fish. Downstairs plays host to regular poker nights; perfect for the serious card-player. But be warned, they have a shoot first ask questions later policy for anyone who cheats.

The Greyhound Stadium

Nevill Road, Hove (01273) 204601, box office 0845 7023 952
Tues, Thurs, Sat, 6.30-10.30pm
Wed 1pm, Fri 10.30am, Sunday 11am
Week nights £4, Sat £6
www.brightonandhovegreyhoundstadium.co.uk

An excuse to don your best tweed cap, dust off *Parklife* and shout yourself hoarse. Sorry, I mean dog. The minimum bet is only a pound; forget trying to figure out how the betting works, just pick the dog with the silliest name, use the touts outside for better odds, watch out for the lasagne and you'll have a terrific night out. Recommended if you fancy a birthday night out with a difference.

The Grosvenor Casino

9 Grand Junction Road (01273) 326514
12pm-4am daily except Thurs-Sat 12-5am
Bar until 3am daily, food 7pm-2am
www.grosvenor-casinos.co.uk

Having long ago moved from its old home by Brighton Station to a swankier residence, this casino has gone decidedly upmarket since the days of grotty psychedelic carpets and a tiny bar. There are now automated roulette tables, a £4,000-jackpot fruit machine, higher minimum stakes, live entertainment some weekends and a bar which stays open longer. True, it's still full of guys with overpowering aftershave trying to impress their white-stilettoed ladies, and swarms of Chinese businessmen with money to burn, but with its massively popular Texas Hold'em poker room, the Grosvenor seems to attract a student crowd as well.

Membership and entrance is still free and as long as you turn up with decent proof of identity you're straight in. The live roulette tables start at 50p a bet, and pontoon and poker at £3, but there are other tables with higher stakes if you're feeling brave. Alternatively, you can just watch the professionals in action and munch on the free sarnies. And did I really hear the desk girl say "*Good evening, Mr Paradise*," to one of the regulars as I was leaving once?

MY BRIGHTON & HOVE

Name: NICK PYNN
Brighton's celebrated fiddler, musician, inventor of the Cocolele and all-round good egg

Brighton, Grandad & Max Miller: a short memoir

Grahame Greene's Pinkie Brown grew up in pre-war Nelson Place, as did my dad in real life, the eldest of five and the son of a Brighton bookie. His mum was a court dressmaker and ex-music hall artiste, and his sisters Joan and Lily were dancers. My uncles Harry and Ted were, respectively, a plumber and a dockhand. I remember staying with my grandparents at 279 Albion Street after family weddings. Grandad would always recommend that I smoke a pipe when I grew up. He was a bit of a gangster, whom my uncles remembered seeing take out a pistol from a desk drawer when about to attend a 'difficult' meeting. He did however open the first legal betting shop in the south of England.

Auntie Lily's wedding.
L-R: Max Miller, Frank Pynn

Music hall performers would attend my grandad's office in Middle Street to bet on a race, before performing at the Hippodrome. Flanagan & Allen, The Crazy Gang, 'Monsewer' Eddie Grey and Max Miller (a close family friend) were all regular customers.

A few years back I was asked to perform with Arthur Brown at the Theatre Royal in a show to raise money for Brighton's Max Miller statue. I asked George Melly, smoking at the stage door, if he'd known Mr Miller, to which he replied, "*I bought him 15 brandies once… he didn't buy me one back*". My uncle Ted told me that Max gave him a guitar in the 1950s saying, "*'ere… my game's finished. Take this and learn it – it'll be the kids with guitars next that'll make all the money…*".

The Music Scene

Let's begin with a few jokes...

Q. How do you know when there's a drummer outside your door?
A. The knocking speeds up.

Q. What do you call a musician without a girlfriend/boyfriend?
A. Homeless.

And while I'm on a roll…
A bass player's girlfriend comes home to find him giving a particularly painful Chinese burn to their ten-year-old son. She begs him to stop and asks why he's inflicting pain on their loved one.
"Because he's de-tuned one of my bass strings," he says angrily.
"But there's no reason to treat him like that!" she exclaims.
"Yes, but the little bugger won't tell me which one."

LIVE MUSIC VENUES

(Upstairs at) The Prince Albert

Trafalgar Street (01273) 730499
www.myspace.com/theprincealbert

While the multi-chambered downstairs bar remains ever popular with edgy, frazzled clubbers and bewildered flotsam, the venue upstairs has found its second wind in recent times. In contrast with the spit-and-sawdust fleapit that is the Hope Live (which is not a criticism, by the way!), the Albert has cabaret-style seating (albeit only a handful of tables), a decent PA, charming star-curtain backdrop, a mirrorball and occasional candlelight. The range of nights here is wildly eclectic and often free, so there are few in Brighton whose tastes and pockets are not well served at some point during most months.

The Brighton Dome, Pavilion Theatre & Corn Exchange

Church Street/New Road (01273) 709709
www.brighton-dome.org.uk

After a £22 million refurbishment quite a few years back, which included the installation of a state-of-the-art sound system and new bar area, the Dome returned from the grave offering classical concerts, world music, comedy events and a plethora of big-name artists from Ken Dodd and Lou Reed (not on the same bill, more's the pity) to Antony and the Johnsons. Just round the corner the cavernous Corn Exchange offers what is, essentially, a rectangular Dome – but with a worse bar set-up and standing-only layout that has seen the likes of The Go! Team, Calexico and Grandaddy (RIP) pack the place. The Pavilion Theatre, however – a great room on the right night – remains frustratingly underused for rock and pop and seems to have faded from the Brighton venue map, except during the festival. Why is this? We need to be told!

The Brighton Centre & East Wing

Kingsway, Brighton seafront (01273) 290131
www.brightoncentre.co.uk

Fancy parting with £50 to see a fat, ageing superstar drag his ravaged organs around an airport terminal? Oh, you do? Then welcome to the Brighton Centre, another of those vile purpose-built conference hall-type venues found in every large town or city, and seemingly designed to sap your very life force with its bleak homogeneity. Talk is in the air, however, of it being ripped down and replaced, so keep your fingers crossed. For good measure, also cross your toes and pray the council doesn't allow it to be replaced with something equally hideous.

Concorde 2

Madeira Drive, Brighton seafront
(01273) 673311
www.concorde2.co.uk

Operating just below the radar of the Dome complex – but still putting on intriguing and up-and-coming acts you actually may have heard of – this is an excellent live venue, even if the view-blocking antique iron posts on the right can mean that you don't see the face of the keyboard player all night. Visiting during the day is not to be recommended however, otherwise you may discover the venue area is actually painted a purple more hideous that

Shane McGowan's teeth.
Top tip: If tickets for your favourite band sell out before you get the chance to buy one, book in for a game of volleyball around 4pm in the open court opposite and you might catch their soundcheck while prancing about in your shorts.
(See *Clubs*)

The Freebutt

Phoenix Place (01273) 603974
www.myspace.com/freebutt

Not a sexual favour, as tediously suggested by just about every visiting US band, but a modestly proportioned venue tucked up a side street behind the Phoenix Gallery. The Freebutt has, over the years, put on thousands of gigs of every musical description, from ska to indie to hardcore, and is the only venue in town where you can see a band every night of the week. Since the Joiners of Southampton took it over and kicked it about a bit it's much cleaner (hooray) but less characterful (boo) and no longer serves Harveys (sob). You still have to strain your neck half the time to see who's on stage, but they ***have*** improved the PA now so that not every band sounds like a Butthole Surfers album being played inside a kettle. If you're in a guitar band and looking for somewhere to play, this will probably be your first port of call. Join the ranks of legends who have helped make this scruff-hole a beloved institution. Upstairs, the Penthouse is a small chill-out room with a bar and the odd shagged sofa, serving as home to uber-hip club nights that are often packed with scruffy young things in need of a good square meal and a hug.

Hope Live

Above the Hope, 11-12 Queens Road
(01273) 325793

While the Hope pub barely merits a mention (and there it was), Hope Live upstairs is a key venue on the Brighton music scene, and sprang from the ashes of the long-defunct Lift Club once run by the crazy American with tattooed autopsy scars on his face and neck. On a busy night you'll find 90-odd skinny-trousered types here to see the latest guitar gods and goddesses strutting their stuff. If you prefer your gigs intimate, this is the place to come. I've always held to the notion that the smaller the venue and the cheaper the tickets, the better the gig. Why spend £100 to stand at the back of a football stadium watching a giant plasma screen when you can spend £6 and actually be able to smell the singer's armpits?

I'm still kicking myself at missing the likes of the White Stripes and Strokes who played here years ago on their first tours. Don't make the same mistake: come to ***every*** single gig they put on and in a few years you'll be able to say: "*Gloria Cycles are playing at the Brighton Centre? Listen mate, I remember seeing them at the Hope. It was only a few quid. And I stood right at the front and got to touch Jen the bassist's kneecap with my rubber glove...*"

West Hill Community Centre

West Hill Hall, Compton Avenue
www.myspace.com/westhill

It'd be easy to spend a lifetime in this town and not know of this venue's existence. The building is hidden down the alleyway of a residential road in Seven Dials, there's no phone number and very little evidence of its existence beyond the odd poster and a MySpace page. After a visit here recently I had the idea to ask one of the organisers to put me on the mailing list. He frowned, ripped the back off a fag packet and proffered it me with a broken biro. I never heard back.

So is it really worth the effort? Actually, yes. While weekdays are, I suspect, given over to yoga, salsa and tupperware parties, at weekends (well, Saturdays at least) the community centre transforms into a kooky, cabaret, *It Ain't Half Hot, Mum* village hall affair with the latest leftfield, weirdy-beardy bands on stage fiddling with theremins, kettles, sitars, banjos and musical saws. If you prefer your music more Robert Wyatt than Robbie Williams, you'll find this beautiful, intimate venue just the ticket, and a good place to meet other local avant-garde musicians. As for finding out what's on and when, try the above website – and if that fails, pop into Edgeworld Records in North Laine and pester them.

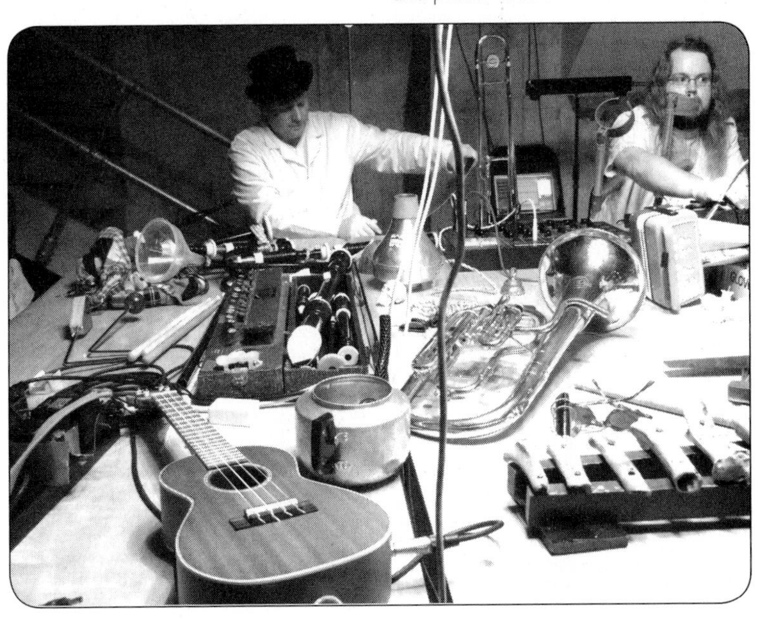

Healthy Concerts

www.healthyconcerts.com

Whatever you think of Nizlopi's JCB Song (and I try to think of it as little as possible), their career has an unusual genesis in the Gigs In Digs scene, where acoustic performers play in people's gardens and living rooms. This concept was invented in Brighton as Healthy Concerts in 1994 by Paul Chi, who wanted literally to bring the artist and audience closer together, and cut out the background noise and fag smoke of pubs and clubs. The idea has since spread across East Sussex, seems particularly popular in the Bristol area and even popped up in the USA under the label House Concerts.

Anyone can volunteer their home as a one-off venue, and there's a BYO policy on booze, although some venue owners are particular about what type of drink you bring, presumably to keep the Special Brew crew at bay. Talking is forbidden while musicians are playing, which you will either view as po-faced and overly reverential or a huge boon that allows you to concentrate on the music. There's also the occasional after-party, which can be, erm, not so healthy.

Wholegrain baguette Flying V

LOCAL PROMOTERS, MOVERS AND SHAKERS

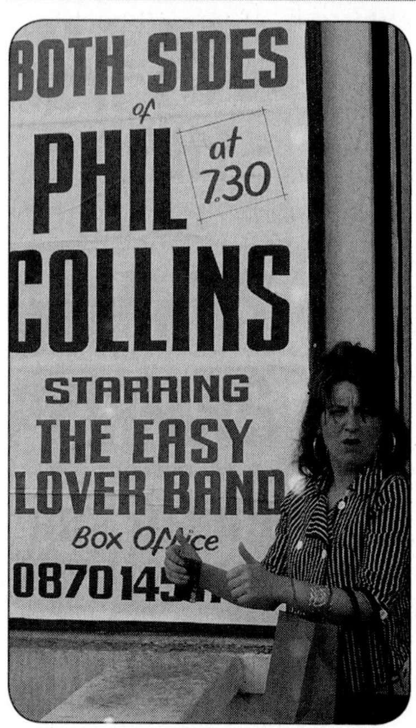

Eee baa gum, Anna Moulsecoomb looks forward to another groundbreaking promotion

Melting Vinyl

Contact Anna (01273) 325955

www.meltingvinyl.co.uk, info@meltingvinyl.co.uk

Groovy Northern lass Anna 'eh-up' Moulson has been beavering away in Brighton for four or five decades now as a top promoter, and is responsible for some of the best gigs in town; everything from garage pop to twisted electronica comes under her wing. To her credit she arranged the first-ever UK shows for the White Stripes (at the Lift, now Hope Live; yes, it was insane) and has put on gigs by such luminaries as Julian Cope, Emiliana Torrini, Howe Gelb and underground Norwegian one-man band Midgetboybaconfjord. As well as doing regular gigs at the

Albert, Concorde 2, the Pavilion Theatre and the Dome, she has put on events in local churches, the Duke of York's cinema and even Fred's old allotment shed in Peacehaven. Go to Anna's events and expect way-out sounds, electronic pioneers, lo-fi, punk and some of the coolest bands on the planet. Support this lovely Yorkshire lady. It would be awfully quiet in Brighton without her.

The Gilded Palace of Sin

www.thegildedpalaceofsin.com

The clue is in the name. Set up ten years ago with the express intention of bringing country-based/influenced music of any sonic approach to Brighton, TGPoS have earned themselves a thoroughly deserved but totally unexpected international reputation. Their care for acts and punters, an acute attention to detail and unnerving passion for the music they promote has won many friends, impressed by their drive to present great-value, top-quality shows. There's a punk DIY ethic, coupled with an obsession with bringing Brighton only the very best of what they see as Americana. They have an uncanny knack of unearthing future legends just as they set off and they heartily support the local scene. You can expect anything from bluegrass to power pop to future folk to acoustic misery at GPoS nights. There's plenty of country, of course, but the church is broad even within that genre. They also have a catch-all offshoot called Be A Ham to indulge much wider passions that have thus far ranged from the avant-orch pop of Efterklang to the visceral punk pop of the Thermals. Always unpredictable and never, ever dull.

POP QUIZZES

I Predict a Pop Quiz

The Iron Duke, Waterloo Street, Hove
Mondays 8.30-10.30pm Free entry

An off-kilter pop quiz where you're just as likely to come across a live bagpipe player performing the songs of Kraftwerk or sitar renditions of hip hop classics as you are more traditional music trivia about who was the tallest or ugliest member of the Beatles.

Hosted by the genially rambling Pete Fijalkowski (former lead singer of Coventry-based Creation band Adorable) the quiz has an emphasis on fun and veers off into Vic And Bob/Alan Partridge territory as well as satisfying the more traditional pub quiz gamer. A good cheap night's entertainment as the quiz is free and every team wins a prize, plus there are the usual free drinks and free crisps rounds. Trust me, it's brilliant.

Full details at *www.myspace.com/ipredictapopquiz*.

LOCAL RADIO STATIONS

FIP 90.5-91FM

www.fipradio.com

While not strictly local (in fact not even British), this cool, Parisian radio station has been broadcasting from a secret location in Brighton for years now. Advert-free and genuinely eclectic, FIP knocks spots off mainstream English music radio stations by offering everything from classical to jazz to underground pop and heavy dub reggae, all interspersed with the occasional lilting tones of a spaced-out Frenchman. The acronym, incidentally, stands for France Inter Paris.

Top tip: While not directly connected with the radio station, Vive La FIP is a club night in Brighton, hosted by Francophiles with eclectic music tastes, stripy shirts and garlic breath. Like FIP, it's really rather good.

DJ, performer, club host and King of Camp, Boogaloo Stu

Juice 107.2FM

www.juicebrighton.com

While daytime playlists are pretty much what you'd expect from a local radio station, in a *Jekyll and Hyde* sort of way, come the evening and weekends Juice turns all hairy and goes on the rampage. Once through the seven o'clock watershed expect anything from the latest dancefloor anthems to cutting-edge indie rock. The undoubted highlight of the week however is Lazy Sunday, running from Sunday 6am to 2am with cracking playlists from Boogaloo Stu, Darius Akashic (known as Mr A to his fanbase of ankle-biters), Tru-Thoughts Recordings head honcho Rob Luis, Lost Idol & La Femme from Cookshop Music, The Roots Garden Sound System and more. The perfect excuse to stay in bed for the whole of Sunday with just a cafetière and bedpan for company.

Totally Radio

www.totallyradio.co.uk

This local online station leaves no musical stone unturned - everything from 60s ska and psych, 70s punk and reggae, 80s hiphop, indie and US hardcore, 90s DnB and electronica and up to date with dubstep, salsa and acid folk though extreme rock, alt country and death jazz – the kinds of music you simply won't hear on your FM radio. On-demand shows are around an hour long and feature such local heroes as Crooked Stylus, Gilded Palace of Sin, Where To Now, AfroBase and Coldcut's Solid Steel. The legendary Mike Bradshaw also has a daily show: a worthy replacement for the late, great John Peel. Recommended.

BBC Southern Counties 104-104.8FM

Local news for local people, Southern Counties offers the tried-and-tested formula of traffic reports, bland music, and Alan Partridge-style presenters. At its best, however, it does probe and discuss local issues and serves the community (well, the Brighton middle classes, anyway). And there is plenty of exposure for local bands through demo panels and live sessions on fervent supporter Phil Jackson's show, so it's not ***all*** bad.

Reverb 97.2 FM

www.radioreverb.com

While the mere existence of this community radio station is to be championed, sadly it seems to have skipped the attention of most Brightonians and desperately needs an injection of funds and advertising to get the listening figures and shows it deserves. Being a station run on a shoestring and largely volunteer-based means that what's on offer ranges from interesting field recordings, avant-garde stuff and a few shows that play some fine music (Bust The Box, Beans On Toast) to the kind of shambolic presenting and amateur DJing that'll make you want to chew the knobs off your radio. Reverb may have a long way to go before reaching the standards of London's community station Resonance, but deserves all the support it can to get it there.

HOW TO FIND OUT WHO'S PLAYING

All the local magazines and websites, particularly www.myspace.com/brightonlivespace, will give you a rundown on who's playing and where. Some of the best places to pick up information are the record shops, which have posters for last-minute and low-key gigs. Rounder Records and Resident should be your first ports of call for information on gigs, club nights and other music events, while Edgeworld Records is likely to have flyers for any lo-fi events that might otherwise be overlooked.

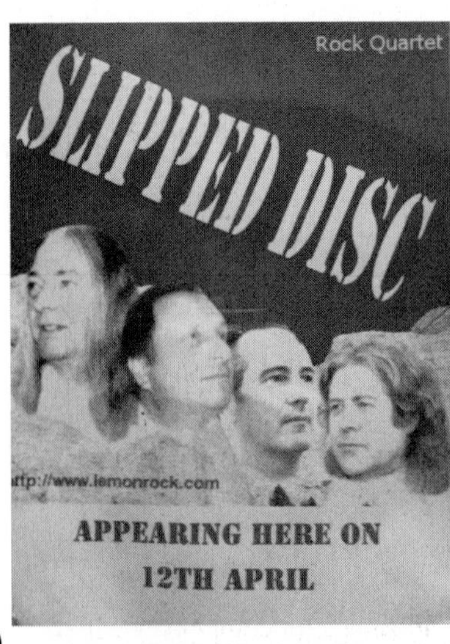

Rock Quartet
SLIPPED DISC
http://www.lemonrock.com
APPEARING HERE ON
12TH APRIL

Former legendary five piece Trapped Wind

WHERE TO GET TICKETS

Rounder Records

Brighton Square (01273) 325440
www.rounder.com

Resident

Kensington Gardens (01273) 606312
www.resident-music.com

The places for tickets and general info on who's playing and when.

Dance 2 Records

129 Western Road (01273) 220023/329459

Tickets for everything related to dance, DJ and club culture, including big festivals and the likes of Beatdown and Devotion.

Dome Box Office

New Road (01273) 709709

For all the bigger events at the Corn Exchange, the Pavilion Theatre and the Dome itself. Also the main ticket office during the Brighton Festival and Fringe.

SO YOU WANT TO BE A ROCK AND ROLL STAR?

Brighton Institute of Modern Music (BIMM)

www.bimm.co.uk

So you want to be a rock and roll star? sang cynical Byrds lead singer Jim McGuinn shortly before joining the Subud faith and changing his name to Roger (they insisted his name had to begin with an 'R'; he suggested Rocket, Retro or Ramjet, they suggested he stop being silly and settle on Roger). But I digress. Here at last is a real School of Rock! Genuine professionals who can teach you the riff from *Stairway to Heaven*, where to buy patchouli oil, how to snort cocaine off a dwarf's head and more besides. But I'm sure they've heard those gags a thousand times. In truth BIMM is brilliant for budding musicians and anyone serious about learning the ins and outs of this sordid but brilliant profession. Through BIMM you can get a diploma in everything from sound engineering and tour management to songwriting. As for how to play guitar with a ciggie dangling out your mouth and *not* getting smoke in your eyes... you'll just have to learn that yourself.

THE POP CELEBRITY HALL OF FAME

It is a well-established fact that, apart from Fatboy Slim, everyone in Brighton is a musician of some sort. With a glut of successful acts in recent years from Bat for Lashes to the Kooks, and with the Brighton Institute of Modern Music (BIMM) attracting popstar wannabes the world over, it seems only right we celebrate the town's euphonious achievements. Below is a helpful guide to the popstars of past and present who at one time or another have graced our city. I must admit, though, some of it may be based on hearsay and an overactive imagination.

Splitting Images
celebrity lookalike agency
Leo Sayer Lookalike

Wonder if he gets a lot of work?

FAMOUS FOR 15 MINUTES

Kirk Brandon *(Spear of Destiny, definitely wasn't Boy George's lover, oh no)*
Electrelane *(now split up sadly, though keep your eyes peeled for a reunion gig in twenty years or so)*
Frazier Chorus (*Anyone remember* Dream Kitchen?)
Peter and the Test Tube Babies *(Still going and still not very famous)*
The Piranhas *(Ska punk outfit best known for their cover of* Zambesi)
Tampasm *(Noisy all-girl band with attitude who appeared once on* The Girlie Show *then settled down to a life of gingham and domestic servitude)*
These Animal Men (NME *darlings who lived entirely off speed and hair dye)*

STILL THROWING TVS OUT OF WINDOWS

Bat for Lashes
British Sea Power
Brakes
Nick Cave
Norman Cook
Gaz Coombes (Supergrass)
The Electric Soft Parade
The Go! Team
The Kooks
The Levellers
Leo Sayer
David Thomas (Pere Ubu)
Emiliana Torrini

MY BRIGHTON & HOVE

Name: BRIAN SATCHEL
local playwright

1. The Whistling Teapot Where else in Brighton could you order bacon and cabbage soup and still have change from 50p? And they show old Laurel and Hardy films in the afternoon. And they still allow you to smoke. Marvellous. Mind you, it did close down in 1978.

2. Shabby's Tweed Emporium The place to buy your second-hand slacks. The gent who runs it is a lovely fellow and often has an old German Shepherd, Bob. He's a nice fellow too. Boom boom! But seriously folks, where else in Brighton could you buy a porkpie hat for under a quid? And they let you smoke. Pity it closed over twenty years ago.

3. Arthur Grumble's Tobacco and Snuff Shop God bless Arthur Grumble. The most cantankerous misanthropic man I have ever met! But he certainly gives a good shag. Boom boom! But seriously, you'll not find a finer purveyor of tobacco this side of the planet. And it's actually still open! Pity I stopped smoking five years ago but then, as the missus keeps reminding me, it is for the good of me health. And besides.... oh eck she's returned. Blast! Better sign off. If she catches me with this pie in me hand she'll, ow, ouch, aagghhh…

The Brighton musician's

Wheel of Life

1. You answer an ad in the Guitar and Amp Shop/Scream Studios and spend the evening with an unhinged alcoholic in his bedsit, listening to demo tracks of his old group.

2. After another year of this you decide to form your own band and bring some purity back to pop music.

3. You audition hundreds of guitarists until you find someone who owns an original 70s Telecaster. Even though he can't play it, you know a cool guitar when you see one and this is way more important.

4. You wait another three years for a bassist and a drummer to come along. When you finally get them it turns out that the bassist is a frustrated guitarist and the drummer is a psychopath who doesn't particularly like music but enjoys hitting things. They'll do for now.

5. At your first gig at the Freebutt the drummer punches the singer of another band, your guitarist fails to notice that he is playing the wrong set and then gets in a strop about it and you have a sneaking feeling that the bassist played slap-bass on one of the tracks. Your friends tell you that you sound a bit like the Stereophonics, which is ironic because you hate them.

6. You record a demo, have 40,000 made, spend a week arguing over the track listing, send one copy to Zane Lowe and put the rest under your bed, where they remain.

7. After six months, the bassist announces that although still committed to the band, he has formed his own band called Funkypanda, playing jazz-funk covers. You are alarmed to notice that he is starting to wear corduroy and grow a goatee.

8. Your demo returns from Zane Lowe with the message "*Sounds too much like the Stereophonics*".

9. The drummer by now has taken to hitting the bass player rather than his drums and the only way to calm him down is with heavy and regular doses of ketamine.

10. You discover the existence of a Swedish synth-pop band with the same name as you.

11. The bassist announces that he is leaving to concentrate on his jazz-funk career, so you hide the drummer's stash of ketamine and unchain him.

12. You read in the paper that yet another Brighton band have just done a Lamacq session.

13. The drummer phones from prison to say that he can't make the next 400 rehearsals.

14. The guitarist comes round to your house, you smoke a joint together, reminisce about the good old days and moan about all the bands you know who have sold out. You jam through a couple of Turin Brakes numbers, then turn in.

15. A month later you have a dream that you saw your old guitarist on *Stars in Their Eyes*. The words "*Tonight, Matthew, I'm going to be Jay Kay from Jamiroquai*" are like daggers through your heart and you wake in a cold sweat.

16. You move into a bedsit, start drinking heavily and put an advert in the Guitar and Amp Shop.

17. The cycle is now complete.

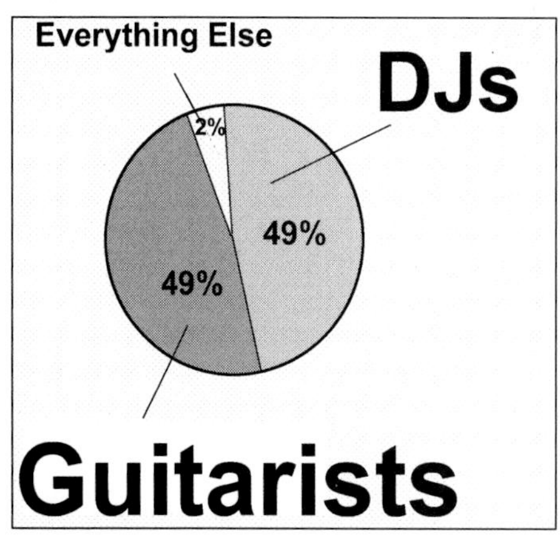

BRIGHTON MUSICIANS PIE CHART

Heroes, Eccentrics & Celebrities

Brighton has always attracted more than its fair share of outlandish individuals, and below is a guide to some of the town's fruitiest and most lovable rogues and mavericks. Far from being branded loonies, these individuals are championed here for their style, courage, humour and lust for life. Saying that, does anyone remember the Bread Man, the guy who used to wander the streets of North Laine between six and seven in the morning with two French loaves strapped to his head like helicopter blades? Now he ***was*** *a loony.*

Drako Zarhazar

Undoubtedly Brighton's greatest eccentric, Drako Zarhazar's life story reads like some improbable work of fiction: he has danced at the Moulin Rouge and the London Palladium, modelled for Salvador Dalì, starred in films by Andy Warhol and Derek Jarman and survived two serious road accidents and comas. Decorated with exotic tattoos and piercings, Drako is a character you simply couldn't mistake, even in Brighton – his forehead sports a tattooed triangle and his face is adorned with bright blue eyebrows, piercings and an impressive Dalìesque wax moustache. A visit to his flat is like stepping into the pages of a psychedelic porn mag: ***all*** the walls, the ceiling, cupboards and even the bathroom are adorned with phallic images. From flaccid to fully erect, there are thousands of them everywhere, some stuck casually onto the wall, some hanging from the ceiling, others accompanied by humorous comments.

Ask him about his movie career and Drako is fairly nonchalant, preferring instead to describe his favourite moment as *"one night in Rome when someone filmed me putting a candle up someone's arse, which I lit and then, with a big whip, whipped out the flame".*

DRAKO RECALLS MEETING DALÌ FOR THE FIRST TIME

"I remember being invited one day to a house on the outskirts of Paris. I walked down the stairs to a pool in the basement, and swimming naked in the pool were two beautiful girls. I remember coming and sitting on a big couch next to Salvador Dalí. He was just wearing a bathrobe and didn't say anything to me but kept watching these two naked girls swimming, when I suddenly noticed Dalí's hand moving up and down next to me. He was looking at these beautiful girls… and he was wanking. And I thought to myself, here I am on the outskirts of Paris, sat next to the famous Dalí, with him wanking over these beautiful girls. Isn't life incredible?"

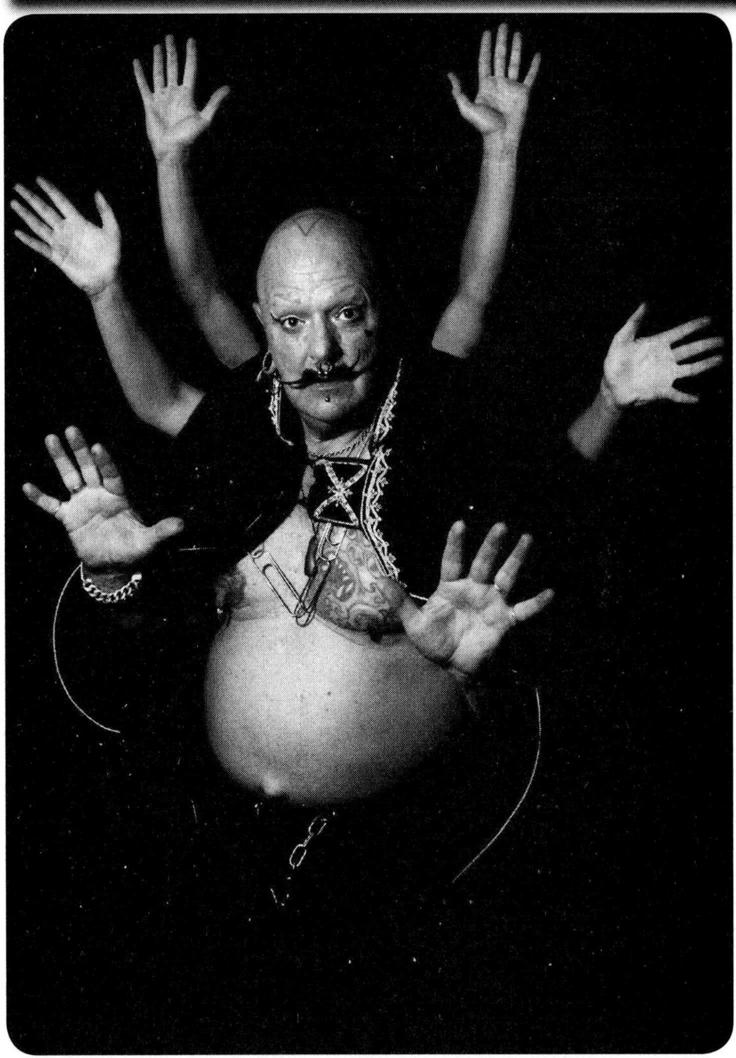

Chris Macdonald

93 Gloucester Road
(01273) 601639
www.chrismacdonald.eu

Chris Macdonald has spent the past fifteen years in Brighton constructing beautiful and strange sculptures out of wood and found metal objects in his studio on Gloucester Road. There is something Dalìesque about the way he juxtaposes curious metal gadgets (such as old camera parts or giant cogs) with beautifully carved wooden items, but the finished pieces themselves are wholly original, the work of a man who fell down Alice's rabbit hole and never returned.

Chris's sculptures can be viewed and purchased from his website or gallery at the address above. If you want to visit the gallery, it's best to phone before, or he'll most likely be dancing around his studio to Talking Heads or dreaming up another work of art.

Charles Webb & Fred

Who'd have thought the novelist responsible for *The Graduate* could be found living in relative obscurity in a small flat in Brighton with a lady called Fred? Having written a book that rejected materialism and middle-class values, Webb went on to practise what he preached, took virtually nothing from the $100 million profits from the book, film and musical and claims that his proudest moment was when one of his sons cooked and ate a copy of the *Graduate* paperback with cranberry sauce. After living in a camper van, illegally home-schooling his kids in California and running a nudist colony in New Jersey, Charles finally moved to Brighton, partly to escape the curse of the success of the book and film. His partner has some lovely eccentricities too, having changed her name from Anxiety to Fred *"to support guys called Fred"*.

Webb has continued to write: the long-promised sequel to *The Graduate* came out in 2008 and his novel *New Jersey* was made into a film. Part of the proceeds were allocated to Fred to create an award for an innovative artistic idea. The result? £15,000 to local artist Dan Sheldon for mailing himself by registered post to the Tate Modern.

Roy Skelton

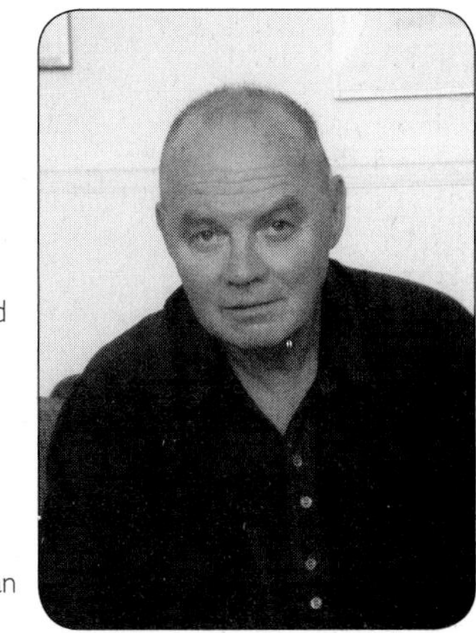

When Kemp Town resident Roy Skelton auditioned for a children's show called *Rainbow* in the early 70s, he didn't figure that it would keep him in gainful employment for sixteen years and turn him and his characters into cult heroes. But after providing the voice of Zippy and George for all these years that's exactly what happened, and Roy still receives sackloads of fan mail every month (most common questions: *"What is Zippy?"* and *"Is George gay?"*)

On top of this, Roy provided the original voice for the Daleks for more than 30 years, tried to exterminate everyone from William Hartnell to Sylvester McCoy, and even played the parts of other universal miscreants such as Cybermen, Monoids, Krotons and David Van Day... Though now in his seventies, Roy is still sprightly and youthful, with more than a hint of Zippy in his smooth round head and bullfrog voice, though whether his alter-ego is a placid camp hippo is another matter.

Sir Ralph Harvey

A well-dressed and genteel man, sporting the fading moustache of a brigadier, Ralph travels the world battling the likes of Vikings and Saxons with military re-enactment societies. He makes regular appearances around the country with his own outfit dressed as the cast of *Dad's Army* – with himself, of course, as Captain Mainwaring.

More surprisingly, perhaps, Ralph is one of the country's leading authorities on the occult, heading his own local Wiccan coven, and is responsible for sorting out much of the poltergeist activity around the Shoreham area. Also an actor, at the height of his fame Ralph played Hercule Poirot on Belgian television, where he became a household name, until the Agatha Christie estate stopped the TV company using the famous detective's name. From then on, even though he dressed the same and played the same role, Ralph had to be known as 'Inspector Sprout', but, somehow, it was never the same.

Look for him as Captain Mainwaring, parading down the seafront during the May Festival, or in town giving lectures on the occult.

Michael "Atters" Attree

www.thechap.net/content/section_news/judge-my-shrub.html
www.ministryofmoustaches.0catch.com

This stylish and singular man about town with a penchant for sartorial elegance and surrounding himself with scantily-clad showgirls can generally be found at local auctions, séances, society dos and the Sussex Fencing Club. However it s his longstanding editorial role as The Chap magazine's "*official moustachioed bounder*" that has made "Atters" (as he is more widely known) not only a caddish hero around Brighton but among 'chaps' and 'chapettes' the civilised world over. He is the youngest committee member of London's famous Handlebar Club, a place whose etiquette demands gentlemanly conduct, the wearing of a Club tie (it's drinks all round if you don't) and, as Atters cheekily puts it, "*an ability to bore all outsiders with tales of the Empire and deceased comedians*".

In 2007 Atters was elected Honourable Chairman of the 2007 World Beard and Moustache Championships held in Brighton, and compered the event, riling judge Nick Cave by introducing him as "*Mr Nicholas Cave*", despite the singer's constant yells of "*My name's Nick!*" As a satirical comic performer his theatre show Atters Attree's Chaporgasmic Terrors screens his risqué magic laptop projections of the supernatural including: A Fossilised Poltergeist, Gym-slip Levitation and The Abominable Gayman. It's comforting to know that, despite all of Brighton's hirsute unwashed, there is at least one bounder who, as he succinctly puts it, "*has the balls to sport the facial topiary worthy of a gentleman!*"

Letitcia

www.brightonbodyworship.com

Self-appointed sex goddess Letitcia has travelled the world, played every brothel from Singapore to Australia, seen the odd willy or two and lived to tell the tales. And very amusing they are too; you can even read them in her candid autobiography *Body Worship*. If the story of the guy who liked inserting other people's dried turds inside himself doesn't have you laughing uncontrollably (or put you right off your dinner), the chapter on men's hygiene will. As Letitcia explains:

"I did have this one client, everything that could be wrong, he had it – dogbreath, the pungent aroma of twenty-year-old sweat… Alarmingly, he produced a medical certificate from his doctor to allay my fears about this strange rash on his chest; I was more concerned that when he took off his underpants he appeared to have elephantiasis of the balls. They were the size of footballs. And as for his feet, well, let's not even go there! I sat him down and drew up a list of things he needed to attend to with regard to his body. It was the kindest thing I could have done."

You can often find Letitcia having a cappuccino in Kemp Town before a busy day ahead. If you want to get to know her more 'intimately', try visiting her website. But guys, if you do give her a call, try and be more original with your opening questions. Apparently, *"can I get a suck without a condom?"* and *"what's the parking like?"* are still the most common.

The Birdlady of St Peters

If you re wandering around town and notice a jabbering flock of several hundred seagulls, endlessly divebombing a shambling woman with gesticulating limbs, don t scamper in to help out   it s just the Birdlady of St Peters, fulfilling her endless quest to ensure the poor birdies don t go hungry. Often accompanied by a supermarket trolley to hold the score or so loaves of bread that are so necessary to keep our unique species of Brighton gull from becoming extinct (they can no longer digest raw fish, having been raised on a diet of doughnuts, candyfloss and used nappies), the Birdlady does the dirty work that the council refuses to contemplate. Her favourite spot seems to be the grass around St Peters Church on Grand Parade but any green space near the seafront will do. Occasionally she fancies a change and you ll see her standing covered in pigeons, looking like a peculiarly ineffective scarecrow.

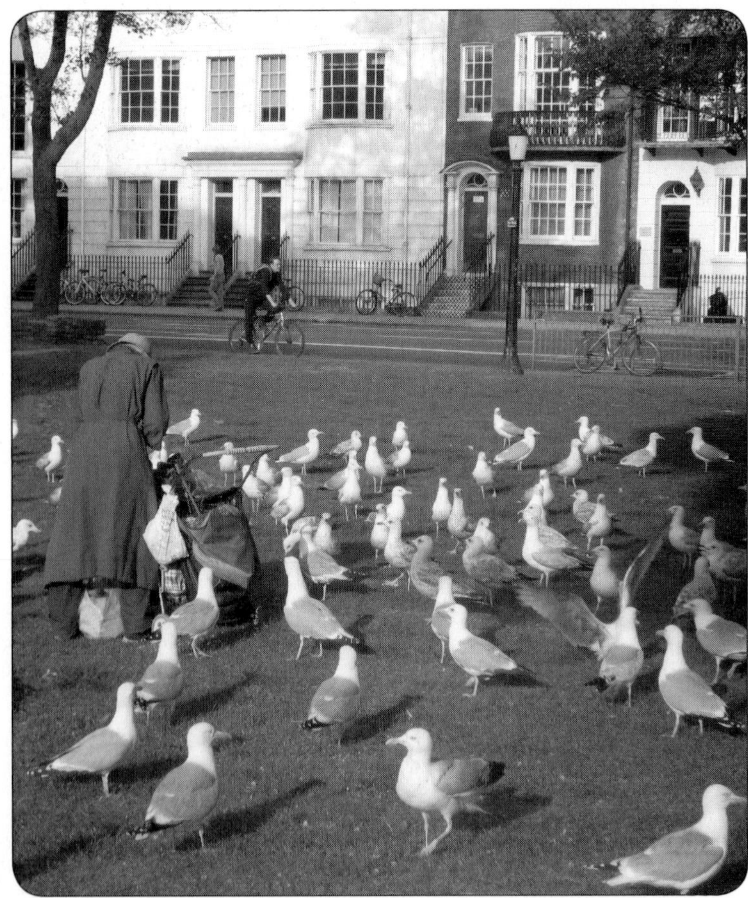

George Birtwell

Looking like a young Prince Charles (without the ugly bits), George's outward appearance and gentle manner belie the beating heart of a philanthrope and adventurer. Not content with being one of the Maydays (a local comedy team who perform one-hour improvised musicals) or sitting outside his house in Hanover handing out free homemade pies and lemonade to passers-by, George is currently on the first leg of a world tour... in an old 80s milkfloat.

In 2009, George and a mate set off round the country in this singular vehicle to raise money for charity. But as it only travels at 8-12mph and needs recharging every ten miles (which takes five hours!), the whole thing seems even more ambitious than Sufjan Stevens' plan to release an album for every US state. Despite Phil Collins turning down George's request to do a charity gig on his float (Phil wanted £250k, apparently) George and co are having a fine old time. According to current calculations George will be back in 2074, aged 93. We wish him good luck and hope he's remembered to feed the cat.

Paul Harrison

Take a stroll round Brighton and it won't be long before you stumble across the work of Paul Harrison: the giant Les Paul outside GAK, the palm trees in the Pavilion shop, Revamp's rubber-clad fetish girl. He even designed the first Body Shop with Anita Roddick. But peruse his workshop in Ditchling Rise, crammed with half-built gadgets, weird musical instruments and mechanical objects of his own design and you'll soon realise that Paul is not just about interior design and sign-making but is a genuine inventor of the Wilf Lunn variety – who can even lay claim to being the creator of the silk flame light. Paul can be spotted busking in town or at festivals dressed in a top hat, crow on his shoulder and making ambient soundscapes with wires, sticks and fingertips, with his own unique creation the X-piano, made from the internal organs of an upright piano! If, like eccentric Oxfordian Bill Heine, you need someone to figure out how to build a giant fibreglass shark and have it crashing through your roof, this is the man to call.

Dolly Rocket

Describing herself as *"successful at the very arse end of the entertainment industry and proud of it!"* singer, club host, burlesque performer and show-off, Dolly Rocket has been wowing Brighton audiences for more than twenty years now, regularly performing at many of the town's longest running and biggest party nights including Dynamite Boogaloo, Wild Fruit and Voodoo Vaudeville.

A champion for the Amazonian woman, she stands some six feet five inches in her heels. This, combined with her larger-than-life character and impressive curves sometimes leads to her mistakenly being called a drag queen, which she is not. She is in fact, *"the kind of woman drag queens are merely emulating!"*

A few of Dolly's career highlights include playing a lesbian pimp alongside Steven Berkoff in the British movie *Nine Dead Gay Guys*, appearing as Boob Woman and Lola Lust in *Electric Blue Adult Video Magazine* (numbers 33 and 34 for those who're interested). She has appeared in the National Portrait Gallery, as well as being photographed by the legendary David Bailey, who told her she had *"beautiful blow-job lips"* (she hastens to add that he didn't get to experience them!) Anyone who's seen her perform will no doubt agree that Ms Rocket is not just a gay icon but a Brighton treasure and one hell of a woman!

Dr Parsons *www.crazycomicclub.co.uk*

Satirical cartoonist Dr "James" Parsons has been punting his often extreme and visceral but nevertheless chuckle-inducing comic books since 2001 when he published *This Is Me by George Bush*, though he no longer touts them round the pubs of Brighton after *"too many freaks and near-fights"*. Tackling modern malaises with titles such as *The Pornography Of Everything* and *101 Ways Diana Could Have Died* is I suppose bound to upset some people, and despite (or possibly because of) his work appearing in a host of respectable newspapers and magazines he has been *"cleaned up by the lawyers plenty"*. Unsurprisingly then, his next book involves the crisis of editorial independence in mainstream media. Though they might not make the ideal Christmas present for granny (unless she enjoys drawings of Michael Jackson undergoing "*gonzo cock surgery*"), James' books often feature delightfully intricate and detailed work that brings to mind a drug-ravaged Heath Robinson or a steadier-handed Ralph Steadman.

Having *"turned to the brainwashing of children"* he now also runs kids' illustration workshops in Brighton and at festivals around the country under the moniker The Crazy Comic Club, and when queried on whether parents should be wary, says *"if they expose their children to my work, the resulting massive psychological trauma is their sole responsibility"*.

www.crazycomicclub.co.uk www.myspace.com/drparsons

Lorraine Bowen

www.lorrainebowen.co.uk

Lorraine Bowen is an eccentric songwriter with a massive organ collection in her loft. The Casio Queen of Brighton is absolutely mad on retro organs from the 1980s and the strains of bossa-nova beats can be heard winding their way up around the vicinity of Brighton Station where she resides.

"It's the auto accompaniments I most love," she sighs passionately. *"It's that little piece of musical history that gets me right there!"* pointing to her nether regions! *"Sometimes the dodgy 80s wiring helps to create that little bit more vibrato than you'd expect from an ordinary organ."*

Her collection mainly involves the Casiotone range but her proudest possession is an original brown 1981 Omnichord that Billy Bragg gave er when she was working with him as piano player/vocal coach in the 90s. Kirsty MacColl had recommended it to him as a songwriting aid but Lorraine proudly declares: *"Billy said it sounded too cheesy for him – but perfect for Lorraine Bowen!"* Lorraine is most famous for her *Crumble Song,* which has now been translated into five languages including Indian. She performs round the world and will accept donations of old organs (especially with dodgy wiring)!

A Spotter's Guide To BRIGHTON CELEBRITIES

Brighton has long been home to an eclectic bunch of celebrities, from world famous actors to popstars. What better way to spend an afternoon than going all gooey-eyed and weak-kneed at having stumbled across that bloke from The Bill *whose name you can't recall, or the bass player from legendary local band Anal Beard?*

NICK CAVE

The brooding Australian singer lives in deepest, darkest Hove (naturally), and can be spotted hanging around outside the King Alfred in a crumpled suit and dark glasses, smoking copious amounts of fags. Either that or he'll be in Toys R Us buying *Mr Bean* videos for his kids.
Worth 50 points (60 if seen in Mothercare)

DAVID VAN DAY

At one time the ex-Dollar singer could be found running his burger stall by Churchill Square. Now, after attempting to kickstart his flagging career through such predictable means as trying to get elected as local Tory candidate, appearing on reality-TV shows, dumping his girlfriend live on daytime telly (classy) and selling his soul to the devil, things appear to be taking off again. Is there no beginning to this man's talents?
Worth 1 point

STEVE COOGAN

A rare spot now his film career has taken off but still most likely to be seen in a boozer. If you're an attractive female it's best to keep your distance or wear heavy protective armour.
Worth 30 points (45 if he doesn't try and mate with you)

FATBOY SLIM

From Quentin to Norman to Freakpower to Fatboy Slim (and a host of other pseudonyms along the way), local hero Norman Cook is still releasing albums, performing the occasional DJ spot at the Concorde 2, and doing his best to support Brighton & Hove Albion. God bless him. And someone buy his records, please, or he'll end up running a burger bar on Western Road and appearing on reality-TV shows…

Worth 15 points

CHRIS EUBANK

Once an easy spot owing to the fact that Chris spent most of his waking hours driving his juggernaut, motorbike or tractor around the Lanes waving at bemused strangers. Since the bankruptcy he's been keeping his head down. Give him time: he'll be back. Probably as the latest face for the *"I'm on the bus"* campaign.

Worth 2 points

PATSY PALMER

The dulcet tones of Patsy Palmer cooing the name of her loved one Ricky in *EastEnders* was once a thing to be cherished. Now she's a Brighton lass, you may think she's gone all poncey but good old Patsy remains true to her genuine Cockney roots. Hang around her home of Kemp Town and you may be lucky enough to hear that lilting warble when she's out walking her pet dog, Licky Micky. Of course you might still hear her even if you live in Hove.

Worth 15 points

HEATHER MILLS

The ex-Mrs McCartney is busy these days spending her hard-earned divorce settlement on such things as her vegan café next to Hove Lagoon. Nip down there on a sunny afternoon and you ll find her feeding five year olds with veggie burgers or throwing mugs of boiling rice milk at tabloid photographers.

Worth 12 points

DAVID THOMAS FROM PERE UBU

Strictly for the music lovers, this one. Look for him striding around Hove like some crazy Ignatius Reilly from *A Confederacy of Dunces*… Hmmm, I feel I've lost a few of you here. Never mind, read on.

Worth 35 points (50 if wearing his red plastic bib)

MARK WILLIAMS FROM THE FAST SHOW

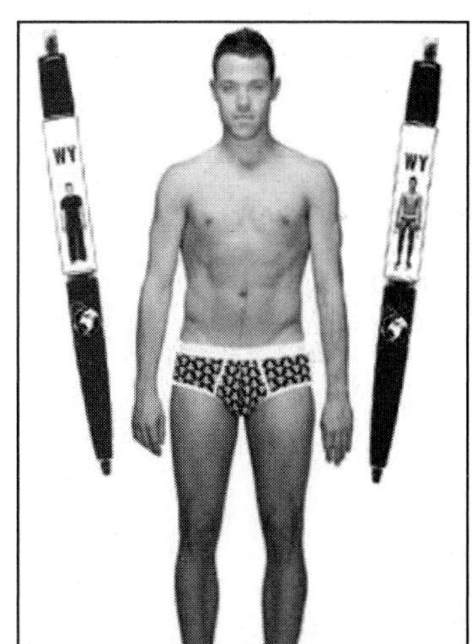

Invariably spotted in a boozer. With a pint or two in his hand. Remember the *Father Ted* episode with Victor Meldrew before you go up to him and say *"Suits you, Sir!"*

Worth 15 points

WILL YOUNG

Tricky to verify owing to his habit of denying he's Will Young and pretending to be Graham Norton, the fame-shy *Pop Idol* winner is most likely to be seen falling off a surfboard down at the beach.

Worth 25 points

If you've been missed out of our *Spotter's Guide* and feel that you ought to be included, please write to us finishing the following sentence:

***I think I'm famous enough to be in your guide because*.................................**

...

Please enclose £10 and a signed photo. If you are Simon Fanshawe or have just been in *Holby City* a few times, this will not be sufficient.

BRIGHTON RIP

After ten years of Cheeky *it seems a good time to celebrate some of the places and people that have long since shut up shop, gone to meet their maker or, worse, moved to Hastings. Below are a few excerpts from old reviews that will hopefully prompt a few smiles of recognition from some readers, and have others kicking themselves that they didn't come to Brighton earlier.*

The Sunday car boot at Brighton Station

One of the strangest stalls is the one selling manky limbs from Victorian dolls. It's always there so logic dictates there must be a regular stream of people who need them. WHO ARE YOU???

(Sent to the Marina to die)

124 Queens Road bookshop

The window display defies explanation and the whole shop looks as if the owner got a huge truck full of books and just emptied them into the shop and said, "*OK, we're open*". In fact he's always reminded me of Michael Caine in *Educating Rita*, after he's had a few. But ask for any title and he'll wander down one of those war-torn corridors, rummage through a pile and somehow find it. Remarkable to behold.

(Now an estate agents with internet café and photocopying service)

DK Rosen Tailoring Church Street

One customer was refused entry to the shop on the grounds that he was wearing the wrong buttons on his shirt, although Mr Rosen did offer to sew on the correct ones if he didn't mind waiting...

(Now empty; Mr Rosen last seen handing out flyers for Pizza Hut in Hove)

Dynamite Boogaloo club night

Two contestants each wear a pair of knickers onto which is attached a parsnip roughly sculpted into the shape of a dildo. A couple of audience members then sit with legs open as goalposts and contestants have to try and knock a potato through the posts using their dildo...

(Now ended)

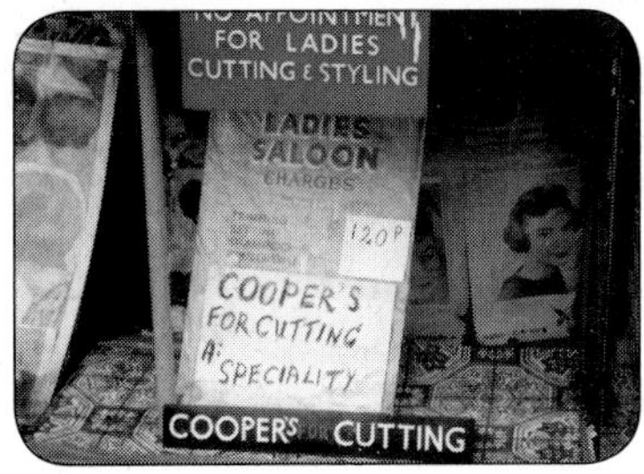

Cooper's for Haircuts Baker Street

He's just like any other 203-year-old desert-rat war-veteran barber who charges 100p a haircut, offers an endless stream of invective about anything, and who cuts bits of your hair actually ***out of*** your head.
(Now a trendy hairdresser's)

Black Chapati restaurant Preston Circus

Brighton's most pompous restaurateur, Steve Funnell, will regularly lecture diners on what they are eating; if anyone is spotted talking during these sermons he'll ask them to share the joke with the rest of the class or, on occasion, use the C word and throw them out.
(Now working with Gordon Ramsay)

The Cheese Shop Kensington Gardens

I asked the woman behind the counter how many times a day someone walked in and quoted the Monty Python cheese shop sketch to her and she answered, "*what sketch?*"
(Now a pet shop specialising in parrots)

The Gloucester nightclub

Some nights it's full to capacity, on others there'll just be a few goths sat in the corner eating jelly.
(Now closed)

Joker Basement comedy club

For the joke competition compere Guy Venables dishes out top-quality prizes ranging from hi-fis to Rolex watches, all pilfered by his mate Dodgy Dave. One month a friend of mine won the home phone number of Brian Sewell.
(Dead but not forgotten)

George Hamilton V B&B Lower Rock Gardens

When the door opened a rather unshaven man emerged smelling of booze.
Me: *Hello.*
Him: *What do you want?*
Me: *I'm writing a guide book on Brighton and...*
Him: *I'm not interested.*
Shuts the door.
The end.
(Last spotted on Britain's Got Talent*)*

Dr Who obsessives Seb and Dunc

"*Women give you a wide berth when they find out what you're into,*" explained Dunc, "*but they don't know what they're missing. We can be sensitive. I cry sometimes. I mean, have you seen* Dr Who and the Green Death?"
(Both still single)

Only in Brighton...

...can you visit your local Somerfield dressed as Elvis and not be stared at.
Guy Lloyd

...could an arts consultant be considered a key worker.
Cara Courage

...would you be walking down a street in Kemp Town and find a burnt-out pair of rollerblades.
Tim Bidwell

...would the seagulls have torn open a neighbour's bin-bags, strewing oversize nappies and other 'adult' baby paraphernalia down the street.
Rowena Easton

..would you get a text saying "*the drag queens are about to start rolling down Devil's Dyke in giant hamster balls*".
Emily Dubberley

...would you find single dads who keep nappies in their record bags.
Anon

...would you be unsurprised when 50+ naked cyclists ride past on a Saturday morning.
Jenny Pickup

...would you find your Hanover neighbour taking his 'pet' K9 out for a walk.
David Bramwell

...would you come across a local Freecycle ad that reads: "*Size 12ish colourful leggings or thick tights wanted for a trapeze performance*".
Fred Pipes

...would you find a drunk man pinned to the ground by a triumphant seagull.
Anon

...does a *Big Issue* seller greet you as if you were a well-known celebrity, eg: "*Hello Neil Tennant, all right mate? Come on Neil, you're a rich bastard, you can spare a couple of quid from all those royalties.*"
Tim Bick

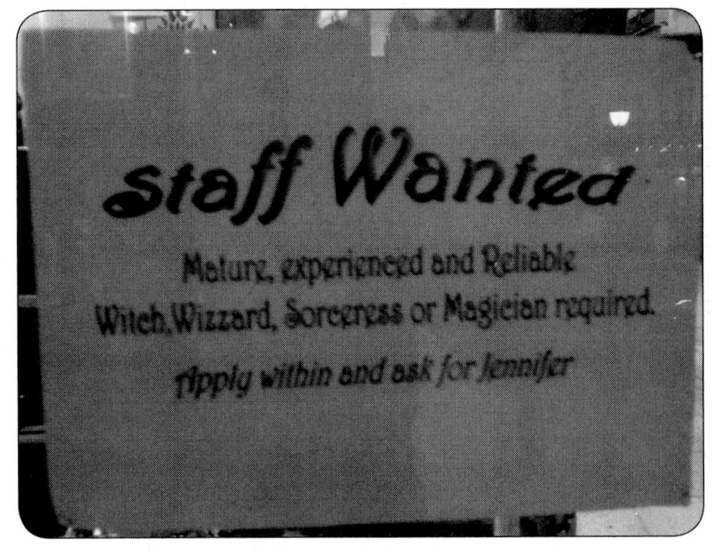

Brighton in Books & the Movies

MOVIES

Brighton Rock

1947 Dir. John Boulting

Discover a Brighton of Bovril adverts and Brylcreem in this classic Graham Greene story set in the 30s, with plenty of fascinating scenes from the Old Lanes, Queens Road, Grand Hotel and the Palace Pier. Richard Attenborough plays Pinkie Brown, an evil small-time gangster who tries to cover up a murder by marrying a young girl who could give evidence against him. While the ending is far better in the book (aren't they always?), this film is a genuinely chilling account of the gangster scene that once flourished in Brighton. If you're a *Doctor Who* fan keep your eyes peeled for a young William Hartnell.

Classic line from the film: *"People don't change; look at me. I'm like one of those sticks of rock. Bite all the way down and you still read Brighton".*

Oh, What A Lovely War!

1969 Dir. Dickie Attenborough

Attenborough's first movie is an over-ambitious and heavy-handed affair, telling the story of the First World War through allegory, mild satire and ***way*** too much singing. The West Pier is the platform for events leading up to the war, and the film does include many fine shots of the seafront, the Downs and Devil's Dyke.

Despite its flaws it's an interesting piece of British movie history, with some occasionally stunning moments. The scene in the trenches on Christmas Day, when the German and English soldiers nervously meet in No Man's Land and share a drink, is genuinely moving. The film also boasts an incredible cast, ranging from thespian gods Laurence Olivier and John Mills to the Fairy Liquid queen, Nanette Newman.

London to Brighton

2006 Dir. Paul Andrew Williams

A gangland thriller based around prostitution, murder and two troubled London girls fleeing to Brighton. Twenty years on from *Mona Lisa*, sixty from *Brighton Rock* and still Brighton seems to incite filmmakers to direct tough, gritty dramas where everyone's effing and blinding and shooting each other. The film apparently took four days to write and four weeks to shoot. Having watched it you may wonder what took them so long.

Quadrophenia

1979 Dir. Franc Roddam

Jimmy, a troubled young Mod, visits Brighton for a wild weekend but gets carried away, takes too many pills, loses his job and is so disillusioned with Sting's acting that he drives his scooter off Beachy Head. Or does he?

The shots of 70s Brighton (masquerading as 60s Brighton) are wonderful – it's all smoky cafes, Triumph Heralds and Wimpy bars. The fight scenes take place down East Street and on the beach (where potatoes were substituted for stones!). If you want to find the famous alleyway where Jimmy and Steph cop off, go down East Street toward the sea. Near the end look for the shop LTS and above it is a sign for an alleyway that reads 'to little East Street'. It's down there. This was once a graffitied Mod shrine, but with the next Mod revival not due for another ten years it doesn't attract as many visitors any more. Yes, the doorway is still there, but it's locked so, no, you can't pop in and have a shag, though countless have tried…

Classic line from the film: *"I don't want to be like everyone else, that's why I'm a Mod see."*

Slade in Flame

1975 Dir. Richard Loncraine

The chirpy Brummie boys with huge lambchops star in this surprisingly sombre film, which charts the rise of fictional Midland pub band Flame from obscurity to glam superstardom. Of course it all goes awry after one too many Babychams and ends with a brawl in the famous Grand Hotel.

Incidentally, Loncraine returned to Brighton in 2004 to film parts of his movie *Wimbledon* here, though why they chose to convert the barbers Headroom near the Seven Dials into a bookies rather than use a normal bookies is anyone's guess. As for the film, if you liked *Four Weddings* then you'll find this a weaker cup of tea from the same pot.

Others to look out for

The Fruit Machine
1988 Dir. Philip Saville

Genevieve
1953 Dir. Henry Cornelius

Jigsaw
1962 Dir. Val Guest

Loot (based on the Joe Orton play)
1970 Dir Silvio Narizzano

Mona Lisa
1986 Dir. Neil Jordan

The End of the Affair
1999 Dir. Edward Dmytrykl

Tommy
1975 Dir. Ken Russel

Under Suspicion
1992 Dir. Simon Moore

To avoid like the plague…

Circus
2000 Dir. Rob Walker

Dirty Weekend
1993 Dir. Michael Winner

Me Without You
2001 Dir. Sandra Goldbacher

CARRY ON BRIGHTON

Carry On Girls

1973 Dir. Gerald Thomas

Where in Brighton?

It all takes place in the pretend seaside town of Fircombe (oooerrr!!) which is, of course, actually Brighton. The film features shots of the seafront, the West Pier and a fleeting glimpse of Regency Square. My favourite bit of the film is near the end, when the contest goes awry and Sid James – chased by a crowd of angry men – escapes down the West Pier in a go-kart. Look out for the outrageous gay stereotypes in the movie – there's the camp film director with the flowery shirt and mincing walk and June Whitfield's sidekick: a humourless, man-hating lesbian who dresses like Hitler. They just don't make comedy clichés like they used to.

The Plot:

Sid James is on the make as usual, this time as the buttock-slapping Councillor Fiddler, who organises a beauty competition only to be foiled by sour-faced women's-libber June Whitfield.

Trivia:

This was the first *Carry On* film that had to be broadcast after the BBC's 9pm watershed, as it was considered far too saucy!

Carry On at Your Convenience

1971 Dir. Gerald Thomas

The Plot:

Hailed as a *Carry On* masterpiece, this tale of industrial strife and romance at WC Boggs toilet factory meant that finally the lavatorial gags could really let rip (ahem). And, of course no *Carry On* movie would be complete without Brighton's own Patsy Rowland (as sex-crazed secretary Miss Withering) trying to get into Kenneth Williams' trousers. I just don't think you were his type, dear. Starring Kenneth Williams as WC Boggs and Sid James as… Sid. Well, why make life difficult?

Where in Brighton?

The gang take a bus trip down for their annual works outing and head for the rides on the Palace Pier.

Trivia:

Alternative title for the film was *Carry On Ladies Please Be Seated.*

Breakfast in Brighton

Nigel Richardson

Having almost made a legend out of one of the least likely pubs in Brighton (The Grosvenor) Nigel Richardson has, with this book, woven together a series of inconsequential but entertaining anecdotes about his relationship with the town. The book's McGuffin is a mysterious painting that Richardson is trying to find out more about, a conundrum that leads him to visit séances and spiritual churches, and meet art collectors, hammy old actors, fishermen and landladies. While the plot is rather scant it's a very personable and revealing insight into the darker, sleazier and wealthier corners of this city.

Brighton Ghosts, Hove Hauntings

John Rackham

The result of five years' investigations and more than 400 interviews with people who claim to have had supernatural experiences in the local area, Rackham's book of true ghost stories starts well – the introductory chapter *What are Ghosts?* shows his open-minded enthusiasm and inquisitive approach to the subject – and goes on to investigate supernatural sightings through the themes of location (Pavilion, churches, pubs, theatres) and subjects (smugglers, Ouija boards). At over 300 pages it's more digestible as something to dip into now and again, rather than read from cover to cover.

Brighton Rock

Graham Greene

(See *Movies*)

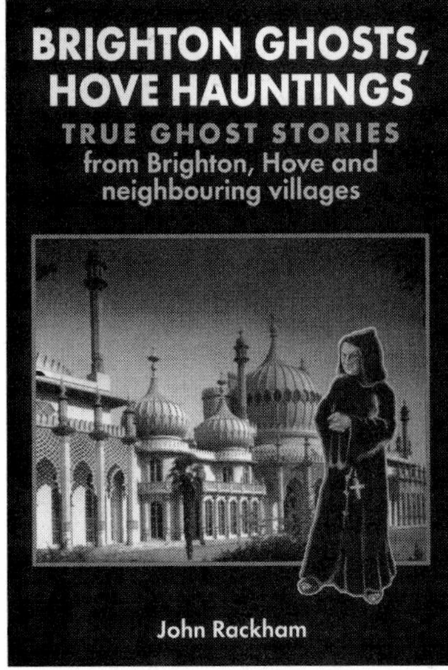

BRIGHTON GHOSTS, HOVE HAUNTINGS
TRUE GHOST STORIES
from Brighton, Hove and neighbouring villages
John Rackham

The Snowman

Raymond Briggs

Christmas wouldn't be the same without this children's tale, brought alive every year through the magic of television and the lilting tones of a Welsh eunuch. Next time it's on the telly look out for the flying scene and you'll see the Snowman and the boy sail over Brighton Pavilion and the Palace Pier as they head south to the errrr… North Pole.

The Illustrated Mum

Jacqueline Wilson

Though the Ray Bradbury reference may be lost on its teenage readers, Wilson's acclaimed novel takes an insightful look into some of the problems surrounding an unconventional modern family and provides humour and compassion when dealing with 'difficult' issues such as a mother's manic depression.

Brighton was the natural setting for Marigold (a single mum with a penchant for wacky clothes and tattoos) and her two daughters, Star and Dolphin.

Hangover Square

Patrick Hamilton

A must for all diehard Brightonians, Hamilton's dark, disturbing novel is the tale of one man's pursuit of large quantities of alcohol and a rather unpleasant lady gold-digger set in late 30s London and Brighton. Our hero is a social inadequate with a private income that allows him to be fleeced continually for whisky funds by his drinking buddies; not an easy character to sympathise with and a rather sombre read, but a salutary warning for Brightonians viewing hedonism as an end in itself.

Almost on a par with Greene, Hamilton is one of the UK's great minor novelists but the tone of this classic book and his own struggle with alcoholism show what a childhood spent in Hove can do for you.

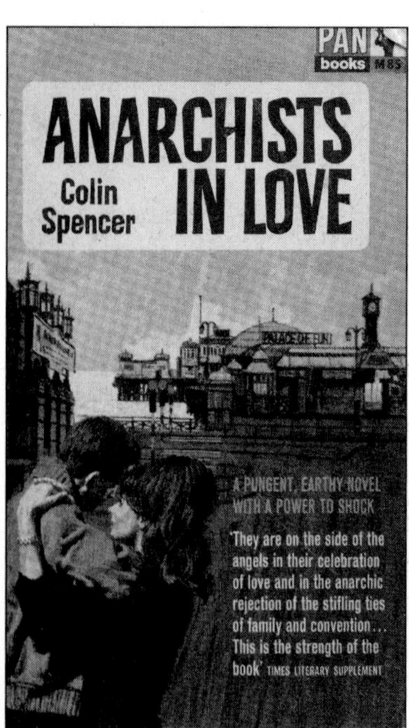

The Vending Machine of Justice & As Good As It Gets

Simon Nolan

Simon Nolan seems to like writing comedies set around Brighton, as these two novels demonstrate. *As Good as it Gets* is a trendy novel about a bunch of twentysomethings who find five kilos of coke and decide that they could find a better use for it than the police, while *The Vending Machine of Justice* revolves around a bizarre case at Hove Crown Court and a few local zombies.

While Nolan's books include some good descriptions of the pub and club culture in Brighton and have some genuinely funny moments, it's all fairly lightweight stuff and may disappoint those with a penchant for quality literature.

The Brighton Book

Released in conjunction with the Brighton Festival a few years ago this is a cornucopia of short stories, recipes, poetry and more by the likes of Jeanette Winterson, Louis de Bernières, Nigella Lawson and various local writers and illustrators all, supposedly, on the theme of Brighton.

While there are some interesting and well-written pieces (and it's great to see work in here by illustrator Woodrow Phoenix), the theme of the book seems to have gone astray somewhere down the line as there is plenty in here that has bugger all to do with the city. According to Amazon, the 'perfect partner' for this book is *Weight: The Myth of Atlas and Heracles* – which is like twinning *Little Dorrit* with the Haynes Renault Clio manual.

The Illustrated Brighton Moment

Succeeding where *The Brighton Book* failed, this is a digestible and thoroughly entertaining collection of stories and artwork that genuinely capture the true spirit of Brighton, not least because they're written by people who actually live here and love the place.

There are tales of seagulls, pebbles, personal ads, trips to séances and Snoopers Paradise to name but a few. Worth buying alone for Annabel Giles's hilarious rollercoaster tour through Brighton's various areas ("*let's pretend that Churchill Square doesn't exist*" or "*Hanover? Big hair, little houses!*") and Tanya Murray's account of the Brighton Transsexual and Bisexual Swimming Club's camping trip to Weymouth!

QueenSpark Books

www.queensparkbooks.org.uk (01273) 571710

QueenSpark Books began life over 30 years ago as a local campaign to save the Royal Spa building in Queens Park from being turned into a casino by developers. The campaigners produced a regular newspaper, *QueenSpark*, which was sold at the princely sum of 1p. Then in 1974 Brightonian Albert Paul sent his life story, *Poverty, Hard Work but Happiness*, to the group and this became the first QueenSpark book, with Albert selling more than 1,000 copies door to door around Brighton. Since then, QueenSpark – set up as a voluntary non-profitmaking community publishing company – has produced more than 80 titles, including individual life stories by local people, community oral histories and the occasional poetry anthology. Gems include *Moulsecomb Memoirs* and *Tales from the Fishing Community*.

Things turn nasty at the monthly meeting of Brighton's infamous book club The Paperback Vipers

Occult Brighton

With Brighton as the chosen resting place of Aleister Crowley, home to famous witch Doreen Valiente, birthplace of the notorious Temple of Psychic Youth and birthplace of Occulture, the world's largest annual occult festival, it seems fairly clear that there's something a bit 'Sunnydale' about the place.

No less remarkable is the fact that the two greatest UK occultists, Dion Fortune and Aleister Crowley, have both written about Brighton in their novels.

It may come as no surprise therefore to learn that Sussex was the last county to convert to Christianity. In 666 AD, no less!

OCCULTISTS PAST AND PRESENT

Doreen Valiente

Described as the mother of modern witchcraft, this remarkable Kemp Town resident breathed life into the rather fragmented rites and rituals contained in *The Book of Shadows* (the bible of Gardnerian Wicca) using her poetic skills. Today, nearly every witch in every coven in the world repeats the sacred invocation *Charge of the Goddess*, penned by Doreen. She is credited with inspiring the current popular interest in witchcraft (though *Buffy* creator Joss Whedon might dispute this) and left several important works on the subject, including the carefully guarded *Book of Shadows*, whose contents are forbidden to non-witches!

Genesis P.Orridge

This singular individual made a name for himself back in the 70s through the group Throbbing Gristle and a series of rather explicit live-art performances with an act known as COUM Transmissions. Like all good subversives Orridge incurred the wrath of the establishment and one Tory MP even went so far as to describe him as a "*wrecker of civilisation*". But the worst was yet to come.

In the early 80s Genesis moved to Brighton and set up the Temple of Psychic Youth (TOPY), a "*Cyberian Anti-Cult*", whose collective of like-minded searchers aimed to explore altered states through scarification, piercing, sado-masochism and sex magick. While this kind of thing is pretty much compulsory in Brighton nowadays, twenty years ago it was enough to cause a witch-hunt in the media. In 1991 a Channel 4 documentary 'exposed' TOPY as a "*sick Satanic cult*" with witnesses speaking on camera of being drugged, raped and forced to eat babies in the basement of Orridge's house in Roundhill Crescent. The police raided the house and Orridge – who was then in Thailand – was strongly advised not to return home unless he wanted his children taken away.

Genesis settled in the US, where he still lives today, despite the fact that subsequent enquiries into the documentary showed it to be a malicious stitch-up by fundamentalist Christians (Orridge's house didn't even have a basement!).

What makes Genesis such a fascinating character still is his ability to constantly re-invent himself and – true to form – he is still courting controversy, having spent the past ten years exploring transsexuality with his partner, Miss Jackie Superstar. The two have been breaking the boundaries of male and female polarity through plastic surgery, adopting each other's characteristics and dressing identically.

As Orridge was fundamental in making Brighton the tattoo and piercing capital of the UK, is he, one wonders, about to spearhead the dissolution of another great taboo with his latest venture? Can we soon expect to see hordes of transsexual clones alighting the train from Hassocks and Croydon every Friday night? We can only live in hope.

Aleister Crowley

As the author of *The Book of the Law*, and dubbed "*The Wickedest Man In The World*", it's only natural that drug fiend and poet Crowley would have a connection with Brighton; and though he died in Hastings in 1947, he sensibly chose to be cremated at Woodvale Cemetery down the Lewes Road.

At his funeral, a selection of Crowley's work was read, as was the "*Hymn to Pan*", which thoroughly shocked the locals and prompted the council to hold an emergency meeting ensuring such a ceremony would never again take place in their town. Don't go looking for him though: he's all blown away by now.

OCCULT AWAYDAYS

Chanctonbury Ring, five miles north of Worthing

This small Iron-Age hill fort, noted for its ring of beech trees (though most, sadly, were lost in the hurricane of 1987) is a beguiling place steeped in folklore. According to legend, if you walk or run seven times around the Ring at midnight, the devil will appear, offering a bowl of milk, soup or porridge (?!). If you accept these comestibles, he'll take your soul or offer you your heart's desire (which is obviously a bit of a gamble for anyone daft enough to risk it).

Long associated with witchcraft, Chanctonbury Ring was described by Crowley as a "*place of power*", while local witch Doreen Valiente revealed it to be the meeting place of an ancient coven. That the place has been used for occult practices is indisputable, as evidence of makeshift altars has been found there on several occasions, not to mention other known occult symbols and artefacts. Whether the Ring is a spot favoured by black or white witches is unknown but, as one Sussex archaeology and folklore website put it, "*being Chanctonbury Ring, it is probably black*".

Chanctonbury Ring is also associated with sighting of UFOs and fairies; there have been countless reports over the years of strange coloured objects and dancing lights.

If you're planning a visit, it's best not to come alone. And certainly not at night.

Former disgruntled customers of Dragon's Gate

OCCULT SHOPS

Dragon's Gate

13 St James's Street (01273) 679992
Mon-Sat 10am-7pm

While the obvious "*hey, this looks like the shop from Buffy*" won't go down well with owner Jennifer Dragon, it's easy to understand why the shop elicits the comparison. Packed to the hilt with charms, occult books, altar cloths, CDs of Aleister Crowley songs, handmade wands, robes, tarot packs (from Thoth to Bosch) and crystals, the place certainly looks the part, despite the pool table in the centre. But while Giles and co were pitched at disaffected teen goths, Dragon's Gate is – according to Jennifer – the real deal: a place for practising Wiccans and witches and those with a serious interest in occultism. Come on a good day and you'll witness Jennifer enthroned behind the counter listening to *Beowulf* in the original Anglo Saxon. On a bad day you may deal with her partner staring vacantly into space and ignoring you.

Dragon's Gate is also a good spot for finding out more about occult events. There's a noticeboard for activities and groups, and adverts for second-hand amulets. And for those who dream of a Hogwarts for adults, be cheered! Jennifer claims to be putting together an Academy of Magic some time in the future, although you won't be allowed to enrol unless you own a pointy hat.

WHERE TO CONTACT THE DEAD

Brighton National Spiritualist Church

Edward Street, opposite Devonshire Place
(01273) 683088
Sunday services 11am and 6.30pm

It all starts off surprisingly similar to a Christian service except instead of God, one gives praise to "*the greater vibration*" or "*spirit*". Expect a bit more chat and a hymn, then things really pick up when the guest clairvoyant comes on. These can range from the commanding presence of an American preacher to a quiet lady from Crawley in a green velvet skirt. There's a pep talk, some fabulous shaky-hands business then, through the clairvoyant, the dead will start to communicate with a few select members of the congregation.

Don't always expect to be chosen but if you are, you should be offered nuggets of advice and information from the spirit world, channelled through the clairvoyant's voice. The one time I was picked I met my grandad (apparently), and his message was *"Stop worrying about your ears sticking out"*.

Having never given much thought to the orientation of my ears, I did wonder what that was all about, particularly as I had never met either of my grandfathers. On another occasion my friend Denise received the word 'biscuits' from a dead grandmother, while a seated nearby couple were advised to tidy up their garden. Seems the dead are just as obsessed with trivia as the living. Afterwards it's cheese, biscuits and a chat, a flick through *Psychic News* and then a well-earned lunch at the Barley Mow.

Séances

If you are serious about wanting to be involved with a séance group email me at the address at the front of the book and I'll pass your name and phone number on to the group. Unless you are staying in Brighton for some time though, this will not be possible.

If invited you will be expected to take the evening seriously, but I can guarantee you will have plenty of fun. It all takes place in pitch blackness and begins with singing a few old music-hall numbers such as *Roll Out The Barrel* and *Daisy, Daisy* to *"get the energy going"*. Then, once the spirits have manifested through the medium, watch out for stuff moving around the room and hope that you don't spend the night with a chair on your head as one lady did.

Do expect to get covered in ectoplasm and have some questions ready for when you meet some of the fantastic characters, such as James the Victorian transvestite comedian. And, if you ask, the ghosts will even tell you who your spirit guide is. Do I get a Buddhist monk or a Native American Indian chief like everyone else? No, I get a chicken called Cyril.

At the end of the night not everyone will necessarily be convinced but it is, of course, something to tell the grandchildre.

Pets get their paws read for free every Saturday at Margaret's

PALMISTS & CLAIRVOYANTS

Margaret

64 Elm Grove (01273) 683623
Tues-Thurs, Sat 10am-11.45pm and 1pm-3.45pm

Step in here and be ready to enter a timewarp taking you back 40 years or more. The walls are littered with fading newspaper articles and curling black-and-white photos showing Margaret on old TV shows. It'll feel like you're in a Rita Tushingham movie, with Margaret looking and playing the part magnificently.

The readings take around twenty minutes in a tiny room at the back of the shop, where Margaret will read your palm or tell your fortune from a pack of cards. Along with the usual stuff like *"you know someone who reads the* Daily Mail*"*, Margaret also said some pretty accurate and insightful things on my first visit. Readings range from £12 to £16. Go on, treat yourself to a seaside speciality from a true professional.

Paul Hughes-Barlow

254 Kings Road Arches, under Brighton Pier 0791 863 7940
Best phone ahead for opening times
www.supertarot.co.uk

Said to be the number-one expert on Thoth tarot, Paul lectures around the world and is the author of *The Magus – Opening the Key of Tarot and Magic*, a book which presents new methods of invoking spirits using divination techniques. He can also be found under Brighton Pier. No, not sleeping off a night on the tiles, it's actually where he operates as a tarot consultant. He is the only palmist/tarot reader in Brighton I know whose room is full of interesting books, rather than gypsy tat and the usual mystical paraphernalia. Friendly and honest about his profession and possessing a good knowledge of the occult sciences, Paul is easy to warm to, and has a reassuringly boyish laugh. A good choice if you're looking for something beyond the usual nonsense. First sittings are a standard £15.

The Gay Scene

Since the first gay herring fair in 1910 Brighton's gay scene has grown to become the largest and most celebrated in the country. Gay shenanigans had been going on well before then however – most of the Prince Regent's male friends were camp as Christmas and the Pavilion is a classic example of what can happen when you let a gay man loose on the decorating.

By Victorian times Brighton had become the destination of choice for the London homoset wanting to get away from prying eyes. Oscar Wilde met his lover Bosie in the Albion Hotel while Gladstone even had his own drag show. It is the town's theatrical tradition that really played the biggest role in creating the scene as we know it today; gay icons like Ivor Novello and Noël Coward lived here, lording it up and down with Laurence Olivier with whom, ironically enough, you can now ride up and down the seafront, should you catch the number 27 bus. And of course with the town already established as a fashionable pleasure capital, and with place names such as Dyke Close, The Queen's Arms and Tidy Street, Brighton really was the obvious choice for the UK's gay headquarters.

From the 60s onwards the gay community developed around Kemp Town, the Old Steine and St James's Street. You'll find most of the best bars, clubs and shops here as this is where the majority of Brighton's gay population still socialises, although truth is, they are now scattered all over the place: they're everywhere!

The original gay haunts in Kemp Town were developed for cruising but as it became so much easier to be 'out' in Brighton, the clubs and bars became less about a quick fumble in the loos and more about just hanging out, posing and socialising (though, believe me, plenty of naughtiness still goes on).

Statistics show that a staggering 23% of adult males in Brighton are gay, with the number still rising fast (which means if you're straight, single and still can't get a girlfriend, you might as well give up). As a consequence Brighton now has gay everything – gay shops, gay clubs, gay saunas, gay coffee bars, gay B&Bs, gay carnivals, gay plumbers, gay estate agents, gay comedians and Simon Fanshawe. And with the advent of the civil partnership act, Brighton is fast becoming the gay 'wedding' capital of the country, with his-and-his peach Audi TT wedding presents to match. So let's raise a toast and be queer and proud. As Emily Lloyd was so fond of saying in the Brighton-set Wish You Were Here, "Up Yer Bum!"

LOCAL BARS

The Aquarium

6 Steine Street (01273) 605525
www.the-aquarium-theatre-bar.co.uk

An unpretentious local boozer, this cosy theatre bar is refreshingly uncruisy and you're more likely to find the locals all perched round the bar eating curry and listening to Greek bouzouki music. Decor-wise it's all jolly homely too, with wooden boarded walls, framed photos of such illustrious thesps as Dudley Moore and Ronnie Reagan, and a pair of pink flamingos perched on the piano. Ben the co-owner, an ex-theatrical agent, is on a mission to bring quality cabaret to the area (they even have drag queens doing impersonations of other drag queens) so it's not surprising that the Aquarium attracts its fair share of luvvies, although they do also get "*non-gay people, like estate agents*".

And if you don't want Taz the dog to knock you off your feet, take your hat off before you go in. He's very particular about social niceties.

Brighton Tavern

99-100 Gloucester Road (01273) 680365
www.brightontavern.com

North Laine's own local gay bar has a nice friendly vibe that's more like a proper pub that just happens to be gay. Lethal free shots occasionally get handed round, and it's worth coming for their Sunday-evening music session, particularly if Rocking Billy is performing: he's a real live Teddy-Boy DJ.

The Bulldog

31 St James's Street (01273) 684097
www.bulldogbrighton.com

31-hour drinkathons, compulsory happy hours and promotions galore, the Bulldog is somewhere to drink and cruise: a place where nobody wants to know your name but everyone wants to shag you. Despite a slight increase in popularity with the younger gay crowd, the lecherous old-school vibe is still predominant; it's populated most nights by 'mature' gentlemen, many of whom prefer staring to speaking. Rest assured this is still a place where you'll only leave alone if you ***really*** want to. **Top tip:** Don't bring your granny.

The Queen's Arms

7 George Street (01273) 696873
www.queensarmsbrighton.com

A fog of dry ice, a drag queen called Betty Swollocks mincing around the stage, monogrammed carpets (god knows how old they are) and a small gang of lesbians in the corner having a heated debate about Gordon Brown underneath a framed photograph of a Worthing DJ from 1985 called Bubbles. Welcome to the Queen's Arms, a classic old-school gay boozer in the heart of St James's Street with more or less constant entertainment every evening and a drag queen or two invariably loitering outside enjoying a fag. It's also home to the world's saddest drag queen – mad, bad and dangerous to know, she's like Arthur Mullard on crack. Increasingly popular with the girls at weekends, too (the pub, not Arthur).

The Zone

33b St James's Street (01273) 624313

Like the Ranelagh this is another of those slightly surreal St James's anomalies. Walk past here any evening of the week and you'll spy a handful of drunk folk dancing like lunatics to a lesbian country band or belting their way through a camp karaoke classic. But with the decor and feel of the place more akin to a David Lynch film than a classic gay cabaret bar, it's like being part of a bizarre drunken wedding party inside a giant glass bottle. You'll either be irresistibly drawn in and end up dancing with a 60-year-old man with no teeth and two paralytic girls in their twenties or stagger on by with an air of disbelief.

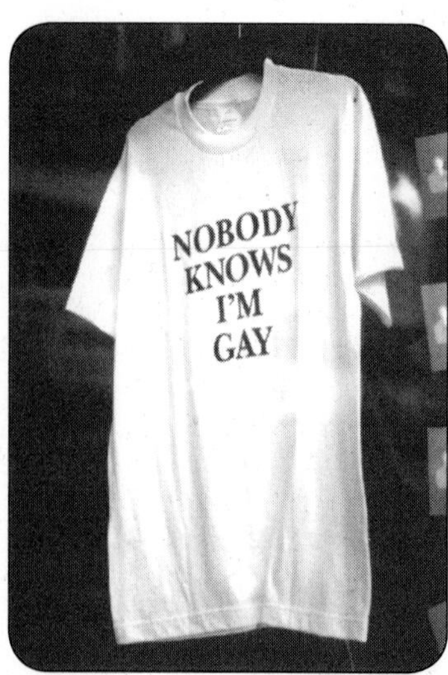

FASHIONABLE BARS

Amsterdam

11-12 Marine Parade
(01273) 688825
www.amsterdam.uk.com

This seafront bar/hotel attracts a mixed crowd (including hen parties) but when the sun's out the terrace is one of ***the*** places to hang out and be seen. While the generic hotel bar decor is nothing to get excited about, the Amsterdam did mark an important change when it first appeared, making Brighton's gay social scene more upfront and visible and not ***just*** about cruising. Saying that, in summer there's bare flesh galore when the sun shines; the huge patio overlooking the sea is a prime spot for sitting in your thong with a mug of Horlicks and a martini while shocking the Hassocks teenagers queuing up for Audio next door.

Charles Street

8-9 Marine Parade
(01273) 624091
www.charlesstreetbar.com

For uber-posers, Charles Street should be first port of call as it is ***the*** place for the early twenties crowd and out-of-towners looking for action. A shedload of cash has been spent making it look like a vast *Star Trek* departure lounge, with a bar stretching to the edge of the galaxy, but the trillions of TV screens advertising drag acts like Lola Lasagne, and an arcade machine where you can win a 'willy lead' bring it back down to earth. Should the earbending din become too much for you then you can always nip downstairs to the spacious vestibule outside the loos; you never know, you might see something you like.

Haemorrhoid-support team training session

Legends

31-34 Marine Parade (01273) 624462
www.legendsbrighton.com

One mega-money facelift later, and we have some posh stools, light panels, and twenty square miles of open floor. Atmospheric is not really the word but this expansive and thoroughly modernised hotel bar is mostly about the sea-facing front terrace and languid sun-kissed posing. Even in winter. The white-walled painting with light approach works much better in the space-age downstairs Basement Club (which doesn't even charge for entry) where you really do feel like you're living in the 21st century. Although annoyingly without the flying jetpack that television promised me I'd have by now. A word of caution: if you're staying in the hotel and value your shuteye, get a room at the back and forgo the seaview – the bar's open till 5am.

r-bar

7 Marine Parade (01273) 608133

Following endless re-incarnations, r-bar (formerly a-bar, b-bar, c-bar, d-bar, e-bar, f-bar, g-bar etc) hit upon a winning formula and now everyone wants to be taken up the r's. You'll find a very young (predominantly) trendy gay crowd here, swanning around the faux boudoir upstairs and gossiping in the doorway as you try to brush past. Surely the highlight of any visit here though is a moment of relaxation in the urinals, which will provide a pleasingly novel experience if you've never peed in someone's mouth.

CLUBS & CLUB NIGHTS

Club Revenge

32-43 Old Steine (01273) 606064
www.revenge.co.uk

Still the biggest gay club on the south coast, open six nights a week with special events, drinks promotions, strippers and cheesy pop nights. It's a little on the expensive side but ranks as one of the best in the UK. Sure, newcomers will find the inevitable cliques, but don't be put off: it really isn't difficult to meet new people here. With all those body beautifuls sweating it out on the upstairs dancefloor, you shouldn't find it hard to get caught up in the contagious party atmosphere.

Top tip: Be nice to the sexy and flirty barstaff – they are your best port of call to find out everything about the hottest bars and parties. Recommended.

The Club @ Charles Street

(Upstairs from Charles Street)
8-9 Marine Parade (01273) 624091

Formerly Envy, the Club stands upon the hallowed ground that many moons ago was heavy metal Valhalla the Hungry Years. For years we joked about it being appropriated by the gay scene and then, suddenly, it was – bringing a whole new meaning to the phrase *"having studs on your back"*. Popular with students and a younger crowd, this is now a gay clubber's paradise, with visits from big-name London clubs and a cavernous space that makes cruising nice and easy. Expect everything from trashy disco nights to the legendary TV night Transister.

Sunday Sundae

(Still resident at Audio at time of going to print)

Long-running gay fest for fit boys, trolly-dolly friends and fag hags. It's no longer a weekly club night though; best keep a look out in the free monthlies for special events.

Wild Fruit

www.wildfruit.co.uk

The big gay daddy of the scene, packed to the hilt with voyeurs and exhibitionists. Wild Fruit is one long night of feather boas, sequins, rubber hotpants and dancefloor anthems. Dress to impress and you'll be beating them off with a stick, or whatever comes to hand. Not to be missed!

Almost everyone in Brighton is gay these days

CRUISING AREAS

Almost the whole of Brighton is a cruising area, so take your pick: Queens Park, Preston Park, Dyke Road Park, Somerfield… just follow your nose and you can't go far wrong (unless you find yourself in Moulsecoomb, in which case – run!) If you want more concentrated trade, however, the following places might be of interest…

Brighton Nudist Beach

Ten minutes east of Brighton Pier

If it's pervs, pebbles, flabby bottoms, curious bi-boys, randy gay men, a plethora of stiffies, lots of parading and a stray drunken hen party you're after, then get yourself down to the celebrated nudist beach. It's even conveniently close to the bushes should you happen to meet a likeable fellow. Straights are welcome in theory but in most cases will feel uncomfortable, especially if they get asked for a poppers-fuelled hand shandy by a tattooed man with a heavily pierced penis and a parrot on his shoulder, as I was.

Duke's Mound

This small, sloping, dense shrubbery ten minutes' walk east of Brighton Pier is the oldest cruising ground in Sussex and comes complete with its own little eco-system and constant stream of lusty men. It affords enough privacy to those who require it, yet is risqué enough for naughty exhibitionists, while those splendid chaps from the Terrence Higgins Trust even come here at weekends to give out free condoms, tea, coffee and oranges at half time.

While not commonly reported, there are occasional stories of people getting mugged after being picked up and taken to Duke's Mound, so take care. There have also been rumours for years of redevelopment at nearby Black Rock bringing an end to the naughty shenanigans, but nothing has happened yet. There *are* plans for a hotel, coffee shop, juice bar, sushi restaurant and Blobbyworld but seeing how long it took the council to build a bloody library, I wouldn't worry just yet.

Hove Lawns/The Meeting Place Café/Behind the King Alfred

A chilled-out seafront coffee bar, the Meeting Place can be a good spot for cruising during the day (though don't get your hopes up on a drizzly February afternoon), while at night the whole area from the Peace Statue to the King Alfred leisure centre can sometimes seem like one long glorious golden mile of talent. It is rather flat and exposed, compared with the bushes, but the beach is dark and can't be seen from the promenade. Alternatively, you can always nip round the back of the King Alfred for a quickie; try not to scare Nick Cave if he's popped out for a crafty fag.

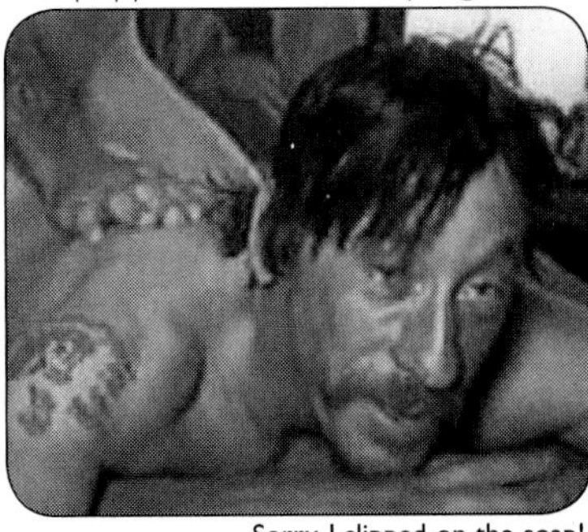

Sorry, I slipped on the soap!

SHOPS

Cardome

47a St James's Street (01273) 692916
Mon-Sat 10am-6pm

A cross between a local craft market, WH Smith's and a sex shop, Cardome lays claim to being Brighton's oldest established gay shop (more than twenty years in the business!) A good place to come for greeting cards (gay and straight), local handmade art, jungle juice and T-shirts with slogans such as "*Some mornings I wake up miserable, other mornings I let him sleep*". While the soft porn in the basement seems to have been replaced by saucy cards of late, friendly owner Mike will answer any discreet questions you may have about all aspects of the sex scene in Brighton (if he hasn't died of joss-stick poisoning, that is).

Prowler

112 St James's Street (01273) 683680
Mon-Sat 11am-7pm

Part of a small chain of gay lifestyle shops that includes one in London and Birmingham, Prowler proudly adds a little culture and sophistication to the formula. Catering mostly for the guys, the shop is perhaps best loved for its large selection of gay literature and 'How to' manuals, as well as the cards, toys, mags, DVDs and AussieBum pants. If you're after something a little more saucy, you'll find it hidden away at the back of the shop. The manager explained, "*we want to be inviting to all. We even had a couple of nuns in the other day looking at cards. That's why it's important to us to keep the contents of the Blue Room separate from everything else. It doesn't have to be thrust into people's faces*". Amen.

SAUNAS

Used as social clubs in Brighton by the gay community, these saunas attract a wide age range and all come with rest room facilities.

Amsterdam Sauna

11-12 Marine Parade (01273) 688825
www.amsterdam.uk.com

Part of the Amsterdam Hotel, this sauna is open to the public and has a steam room, shower and many dark rooms. And with the closing of the Oasis a couple of years ago it's now the only exclusively gay sauna around Kemp Town.

Denmark Sauna

86 Denmark Villas, Hove (01273) 723733
www.denmarksauna.com

A good-quality sauna, popular with Hove residents. Parties held at weekends. Expect the odd stray blue-rinse granny who's wandered in looking for a perm.

Bright 'n' Beautiful Sauna Club

9 St Margaret's Place (01273) 328330

At the foot of the tallest building in Sussex is the oldest sauna in Brighton, boasting a bubbling water feature and a semi-naked gladiator with a saucy glint in his eye.

There's also a large steam room, huge relaxing TV lounge and nearby shops should you need to pop out for a jock strap, lube or a packet of mints.

Pride: a recipe for excess

Early August and March www.brightonpride.co.uk

Take 110,000 highly-charged gay folk; dress them up in as many feathers, sequins, leather jock straps, masks, ribbons and glitter as you can; stir in every intoxicant known to man; pour on the sunshine; march them up and down the streets of Brighton and finish off in a huge park with dance tents, funfairs and more wildlife and antics in the undergrowth than a BBC nature programme and you're beginning to get an inkling of the utterly fabulous, depraved carnival that is Pride.

From just 103 people at the first angry, political Pride demonstration, this event has grown to become ***the*** event in the British gay calendar. The week-long arts celebration culminates in a huge carnival procession and parade with stunning floats, dancers, drag queens, classic cars and scantily-clad people of all types, enveloped by pumping music ranging from camp disco classics to present-day pop. The parade starts in Madeira Drive at 11am and then dances, shouts and camps it up all the way to Preston Park, stopping only for a sandwich and a glass of fizzy pop at PC Pickles café in the Open Market. And if you think the huge fireworks display marks the end of it, think again. It's followed by a weekend street party in St James's Street which, in the past few years, has just got bigger and wilder. Oh, and there's now a second outing in early March! Just remember you might need to bring some warm winter woollies to wear over those rubber pants and feather boas. Pride is simply fantastic, not to be missed.

THE LESBIAN SCENE

For years the lesbian scene in Brighton was almost non-existent, save for a group meeting at the Dorset and a weekly disco at the Hanbury. And although, in principle, most of the gay bars welcomed lesbians, understandably few took up the offer – all that Kylie would put anyone off. Recently, however, a social scene for lesbians has been growing rapidly. There are now lesbian speeddating nights and lesbian diving clubs (called Muffs… no, really!), not to mention the fabulous Marlborough pub, PV and uber-cool Ghetto.

Ghetto

129 St James's Street (01273) 622424

Originally the hugely popular Candy Bar (whose disappearance from the scene remains a mystery), while still attracting a lesbian crowd this small basement club is more a place where hip young fashionistas, straight indie kids, students and the gay scene collide for trashy pop and messy dancing. As a consequence it's destined to become one of *the* hangouts in Brighton or will close down yet again after six months, have another refit and turn into an S&M dungeon for rent.

The Marlborough

4 Princes Street (01273) 570028

Just off the Old Steine, Brighton's long-established lesbian pub attracts a young crowd of gay women, from the civilised to the downright lairy. There are two bar areas: a lively one – usually occupied by feisty dykes monopolising the pool table – and a quieter one next door which has wooden panelling and leather chairs and feels a bit like a Victorian living room. The Marlborough is a good place to pick up gay magazines and information and

"So that's where you hid the soap!"

is also reputed to be one of Brighton's most haunted buildings – the ghost of Lucy Packham occasionally appears, gets her boobies out for the girls and then rolls them along the floor just for fun. There's even a gorgeous theatre upstairs, woefully underused.

The Princess Victoria @ The Jury's Out

161 Edward Street (01273) 687090

When this lesbian-run bar disappeared in 2008 from Upper North Street half of Brighton (well, me anyway) thought it'd simply closed shop. Not so. And despite being now located in something of a no man's land (no irony intended!) on Edward Street opposite the law courts, there's still the same vibe, quizzes, good Sunday lunches and lively crowd. As soon as you walk in and see the full-sized, bare-breasted Princess Victoria figurehead with tequila-squirting rubber nipples, you'll know you're in safe hands.

She likes a bit of ruff

UNDERSTANDING THE LINGO

The old gay dialect Polari was first developed back in the 1930s when homosexuality was still illegal (unless you were involved in theatre, where it was compulsory). This secret language enabled gay folk to get on with matters at hand without fear of persecution. It was later popularised by Julian and Sandy on the radio show Round The Horne *and by the 1970s had evolved into such an esoteric and bizarre tongue that Oliver Postgate used it in* The Clangers *to send secret messages to many of his male lovers* ‹

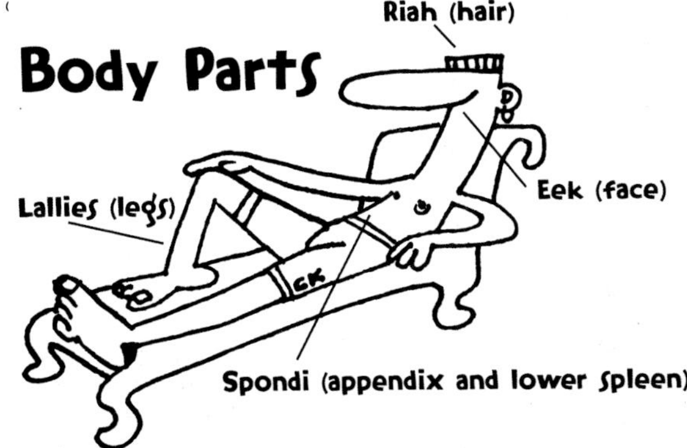

Bona polone/homi
Dictionary definition - Good looking woman/man
Eg. That bloke from the Cheeky Guide, what a bona homi!

Chicken
Dictionary definition - Waif-like young man
Eg. Check out the chicken in Somerfield.

Cruising
Dictionary definition - Sail to and fro for protection of shipping, making for no particular place or calling at a series of places.
Hmmm, that just doesn't seem to be what's going on in the bushes.

Trade
Dictionary definition - Sex/Your pick-up for the evening
Eg. Take your trade home and give him something to remember you by.

Varda/vada
Dictionary definition - To check out
Eg. Varda the legs on him/her/that lovely Regency sofa.

Others still in use
Kamp: Effeminate (Known As Male Prostitute)
Naff: Ugly/bad (Not Available For Fucking)
Omi-polone: Gay man
Lallies: Legs
Plate: Feet/to suck off
Scarper: To run off
Sharpy: Police
Troll: Walk about (looking for trade)

Example:
"Varda the naff lallies on the omi-polone! I've trolled for trade but it's scarpered 'cos of sharpy."
Translation: *"Ey-up, looks like another bloody evening at 'ome, tugging me'sen off."*

SERIOUS STUFF

Safe sex

Condoms are given free almost everywhere, from dispensers in bars and clubs (if you can't see any ask the barman) to 'glow boxes' on the cruising grounds and beaches. You've really no excuse not to use them. Syphilis, hepatitis and HIV infection rates continue to rise and the old "*it won't happen to me*" excuse is still as evident as folk trying to get an appointment at the clap clinic. Thankfully, most gay prostitutes in Brighton do enforce the condom rule. Just remember, sex is as safe as you're prepared to make it, so wrap up your peckers, guys.

Violence towards the gay community

Despite the fact that the gay community is a huge part of city life and most people in Brighton are totally cool and supportive of it, there *are* still plenty of attacks. Although it's sad to have to say it, be careful when you are out at night. Avoid snogging in the middle of West Street at 2am and you should be OK. The local police are both supportive and helpful if you have suffered homophobic or transphobic attack or assault. Get hold of one of the fantastic *True Vision* reporting packs and report any hassles, verbal or otherwise, that you may experience.

THE GAY WEB

The internet forms a bigger and bigger part of gay life these days, so keep up to date and in the know, see what you really did last night and look up a hot date before you even make it out the door. Good websites to check out for events, sexual health, gender issues and dating include:

www.brightonourstory.co.uk
www.gaybrighton.com
www.gaydar.co.uk
www.realbrighton.com
www.womenscentre.org.uk
www.brightonsexualhealth.com

MY BRIGHTON & HOVE

Name: STELLA 'QUEEN OF BURLESQUE' STARR

The Dickensian little fish bar by the Fishing Museum There's something just perfect about the way the old guy who runs this place throws a freshly caught fish on the griddle; you eat your fish-in-a-roll outside – simple and delicious. As a quick fishy stop-off, there's none better!

The Racecourse If you really want to get a taste of the Graham Greene spiv side of things, come here. The building is tacky and municipal but this racecourse high on the hill, with its amazing panoramic views of Brighton, is quite something. The best thing to do (as I did as a kid) is stand by the fence as all the horses come galloping round – exhilarating!

Bali Brasserie in Hove The nearest we'll get (for now) to a Tiki bar in town. Marvellous kitsch bamboo décor and the entrance hall (the ground floor of a 60s block of flats) is worthy of the old Cunard cruise ships! If you want proper cocktails though, go to the very suave Valentino's bar next to the Theatre Royal.

Sex, Fetish & Body Modification

Brighton has long held the tradition of being the place for fat London bosses with hairy bums to bring their secretaries for more than just a telesales conference. And, being a fashionable resort and the perfect short break from the big smoke, it's easy to see why Brighton has earned a reputation for dirty weekends and countless indiscretions. Even the Prince Regent was at it, having secretly married Mrs Fitzherbert here (the passageways connecting his Pavilion bedroom to her place were a means of ensuring their midnight rendezvous were kept secret).

There are even rumours that Brighton has its own dogging scene up at Devil's Dyke, which – if you're unfamiliar with such antics – involves randy couples, cars and the odd voyeur (I'm sure you can piece the rest of the jigsaw together for yourself).

Brighton's saucy nature today comes more from the liberal nature of its citizens than anything else. It's a good place to live for anyone who wants to come out of the closet and feel relaxed with his or her sexuality. And as this town is home to everyone from fetishists to drag queens, you can feel secure in the knowledge that, in your very neighbourhood, there'll always be someone kinkier than you.

BRIGHTON SEX TOURS

BY SEX GODDESS LETITCIA

Inspired by a news article about Thomas Cook's red-light tours in Amsterdam (no really, it's in their 2010 brochure), I am a self-appointed Brighton & Hove sex tour guide. In conjunction with the open-top tour buses, I will be the fearless leader guiding you into temptation. All aboard! You may jump on and off as many times as you like, though this may not be the case with the luscious ladies… so be warned.

Down the side streets of Western Road there are, of course, more parlours than you can shake a stick at, though you will need a Russian and Ukrainian translation manual and don't forget to ask for proof of age. Highlights include the bottom of Preston Street where you'll find thinking man's crumpet 'Debbie', who is proficient in English ***and*** Italian. For gentlemen who prefer the ladies to be in charge, at Holland Road you can sample the delights of 'Spankyouverymuch'. It's worth knowing that there's a chemist next door for Germolene or arnica if she's over-zealous.

Climb aboard once more and you can visit the minxes of Marine Parade (myself included). Continue on to Marina Village and, frankly, if you knock on any door there will be a hooker behind it.

On your journey back, if there are gentlemen… ahem… 'light in the loafers' you can disembark at Duke's Mound. Stroll nonchalantly down the path and the most you will have to pay is the price of a packet of fags. Even condoms are thoughtfully provided here by the local Outreach project.

Feeling thoroughly besmirched, stagger back along Marine Parade and there's just one last stop. That's right, the Claude Nicol Centre at the Royal Sussex on Eastern Road. Er, clap clinic, to those itching to know.

Letitcia with an 'old friend'

SHOPPING

Lust

43 Gardner Street (01273) 699344
Mon-Fri 11am-7pm, Sat 10.30am-8pm,
Sun 12noon-6.30pm *www.lust.co.uk*

Located in the heart of the North Laine amongst trendy boutiques and eateries, Lust really has proven once and for all that Brighton is the most liberal place in the UK. The city's biggest and newest sex shop, Lust offers three floors of goodies. While their companion shop Taboo is stocked more for the professional fetishists and porn-lovers, Lust offers a wide range of stock from games, books and playthings for the cheeky stag / hen parties to quality sex toys, beginners' S&M kits, bondage equipment and strap-ons. On the third floor you'll find a modest collection of pvc, rubber and uniforms aimed at those dipping their toes for the first time into the world of kinky glamour-wear. For those already sexually sated, there's even jewellery, funky gifts and quirky homeware to tempt you.

Like Taboo, everything is well displayed, the dressing room suitably seductive and staff well-informed and eager to please (as are the ladies indulging in a spot of lady love on the TV screen on the first floor). At last, a sex shop for the 21st century.

Tickled

59 Ship Street (01273) 628725
Mon-Sun 10.30am-6pm
www.tickledonline.co.uk

Exclusively run by women for women (and with a strong lesbian following) Tickled offer an excellent, upmarket range of sex toys combined with friendly and discreet service. They are also the only place I know of that offer advice on sexual health.

NB: For those who can't keep up with the changing locations of Brighton sex shops, Tickled is no longer in Gardner Street but has moved to the former site of sex shop Nua.

Taboo

2 Surrey Street (01273) 263565
Mon-Fri 9am-7pm, Sat 9am-8pm,
Sun 12noon-5pm, adults only
www.tabooshop.com

Leave the furry handcuffs behind and enjoy a sex shop that sells the real McCoy. Brighton's only proper licensed sex shop, Taboo stock quality bondage equipment, the best selection of latex and pvc clothes in the city, a good range of sex toys, fetish books and magazines, and an entire room full of DVDs that vary from straight porn to girl-on-goat action.

They also operate an exchange policy offering a £10 trade-in on returned films once you've, ahem, finished with them. Taboo is welcoming, friendly and doesn't have that intimidating atmosphere you find in most Soho sex shops. Also a good spot for finding out about local fetish nights, sex clubs and other kinky events.

No surprise it's been winner of Sex Shop of the Year. Highly recommended for those looking for quality over quantity.

She Said & Impure Art

13 Ship Street Gardens (the twitten between Ship Street and Middle Street)
(01273) 777822 / 732246
Tues-Sat 11am-6pm, Sun/Mon 12noon-5pm
www.shesaidboutique.com
www.impureart.com

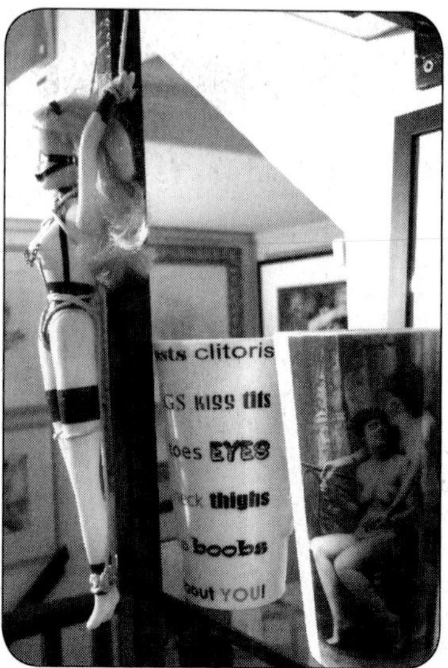

The creation of Nic Ramsey, She Said offers alluring and exotic lingerie, superior quality toys, sexy knickers, stockings, glamorous evening wear and a large range of corsets. Downstairs there's more: a fine selection of dildos, the Alan Titchmarsh-endorsed We Vibe, floggers (from horsehair whips to bejewelled crops), restraints, collars, nipple tassels and "*I Love Anal*" cards for Mother's Day. It is the elegant touches, though, that make She Said the Marilyn Monroe to Ann Summers' Jordan – the decor is beautiful and stylish and the staff, too, dress to impress. A kinky and mischievous version of the shop that Mr Benn used for his psychedelic travels (though where he'd have ended up dressed in exotic underwear and a corset is anybody's guess), with its sassy staff, sexy lingerie and elegant layout, She Said must surely lay claim to being one of the most glamorous boutiques in England.

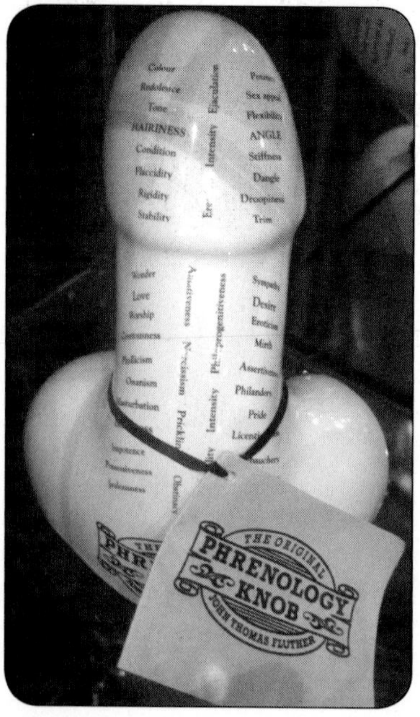

Next door you'll find another of Nic's ventures: Impure Art, the UK's only permanent erotic art gallery, exhibiting Brighton's naughtiest artwork from Fran Duncan's mythical nudes to Eve Poland's kinky ladies.

Brighton Body Casting

7 Ship Street Gardens 0796 133 8045
Prices from £15
www.brightonbodycasting.com

Established by award-winning sculptor Jamie McCartney, Brighton Body Casting offers a highly unusual service: that of turning any body part into a piece of art. From torsos and faces to pregnant bellies and baby's hands, you name it, Jamie has cast it. He's even done a death mask so it's a cradle to grave service! Celebrity parts he's had

his hands on include Jackie Chan's face, Trinny & Susannah's bums and Lisa Rogers' foofoo. So yes, all nether regions are covered too; this ***is*** the Naughty Little Alleyway after all.
In fact, having taken the challenge to get my John Thomas cast, I can vouch for Jamie's good humour, conviviality and erm... hands-on approach. The process is in fact, relatively simple: the part in question is covered with blue goo (as used by dentists for casting teeth) which sets into a flexible rubber within two minutes. The cast is then lovingly hand-made in your desired material – anything from plaster to bronze, glass or solid gold. Um... actually, even rubber is an option, leaving you to do with it as you please. As well as making ideal gifts for loved ones this really is an experience you won't forget in a hurry. At the time of going to print Jamie was still after volunteers for his outrageous *Design A Vagina* wall sculpture too. Go on, nobody will know it's you…

TATTOOS & PIERCINGS

In the past fifteen years, Brighton has seen a real boom in tattoo parlours and body-piercing studios. The following studios are only a small selection of what's on offer but are recommended because they take the art of body modification seriously.

While tattooing is a widespread skill, bear in mind that design and style are very individual. If you are tempted, I'd recommend you make an appointment first with the artists below. Go in person to see if you feel comfortable with them and what you think of their work. All good tattooists should carry a portfolio.

One last thing – if you're having something written, make sure your tattooist is clear on the spelling. One local tattoo parlour, which shall remain nameless, used to have a big sign outside that read: "Come inside, we have 1000's of desings". *Enough said.*

Angelic Hell

2 North Road (01273) 697681
Mon-Sat 11am-6pm, Sun 12noon-5pm
www.mantas-tattoo.com

One of the best established tattoo purveyors in town, having notched up nine years of etching the likes of the Brighton & Hove Albion team and one of the Kooks. They've even put Steven Hawking's face on someone's leg, which has already carried off a couple of trophies – the tattoo that is, not the leg. Artist Ilona does a particularly good line in cover-ups, so while your ex-girlfriend's name may not be erasable, it can be converted into a series of farmyard animals. If you're the sort who acts on impulse you'll be pleased to know that they do walk-ins as well as appointments, plus there's a massive picture window through which your friends can wince and watch the work in progress (there's also a blind that can be drawn if you're shy).

Guru

4a Kensington Gardens (01273) 679504
Mon-Fri 10am-5.30pm, Sat 10am-6pm,
Sun 10.30am-5pm
www.guru.uk.com

This family-run jewellery shop has been here since the mid 90s, when North Laine was better known for metal hardware of the shelf bracket and pack of number nine screws variety. As well as competitively priced silver that you ***can*** display when the vicar's round for tea, there's a huge range of body jewellery including the largest stretching pieces you can find anywhere and various quirky little one-offs. Don't forget to say hello to the cheeky pierced ducks in the window.

Into You Tattoo

4 Little East Street (01273) 710730
Tues-Sat 12noon-7pm
www.into-you.co.uk

When the most renowned tattoo studio in the country opened here in June 2005, it finally nailed Brighton as ***the*** tattooing centre of England (and quite right too, seeing as we are also the most tattooed population in the UK).

Boasting the internationally famous Alex Binnie and Jason Mosseri among its artists, Into You has an undisputed reputation, particularly for large-scale custom work and hand tattoos from specialists like Adam Sage. As well as tattoos, they sell tattoo-related jewellery, books, clothes, Sailor Jerry and a few silly things like the Gangsta Rap Colouring Book. Of course, quality doesn't come cheap – prices for tattoos start at £50 for a simple letter or name while hourly rates here are £70. But for something as permanent as a tattoo, why settle for anything less than the best?

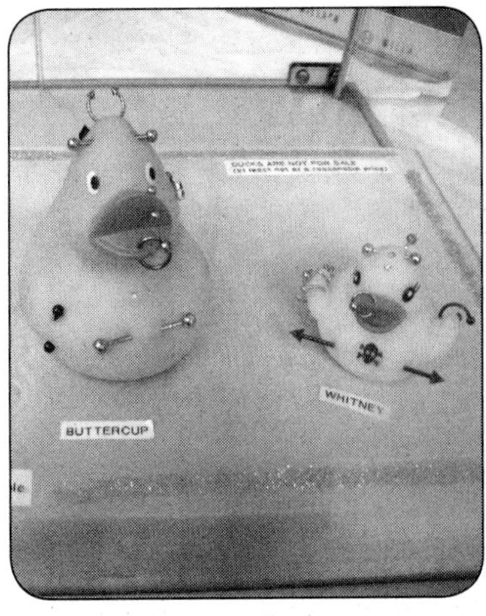

Nine

9 Boyces Street (01273) 208844
Tues-Fri 12noon-6pm, Sat 11am-6pm,
Sun 12noon-5pm
www.nineboycesstreet.com

Formerly Temple Tatu (owner Lester has gone on to other things) and now Nine – a name which may conjure up some insipid boyband supergroup, though nothing could be further from the truth. This impressive tattoo studio is located just off West Street, and its four resident artists (Ade, Nige, Sergi and Jack) come with years of experience, a deep knowledge and understanding of the history of tattooing and hardly ever go around dressed in white, dancing and singing close harmonies.

Newcomers are made to feel at ease by discussing all the processes involved over a cup of tea and the reception room, decorated with artwork by the resident tattooists, is elegant and inviting. Their portfolios are varied and they're particular about researching every design, so you can even find out what the tattoo you're about to get really means.

Top tip: Appointments essential.

Punktured

35 Gardner Street (01273) 688144
Mon-Fri 10.30am-6pm, Sat 10-6pm,
Sun 12noon-5pm *www.punktured.co.uk*

If you could get qualifications in piercing, Punktured would be all grade As. Bringing a friendly, open and caring approach to a profession which still has an image of domination by gloomy monosyllabic hairy types, owner Julie and the gang demonstrate their skill and dedication through little touches such as the giving of aftercare solution and written instructions after all piercings, and training their receptionists in first aid in case anyone feels a bit wobbly afterwards. Not averse to a bit of publicity, Punktured have been filmed by Channel 4 and MTV, featured in *The Times*, teen mags, and on BBC radio, and Julie even played Bjork's body double in the *Pagan Poetry* video. There are five resident piercers here, men and

women, all with years and years of experience, offering scarification, ear scalpelling, dermal anchors, sub-dermal beading, dermal punching and even ear piercing (though their oddest request has to be from the woman who brought in her false nipple to be pierced!) If you want your labia pierced by a grizzly old git high on ketamine try Angry Allan in Portslade; if it's friendly professional treatment you're after, this is the place.

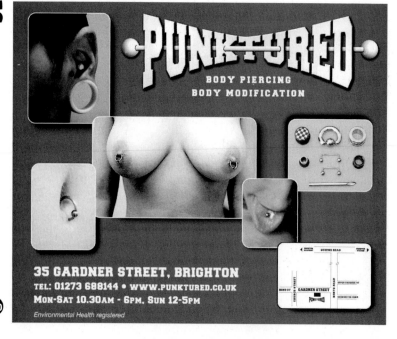

Wildcat

6 Gardner Street (01273) 606489
Mon-Sat 10am-6pm, strictly over-18s
www.wildcat.co.uk

Not content with being the largest suppliers of body jewellery in the world, Wildcat stocks the very latest in genital stimulation, from the world's biggest steel dildo to butt plugs, glass vibrators, labia spreaders, ball crushers and even a urethral vibrator that stimulates the anal G-spot via the bladder (!). Understandably, they keep this stuff downstairs away from the prying eyes of young-uns and *Daily Mail* readers. Fans of Vince Ray will be pleased to know they've got a good selection of his art on crockery, T-shirts and bathroom tiles, while for the man/woman who has everything, how about some fossilised Siberian woolly-mammoth-ivory body jewellery?

Enjoy a good natter with the friendly staff in here, pick up flyers for fetish-related events around town and, if you can, try and persuade them to play some gentle music now and again. **NB:** Wildcat DO NOT do piercings and tattoos but get asked so often that they recently celebrated their one millionth request by having the customer stuffed and wall mounted.

Emily Dubberley's Top 8 reasons Brighton is the sexiest place to be!

Pic: Sam Eddison

1. Sex on the beach is a common fantasy and, unlike most beaches, Brighton doesn't have sand to get into all those hard-to-reach places and ruin the moment.

2. Impure Art Gallery is the only specialist erotic art gallery in the UK.

3. If you fancy a bit of fetish there is Torture Garden at the Ocean Rooms and Tainted at the Caroline of Brunswick. Watch out for pre-parties and after-parties.

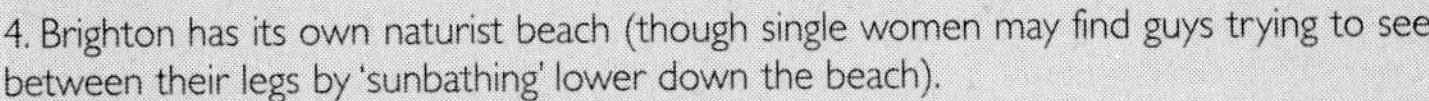

4. Brighton has its own naturist beach (though single women may find guys trying to see between their legs by 'sunbathing' lower down the beach).

5. Burlesque is so ubiquitous about every third woman you meet is a burlesquer!

6. You're never far away from a lapdancing club. The Pussycat Club boasts 25 girls; Grace and Spearmint Rhino aim at the more glamorous end of the spectrum.

7. Brighton has one of the highest populations of singles in the UK, both gay and straight, and a large student population; it's never that hard to get casual sex.

8. Brighton Pride is one of the sexiest celebrations ever, with people of all sexualities getting together to party.

Emily is a sex writer and founder of www.cliterati.co.uk

Dolly Rocket by Eve Poland

SEX PARTIES

The best place to find out about swingers parties and the like is the *Blue Guide*, found in most of the shops reviewed in this section. Events like Club Joy, the F Club, Saucy and Sensual can be found listed in here, or on the net. They welcome couples, go nuts for single women and try and put off any poor single males who happen to be past their prime, sport ponytails or wear socks and sandals.

FETISH NIGHTS

Vinylla

www.vinylla.co.uk

Long-running local fetish night that crops up at irregular intervals for social events and full-on parties.

Torture Garden

www.torturegarden.com

TG has been away from Brighton for years; now it's back every few months or so. The biggest, the showiest and the shiniest.

EROTIC ARTISTS

Eve Poland

www.evepoland.com

Playful, humorous and erotic, Eve's paintings and screenprints range from spooky-looking, mischievous cats to kinky ladies with whips (who seem to bear more than a passing resemblance to the lovely Eve herself). Not surprisingly for Brighton, the fabulous kinky ladies have garnered much attention; they've been exhibited in numerous galleries and sex shops and formed the basis of collaborations with the likes of luxury knickersellers Lascivious and local celebrity tailor Gresham Blake. Eve accepts commissions to paint whatever sordid fantasies you may have, though she draws the line at anything involving David Van Day.

LAPDANCING CLUBS

The Pussycat Club

75 Grand Parade (01273) 689503
www.pussycat-club.co.uk

Grace of Brighton

51-52 North Street (01273) 733212
Admission, £10-£20 Special weekday events include a fantasy dress-up night, free lapdance with student card and a lecture on biochemistry.

Men, if your idea of a good night out is having a girl rub her voluptuous breasts in front of you, then you may want to pay one of these places a visit. Attracting stag nights, rugby teams and visiting businessmen by the coachload, the clubs offer a chance to enjoy lapdances, poledances, VIP dances (behind a curtain), and a range of overpriced drinks. If you don't know the law, strictly no physical contact is allowed between customer and dancer but popping to the loo afterwards to give yourself a hand shandy ***is*** permitted.

Mind Body Spirit

From Yoga and Tai Chi classes to Buddhist centres and homeopaths, Brighton has the lot, and in abundance. Look in the corner of every park and you'll find someone practicing Qi Gong, meditating, doing yoga or (more typically for Brighton) reading about it. If you're curious about what day courses are on offer, or need somewhere to meditate or practise headstands, your best starting point is to pick up any free listings magazines from the shops and cafés in the Lanes.

Since living in Brighton I have developed many new interests, and probably wouldn't have discovered things like Ayurveda without being in the town where anything goes and where so many different lifestyles co-exist. Sure, there's the usual mystical crap, places where your cat can have its aura cleansed, but if people believe in it, what's the harm? I love the fact that Brighton people are, on the whole, tolerant and open-minded. After all, why shouldn't you enjoy meditating and chanting as well as, say, clubbing, carpentry and fisting?

SHOPPING

Angel World

5 Brighton Place (01273) 728398
Mon-Sat 10am-5pm, Sun 10am-4.30pm

Satisfying both your religious and mythological leanings in one fell swoop, there're enough angel and fairy figurines in here (some, it has to be said, with slightly scary faces) to fan the flames of whatever belief system you buy into. Tarot cards and other instruments of the paranormal should enable you to put Colin Fry in his place next time he's wailing about your dead mother when in fact she's sipping tea in a café in Cleethorpes.

Bell, Book & Candle

38 Gardner Street (01273) 572212
Mon-Sat 10am-6pm, Sun 11am-5pm
www.bell-book-candle.co.uk

A fetching log-cabinesque interior housing a predictable selection of spiritual cards, books, candles and models of your favourite deity. Now amalgamated with the mothership Hocus Pocus, they push the spiritual envelope a little further with Hindu figurines made from River Ganges mud for the more discerning shrine, and plenty of Jewish accessories such as riddush cups, Torah scrolls and gefilte fishfingers.

Greenwich Village

18 Bond Street (01273) 695451
Mon-Fri 10am-5.30pm, Sat 10am-6pm, Sun 11.30am-5pm

Think of Camden Market circa 1992 and you're not too far off the mark. These two thin passageways in Bond Street actually open up into a wealth of different stalls which, against the odds, seem to have survived the backlash against all things tie-dye. If you're the kind of person who likes Native American dream catchers, handicrafts from Thailand, sparkly flip-flops, windchimes, batik cards or clothes for that classic Stevie Nicks look, welcome home.

Neal's Yard

2a Kensington Gardens (01273) 601464
Mon-Sat 9.30am-5.30pm, Sun 11am-4pm
www.nealsyardremedies.com

A franchise of one of London's original herbal emporiums, this place has become Brighton's de facto alternative doctor's surgery. With a veritable armoury of herbs, oils, tinctures, vitamins and homeopathic remedies, Neal's Yard also has at its disposal some very clued-up staff (all naturopaths, homeopaths and herbalists) who can help you make informed choices about what you might need. Self-help books are also on hand, as are all the obligatory pampering products should you be suffering from nothing more than a prolonged bout of self-indulgent whinnying. The most usual complaints they deal with are still colds and hayfever but once some guy came in for herbal hormone replacements for his dog. Typical Brighton.

Lose weight holistically – and get a free perm – with the Tie-Diet

Two Feathers

11 Kensington Gardens (01273) 692929
www.twofeathers.co.uk

For too long Brighton has suffered under the oppressive yoke of Eastern mysticism, so why not try some Western mysticism from the Navajo Indians? Here's a shop stuffed full of all the tools your friendly neighbourhood shaman needs to get the job done, including carved animal totems, kachina dolls and rattles for shaking at evil spirits, and even bows and arrows for when they absolutely refuse to lay down. They also have a dizzying array of herbs both smokable and brewable (I'm not sure exactly what they do but don't blame me if you wake up thinking you're a bald eagle and try to fly out the window) and a Native American fashion range that's most definitely not for vegetarians – cow hide and big chunks of bone rule the day. At the back of the shop there's a calming contemplation pool to stare into, which might come in handy on a Saturday morning when you need to escape the crush of North Laine shoppers.

Messianic condensation therapy bags: the latest must-have treatment in Brighton

A warm welcome awaits you at Winfalcon

Winfalcon Healing Centre

28/29 Ship Street (01273) 728997
Mon-Fri 10am(ish)-5pm, Sat 10am-6pm, Sun 12noon-4pm
www.winfalcon.com

Brighton's no-holds-barred New Age shop, Winfalcon stocks every crystal, stone and karmaceutical known throughout the cosmos. Upstairs, it runs workshops in things like *Psychic Development* and *Know Your Inner Butterfly*, and offers the opportunity to have your aura photographed, so bring a comb. Here is the place to purchase things even the most green-eared hippies might think twice about – unicorn posters, books called *Full Esteem Ahead* and stickers saying "*It's A Druid Thing*". But, for a shop of this nature, it seems all the more bizarre (and unintentionally funny) that the bloke who runs it is a right miserable bugger.

THERAPY & BODYWORK CENTRES

Brighton Buddhist Centre

14 Tichborne Street (01273) 772090
Weekdays 12.30-2.30pm for visitors
www.brightonbuddhistcentre.co.uk

This group is part of The Friends of the Western Buddhist Order and their centre has two stunning meditation and yoga rooms and a library. The Order members wear strange little white collars, are very friendly (try asking *"how will I know when I've reached enlightenment?"* and marvel at their patient response) and make a decent cup of tea. Look out for more unusual stuff going on here too, like theatre and lectures. I went to a great talk during the May Festival one year where a Buddhist theatre director talked about the genius of Tommy Cooper and Frankie Howerd. Sunday school was never like this.

Bodhi Garden Dharma Centre

7a Ship Street Gardens 0779 298 1029
www.bodhigarden.org

Tucked away in a skylit quiet ex-art gallery is this sacred space, dedicated to Buddhist meditation and study. Described as a "non-denominational Dharma centre" and operating as an umbrella space for numerous Buddhist groups (Theravadin, Tibetan, Zen, Gaia House etc), the Bodhi Garden organises drop-in evening meditations, talks, quality courses and weekend day retreats for Brighton's burgeoning Dharma bum scene. As a charitable concern, it walks the Buddha's walk by relying on donations for many sessions, although I noticed a slight limp in his gait now that workshops are being charged at upwards of £20 .

The Clinic Upstairs

Above Bell Book & Candle, 38 Gardner St
(01273) 572204/572101
£15 weekdays, £25 weekends for an hour in the tank

Follow the shop's spiralling incense upstairs to discover this little-known world of shift-working tarot readers and karmic art. But the real gem here is the flotation tank, offering that unique opportunity to switch off your mind, relax and float, gravity-free. Ideal, in fact, for accelerated learning (play

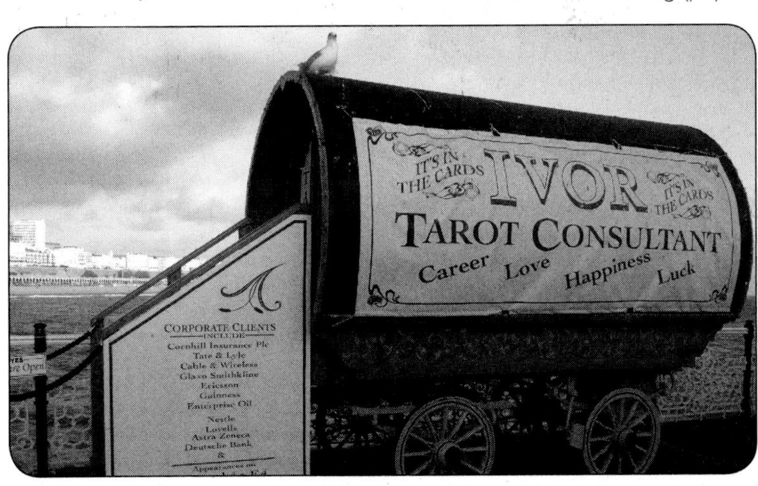

a language tape and you'll be fluent in no time), hypnosis (available upon request), creative thinking, meditation and planning the perfect bank job. Please don't start playing with yourself though: you'll get the water all messy.

Natural Bodies

28/29 Bond Street (01273) 711414
www.naturalbodies.org.uk

Set up by Gary Carter (known to make the ladies swoon), this is definitely one of Brighton's more capable yoga centres. Classes are mostly drop-in, cost around £8 and run throughout the day, with workshops at weekends. Follow the screams and you'll find them on the first floor. I can thoroughly recommend these classes as I've been coming (sporadically) for about five years now, and my mum doesn't tell me off for slouching any more. Be warned: they ***never*** answer the phone, so get a programme and find out when to come.

North Laine Holistic Therapies

1 Kemp Street (off Gloucester Road)
(01273) 681794
www.nlhtherapies.co.uk

A tiny five-person co-op with commensurately lower prices than are often found around town, it's a cosy single-treatment-room concern offering reflexology, reiki, hopi ear candles and massage flavours from aromatherapy, reiki, Thai and Swedish through to the full English with a fried slice. They also make their own bodycare products such as moisturisers and lip balm from wholly natural ingredients, so if you can't be bothered to walk all the way to Boots or you tend to fret about your skin's absorption of heavy metals, this is the place to come.

Revitalise

86 Church Road, Hove (01273) 738389
www.revitalise-u.co.uk

Previously the hippy-dippy Planet Janet and now unfortunately rebranded in a noughties manner, there's a healthy options-type café and Osho-orientated shop on the ground floor, plus nine consulting and group rooms. Depending on who is renting which, you will generally find an entertaining cocktail of Chinese kickboxing, oneness meditations, chakra dancing classes, tai chi and astrological counselling. The rooms are now named after fruit instead of planets, although reports that the Pineapple Room is used for colonic hydrotherapy remain unconfirmed.

Subbuteo girl

A CAUTIONARY MESSAGE FOR YOGA VIRGINS

While Brighton has some truly excellent yoga teachers in its midst (including the legendary Peter Blackaby), there are a small minority of practitioners in this town who, quite frankly, are clueless and still seem to be operating on that ludicrous 80s principle of "*no pain, no gain*". Should you find yourself at a beginners' yoga class where the teacher launches straight into difficult and demanding poses (and without bothering to check if anyone in the group is pregnant or suffers from high blood pressure or back problems) you are well within your rights to advocate that he/she be tarred, feathered and torn apart by wild dogs for their negligence. And don't be afraid to ask how your teacher was trained. Most training of any repute lasts a minimum of two years, while you'd expect a teacher to have done at least six years of yoga practice themselves before even considering taking a class.

Finally, if you're interested in giving yoga a try, but feel confused by all the different styles out there (hatha, astanga, iyengar, jenga, menga, mango etc), the drop-in classes at Natural Bodies make a perfect starting point.

Samurai

69 North Road (01273) 570940
www.shinjindojo.co.uk

Housing a shop at street level where you can pick up those stray weapons from your shopping list like swords, staffs, whip chains and nunchaku, this underground martial arts centre focuses on jujutsu and the art of the ninja. Done up to resemble a traditional Japanese dojo, its sprung and padded floor makes injuring yourself difficult; disappointingly they've never had any serious sword wounds occur, although they claim mysteriously, "*we do have the means to deal with it*". If you fancy turning your adorable five-year-old into a trained killer they also run mini-ninja classes.

The Treatment Rooms

21 New Road (01273) 818444
www.thetreatmentrooms.co.uk

While there is no denying their expertise, there's an element of the geisha about this gorgeously decorated salon, where you feel the only ugly people allowed on the premises are the customers. Massages, body wraps and facials are the main items on the menu here, and for premium prices you get premium pampering: fresh robe and fluffy slippers, your feet gently washed in candle-lit rooms with soothing music, a post-treatment relaxation area with Moroccan recliners, and a glass of herbal tea. You'll walk out of here feeling as light as your wallet, but delighted to be alive.

Unit 4

20-26 Roundhill Street
www.aiyp.co.uk
peteblackaby@aol.com

Perched serenely above The Level on the summit of Roundhill is this centre of yogic excellence. Started up by Brighton's legendary yoga guru and Kinks fanatic Pete Blackaby, it is almost entirely devoted to yoga of the Scaravelli style, along with more specialist stuff such as yoga for pregnancy, teacher-training courses, and Feldenkrais treatment.

Kids' Brighton

Brighton haS aLways bin a grate place for kidZ. With scaRy rides oN the peer, sPeshul theerter and sinnyma events, paddling poos and the seefront, there's always plenti of mischEEEf for uz to get up to (OK, so we downt hav a beech sootaBle for Bukets and spaides but at leest me dad can be spard the time-onnered fate of being Berried up to is nek in sand). And wen its chucKing it down in the middel of Orgust, their is ~~inumberabable enoomerrible~~ lots of famly-fiendly cafays, bars and restyrants were uz Ankel-bitters our free to run a rownd, scream and be sick. Fact is, nearlee evrythin in BrIghton apart from the nitelife is kidz-frendly. But then, tHeres alwayz Oceana...

WEIRD & WONDERFUL THINGS TO DO

Junior Dukes

Kids' films at the Duke of York's cinema
Preston Circus (01273) 626261
(Children over eight can stay without parents' supervision)
www.picturehouses.co.uk/site/cinemas/Brighton/local.htm

With its own hardcore cult following of diminutive movie buffs, Junior Dukes is, if nothing else, the cheapest babysitting facility in town. As well as showing new and old children's movies every Saturday, its organisers host a raffle for the kids, hand out sweets and, if it's someone's birthday, let him/her press the button to 'start' the film (OK, it's a con, but it makes them happy).

At the end of the movie there's even time for the children to draw pictures inspired by the film. According to one girl who works there, *"some are quite disturbing: recently, one kid drew a microwave that turned 'packets' into 'proper food like McDonald's'"*. Have a look behind the bar next time you're there – that's where they stick the best ones. Highly recommended.

Drusillas Park

Alfriston (01323) 874100
Adults and kids 2+ approx £12-13
www.drusillas.co.uk

About 30 minutes' drive from Brighton. Drusillas is a great place to keep the kids happy for a day as they feed the squirrel monkeys, otters and penguins, nag you to let them adopt an animal (don't worry, you won't have to bring it home with you), ride the Safari Train at breakneck speeds of up to 3mph and squirm at all the creepy-crawlies. My favourite bit is the meerkat compound where you get to go through these tunnels underneath and pop up in the middle... meerkat style!

Middle Farm

A27 between Lewes and Eastbourne
(01323) 811411 £3
www.middlefarm.com

Great tearooms, a food shop, animals to fondle, cows to milk and the marvellous English Cider Centre where, after sampling a few brews, you'll be on your back belting out a few old Wurzels tunes.

Coombes Farm Tours

Church Farm, Coombes, near Lancing
(01273) 452028 £3/£2
www.coombes.co.uk

A real working farm with tractor and trailer rides. Come between March and April and the kids can even see lambs popping out of their mummies' bottoms. Yum.

Heaven Farm

On the A25 between Dane Hill and Sheffield Park (01825) 790226 £3.50/£2
www.heavenfarm.co.uk

Enjoy the famous Heaven Farm nature trail with bluebells in season. Come and see the large family of wallabies and their joeys in the magnificent parkland surrounding this ancient farm. Organic farm shop, stable tearooms. Unique farm museum.

Typical Brighton dad

Holmbush Farm World

At Faygate on A264 Crawley-to-Horsham road – just 30 minutes from Brighton
(01293) 851110 £6/£5.50
www.holmbushfarm.co.uk

Two spanking new jumping pillows, cuddly miniature donkeys (though they might kick you in the goolies if you actually try and hug them) and even more woolly pigs! Plus the usual attractions, animal handling, tractor rides, tearooms and gift shop.

Museum trips

(01273) 292818

Brighton & Hove Council runs lots of activities at the museums and libraries throughout the year, especially in school holidays. For full details call the number above and check museum reviews in *Weird and Wonderful Things to Do*, which I've just realised is confusing as this section is also called *Weird and Wonderful Things to Do*. I was trying to be clever by doing a mini-version of the book within this chapter but it's all backfired.

Pottery

There are lots of places now that offer pottery workshops, which are great fun if you've got kids (or even if you haven't). Why not put your baby's handprints onto a plate or let them paint a mug or a vase? I spent a terrific afternoon with my nephew at Painting Pottery Café last year and he made me a plate with a picture of me on it playing the guitar, which was really sweet. (But between you and me, the picture was rubbish. ***No-one*** has hands that big...)

Paint Pots

39 Trafalgar Street (01273) 696682

Painting Pottery Café

31 North Road (01273) 628952
www.paintingpotterycafe.co.uk

The Pottery House Café

175/177 Portland Road, Hove
(01273) 773697

SHOPS

The Book Nook & the Little Nook Café

First Avenue, Hove 0779 307 3978

Brighton & Hove's only independent children's bookshop, offering the widest selection of books for children aged 0–16 set in a safe child-friendly environment. Perfect place to meet and have coffee with like-minded parents.

Klodhoppers

103 Blatchington Road, Hove
(01273) 711132
www.klodhoppers.com

Cool shoes for cool kids, school shoes, plimsolls and wellies always in stock.

Wigwam & Wigwam Baby

267a/93 Preston Drove
(01273) 505504/554056
www.wigwamstore.com

While their baby shop specialises in nursery goods and developmental toys, their (elder) sister sells clothes, wooden toys and a fruity selection of slogan t-shirts including Enjoy Milk, Future DJ and Made in Brighton.

You're not really supposed to let them inhale too much pottery paint

RESTAURANTS

While the following places don't offer crap plastic toys and Klassic Kids Menuz (ie. dogburger and chips), they do have quality food, are welcoming to families and don't mind the odd bit of yelling and dribbling (from the kids, that is).

Bardsley's (fish and chips)

22-23a Baker Street (01273) 681256

Dorset Street Bar (café/bar)

28 North Road (01273) 605423

Food for Friends (vegetarian)

18 Prince Albert Street (01273) 202310

Lee Cottage (Chinese)

6b Queen's Road (01273) 327643

Oki-Nami (Japanese)

6 New Road (01273) 773777

Piccolo's (Italian)

56 Ship Street (01273) 203701

Tootsies

15 Meeting House Lane (01273) 726777

Woodies Diner

366 Kingsway, Hove (01273) 726777

PUBS

The places below will generally provide a warm welcome and some scoff until early evening, giving the nippers free rein of the garden or family room. Harumph, in my day we were locked in the car with a packet of cheese-and-onion crisps and told not to play with the handbrake.

The Ancient Mariner
Junction of Coleridge Street and Rutland Road, Hove (01273) 748595

The Battle of Trafalgar
Guildford Road (01273) 327997

The Dover Castle
Southover Street (01273) 688276

The George
Trafalgar Street (01273) 681055

The Lion and Lobster
Sillwood Street (01273) 327299

The Open House
Springfield Road (01273) 880102

Pub With No Name
Southover Street (01273) 60141

Aaaaah, look, he's rolling his first fag

Er, can I give it back now please?

INDOOR PLAY AREAS

Jumping Gym at Carden Tots
Old Boat Corner Community Centre, bottom of Carden Hill, Hollingbury (01273) 540779

Brand new kiddies' gym open Mondays and Thursdays 10am-2pm.

Kids Fit Skool
(01273) 202226
www.kidsfitskool.com

New in 2009, this brand new play and fitness facility for children and parents featuring soft indoor activity centre, smoothie and snack bar, toddler training, teen gym, and personal training for parents while your progeny play. Or you may prefer just to watch a good slasher flick on your iPhone.

Little Dippers
Upper Gardner Street 0844 482 0222

Babies-only swim centre. Basically you just lob them in and see if they float. Be ready to dive in pronto if your baby turns out to be a sinker.

Toddler Gym Sessions
Portslade Sports Centre, Chalky Road, Portslade (01273) 411100

Under-fives' supervised play area with trampolines, bouncy castles and gym equipment. And, no, you can't have a go, it's strictly for the kids.

PARKS/ OUTDOOR PLAY AREAS

Blakers Park
Southdown Road

A quiet park with good play equipment, sandpit, tennis courts and a great café that's open all year round. Great fun at Halloween with prizes for best pumpkins! And hot toddies for parents.

Hove Park
Old Shoreham Road

One of the two parks worth a visit in Hove. It's a large, open area loved by squirrels and offering bowls, a fantastic playground, static climbing rock, a miniature railway and café. Keep an eye out for the wallabies and old ladies that breed prodigiously in this part of town.

Kings Road Play Area
Brighton seafront, near the West Pier

Brilliant play area, right on the seafront, with lots of fun equipment. Always rammed in summer with thousands of trendy Brighton parents sitting around and sharing muesli recipes.

Top tip: This is *the* place for flirting if you're a single parent.

Queens Park
Queens Park Road

Something for even the most intractable child, including a playground, lots of open space for ball games, a stream with waterfalls to explore, and a small shallow lake where they can chuck marmite sandwiches at the ducks and gulls.

WEBSITES

These two have loads of useful info and, seeing as your sprogs are probably more adept with a browser than you, it makes sense to get them to do the hard slog of looking things up.

www.abcmag.co.uk
www.brighton-hove.gov.uk

BRIGHTON & HOVE COUNCIL SERVICES

Childcare/crèches
Family Information Service (01273) 293545
www.brighton-hove.gov.uk/fis

For information on all types of local registered childcare provision, nurseries, holiday and after-school clubs, call the number above. Every summer they also organise outdoor events for families all over the city. Ring for a free brochure.

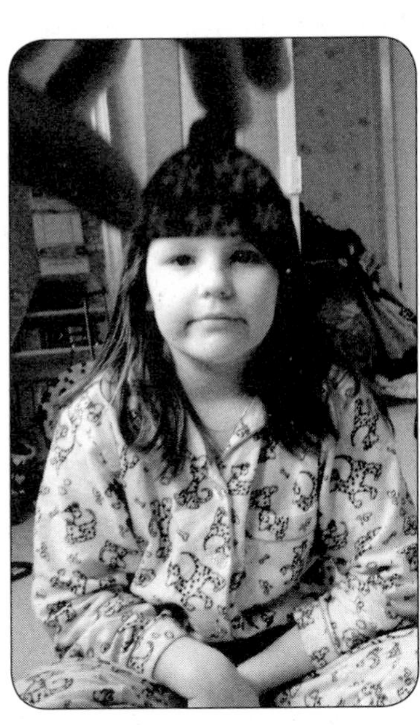

What's On

DIARY OF EVENTS

Isn't it only right that the town that likes to party should be host to the biggest arts festival in England? Not only that but throughout the year Brighton plays host to food, film and comedy festivals, car rallies, bike rides, two Gay Prides, Burning Of The Clocks, several music festivals, the Children's Parade and a firework display every two weeks or so. And with numerous political party conferences, where else could you combine a lovely seafront environment with the pleasures of egg throwing?

Brighton Science Festival

Last week of February

www.brightonscience.com

For five days every February the streets of Brighton become a sea of corduroy as thousands of bald-headed and bearded men and women descend upon the town. When not wandering round the Lanes talking to themselves they can be found lecturing and doing live experiments at various city venues. This festival, the brainchild of author Richard Robinson, has scientists teaming up with local schools, colleges and museums for open days. You can also

catch them letting their hair down at local debating nights Café Scientifique and Catalyst Club, where lively late-night lectures inevitably turn into a load of drunken eggheads in lab coats doing the can can. See website for details.

The Brighton Festival & Brighton Festival Fringe

May
www.brightonfestival.org,
www.brightonfestivalfringe.org.uk

In May Brighton goes bananas. For three weeks the whole town is packed with comedians, novelists, opera singers, dancers, circus acts, street performers, artists, musicians and thousands of blokes on stilts trying to juggle. This is the largest arts and entertainment festival in England and brings performers from as far afield as Peru, China and New Zealand, and audiences from as far afield as Hollingbury. If you want to see the town at its most vibrant and colourful, this is the time to visit. One unmissable event was Streets of Brighton: for one weekend, weather permitting, the roads were packed with strange cabaret acts, bizarre costumes, troubadours, minstrels and silliness. Funding and other issues have put a stop to that the past couple of years, so pray that it returns and we don't just end up with the bloke who plays the violin badly while balanced on a trapeze wire (although his playing does seem to have improved recently).

Alongside the main festival runs the Brighton Festival Fringe, offering more homespun and contemporary performances from DJs, bands, comedians and theatre groups in numerous smaller venues, theatres and pubs in town.

An important part of the Fringe are the Open Houses, where artists all over Brighton and surrounding areas open their homes for several weekends and everyone finally gets a chance to nosey around other people's houses, clock a few ideas for what to do with their kitchen and pretend to look at the art.

Two stunning additions to the Festival in recent years have been the Spiegeltent, and St Andrew's Church

in Hove, hosting some fantastic burlesque cabaret, gigs, comedy and dance. During Brighton Festival you can expect everything from guided tours of old cash-machine sites (no, really!) to special club nights, experimental theatre, street parties and parades. More than 700 events, two festivals rolled into one, and an inevitable free fireworks party or three. Unmissable.

The Great Escape

Weekend mid May

www.escapegreat.com

And lo, for three days and nights God did smite Brighton with a plague of shy indie kids with dyed black hair, skinny-leg jeans and retro footwear who did impose on the good folk of the city and say things like, "*excuse me, I'm trying to get to see Duh, Yeah? play at Audio and I don't know where the sea is, but it's near there?*" And, "*help, I seem to be trapped inside my trousers, would someone call my mum?*"

And the good folk of Brighton were mildly afraid, but only because it reminded most of them that they weren't teenagers any more and still secretly liked the Levellers...

Three manic (and brilliant) days of gigs all over the city from the latest asymmetrically haired upstarts and a few older acts that ***still*** hardly anyone's heard of. If you've not got a VIP pass, though, be prepared to stand in some long queues outside venues.

London to Brighton Bike Ride

Mid June

With the mean-spirited idiots who run our railways having banned bicycles on trains between London and Brighton back in 2005, the poor buggers who cycle the 50-odd miles down here for the annual bike ride now have to get a long-suffering relative to come and pick them up in the car. Or there's always the option of catching the giant pedalo from the end of the pier that winds its way round the Kent coast and back down the Thames Estuary.

Brighton Carnival

July

www.brightoncarnival.co.uk

Brighton Carnival winds, grinds and bops through the city streets in July every year from the Lanes down to Madeira Drive for a Caribbean goat curry and still more partying.

Steel drums, samba bands, 38,000 drummers and Mardi Gras style brass all compete for air space, causing a

racket loud enough to make your teeth fall out. And outré dress is of course compulsory: there might be giant flowers, huge pineapples, twelve-foot-high peacocks, mega dinosaurs or Japanese warriors and for paraders of retirement age, bikinis, bare flesh, bodypaint and many a flamboyant feathery headdress.

Pride

Middle of the second week in August, and mid March
Preston Park

(See *Gay* chapter)

Loop Festival

Mid July, Victoria Gardens
www.loopbrighton.com

Usually held on the second or third Saturday in August this mini festival (originally a one dayer now expanded to two) is a celebration of cutting-edge electronic music. No bloated has-beens peddling their tired four-chord songs here, it's all the latest new, shiny sounds that have been provided in the past by the likes of Grasscut, Caribou, New Young Pony Club and Four Tet. And if it's raining, they've got it covered. With a couple of giant tents. Recommended.

Beachdown Festival

Last weekend of August, Devil's Dyke
www.beachdownfestival.com

While still finding its feet, this four dayer (is it just me or are festivals getting longer and longer? I usually want to go home for a bath and a box of Jaffa Cakes by the third day) is a proper do hosting the likes of Super Furry Animals and The Magic Numbers, as well as Brighton-based acts and a bunch of scrumptious local food suppliers instead of the same old noodle and square-pie stalls you get at every other festival. You won't see the beach from up on the rolling downland but you can see the sea, and the chalky hills mean that you won't be wading through slurry even in monsoon conditions. I'd take a hat though, it gets a bit breezy up there.

Food & Drink Festival

September

This month-long event, organised by a collective of Brighton's restaurant owners, offers special cookery courses in the kitchens of some of our finest restaurants. You'll find weekend food stalls in the city centre and special events including wine tasting and banquets at the Pavilion, all culminating in a huge food fight.

Brighton Comedy Festival & Comedy Fringe

Beginning of October
www.brightoncomedyfestival.com
www.brightoncomedyfringe.co.uk

Every October the big names in comedy descend upon Brighton and perform their latest shows over an intensive fortnight at the Brighton Dome and Corn Exchange. Ticket prices can be a little intimidating (often £15-20 for just an hour's stand-up) but as long as you avoid Phill Jupitus you'll be fine.

For those who prefer to check out the rising stars of the comedy scene as well as the less glib and unshiny suited, look no further than the Comedy Fringe, set up in 2006 by the good folks at Otherplace Productions (see the review of Upstairs at Three and Ten in the *Entertainment* chapter). These guys really have their finger on the pulse, and with tickets about half the price of those in the main festival, combined with the intimacy of this magical 40-odd-seater venue, you'd be a silly bugger not to give it a try.

Brighton Live

October

One long weekend, 100 gigs, more than 250 Brighton bands, lectures, seminars and other events. All free.

John Lidbetter All-Weather Open International Stone Skimming Competition

Sunday afternoon, mid to end September
(Check press for exact date and time)

Simple, silly, free to all and utterly pointless, this fabulous competition was dreamed up and organised by man-about-town John Lidbetter. The rules are simple – each contestant is given three stones for three skims, has to choose a skimming name (FatBoySkim being the most obvious!) and tries their best. Whoever scores the highest is the winner. The prizes include a bottle of champers for best style and a cup for the outright winner, which is kept on display in the Lion and Lobster pub. Of course, with Brighton woefully barren of flat stones I'd recommend starting your search now for those three perfect bouncers, and I'll see you in September for the skim-off.

Lewes Fireworks

5 November

Still upset about a bunch of Protestant martyrs who were burned here centuries ago by the wicked Catholics, the people of Lewes remember the occasion by hosting the biggest and most phenomenal Bonfire Night celebration in the UK.

Along with the procession of carnival-style floats, you'll get the chance to see the townsfolk dressed up in Freddie Krueger jumpers, marching down the streets holding flaming crosses and throwing bangers. Around 8pm, the crowds head off to bonfires in different corners of the town where, some years, loonies dressed as cardinals stand on scaffolding and encourage the audience to hurl abuse (and fireworks) at them. A few effigies of the Pope, political figures and crappy celebs are then ceremoniously blown up for good measure, followed by huge firework displays.

The whole event has a very dark, anarchic, pagan feel to it; there are definite hints of *The Wicker Man* in there too. It's only a short train ride from Brighton but I recommend getting there no later than 6pm if you want a good view of it all. Best not to take any pets, especially potbellied pigs, since the townsfolk are notoriously carnivorous.

Top tip: Waiting to get the train home after the fireworks can be a long, gruelling wait. Make for the station once they've began; you can still enjoy them as you leg it for the train.

London to Brighton Veteran Car Run

First Sunday in November

Not being a car nut I find it hard to join in the excitement of the enthusiasts who congregate down at Madeira Drive, share notes on the pros and cons of tungsten-drive camshafts and then disappear back to their stately mansions. But, as one of my friends put it, *"surely the sight of a lot of lovely old cars putt-putting away stirs the little boy in you?"*

Cinecity: Brighton Film Festival

Late November
www.cine-city.co.uk

The city's annual celebration of celluloid, Cinecity was established in 2003 and presents a packed programme highlighting the best cinema from around the world. The festival's home is of course the Duke of York's, but Cinecity screens in all the city's cinemas and in a range of unusual locations – whether it's projections onto the Pavilion or in the cells of the old police station. Past events with a Brighton flavour include Hove resident Nick Cave selecting his favourite Berlin-set films, and a 25th anniversary screening of cult classic *Quadrophenia,* with the cast and crew given a Vespa escort to the Grand.

Burning Of The Clocks

Winter Solstice (around 22 December)

While most seaside towns go into hibernation for the winter, Brighton celebrates the shortest day with this fantastic pagan procession along the seafront, culminating in a huge bonfire and fireworks display. Expect hundreds of strange and beautifully designed paper lanterns around the theme of time, and lots and lots of candles. The whole event evokes that perfect, dark wintry spirit, mixed with the excitement of knowing that Christmas is just around the corner. One of my favourite events in the Brighton calendar. Highly recommended.

Christmas Day Swim

11am Christmas Day

(see Brighton Swimming Club in *The Sea* chapter)

EVENTS WEBSITES

For what's on and daily listings:
www.whatson.brighton.co.uk
www.visitbrighton.com
www.brightonlife.com
www.theargus.co.uk/whatson
www.ents24.com

www.myspace.com/brightonlivespace

The most comprehensive live-music listings for the town, written by people who actually seem to go to most of them, with occasional gig reviews.

www.mybrightonandhove.org.uk

This community website contains quirky and little-known aspects of local history, together with people's memories and photographs. Regularly updated by volunteers, the site publishes local knowledge and answers enquiries about Brighton & Hove past and present. The group is affiliated to QueenSpark Books and supports its aims of giving local people a voice.

BRIGHTON PEERS
by Cool CHEESE

TRAFFIC WARDEN

LIVES:- NEAR WITHDEAN WHERE SHE USES THE 'PARK AND RIDE' SCHEME TO GET INTO WORK

SPOTTED:- PATROLLING YOUR STREET EVERY FOUR HOURS, SEVEN DAYS A WEEK

Places to Sleep

Brighton has hundreds of places to sleep, from hotels, B&Bs, guesthouses, hostels and hotels to that old mod favourite – under the pier in a sleeping bag. And since the arrival of such themed places as Drakes, the Pelirocco and Blanch House, some visitors can even expect to find their room decorated by their favourite bands, dressed up as a Moroccan harem and kitted out with DVD players, PlayStations and even the odd porn film. With the growth of all these new stylish places, however, the price of a good room in town has increased considerably. So, in our efforts to bring you a flavour of what's out there, we've tried to cover a range from the priciest to the cheapest, the friendliest to the rudest, and the simplest to the most outrageous. A word or two of warning though: booking only one night at weekends can be next to impossible (try www.laterooms.com), and Brighton is a noisy place for most of the night so for heaven's sake bring some earplugs.

The Grand

Kings Road, Brighton seafront
(01273) 224300
www.devereonline.co.uk

The most famous hotel in Brighton and, at £1,500 a night for the Presidential suite, far and away the most expensive. This ***may*** seem a bit steep, but it's worth bearing in mind that Ronald Reagan and JFK have flossed their teeth ***in this very room***.

Sadly, despite the opulence of the lobby and the doorman standing outside in a big hat, they no longer do valet parking, and many of the rooms are on the comatose side of tired. Even the health spa and pool are now closed and the staff seem unclear about whether they are due ever to reopen.

Rumour has it that Barack Obama recently cancelled his weekend getaway here when told that he wouldn't be allowed to smoke on the balcony.

Dress code: Armani, Nicole Farhi etc. Although if you're just popping in for tea they don't care if you're wearing trackie bottoms and a vest.

Singles £100-160, doubles £120-240

The Hilton Brighton Metropole

Kings Road, Brighton seafront
(01273) 775432
www.hilton.com

Another swish affair situated right on the seafront between the two piers and, again, catering for the more affluent ladies and gentlemen. But while the rooms and decor may be swanky, the service and quality of food and drink do not always match. Having had friends stay for a weekend recently the verdict was: food disappointing, service varied and ordering a drink after 11pm an unnecessary palaver. And when you order overpriced nachos and guacamole you'd expect more than a thimbleful of guacamole, especially after the first time it arrived it was just a bare plate of nachos.

Rooms £80-180 without meals, suites £220-280

Drakes

43-44 Marine Parade (01273) 696934
www.drakesofbrighton.com

If you fancy soaping your rude bits while enjoying one of the best sea views in Brighton, the majority of the rooms in this sexy and sumptuously designed twenty-room hotel actually come with a freestanding bath in the bedroom, right in front of the window (if you're on the right floor you can wave your loofah at top-deck bus passengers). The pampering extends to wet rooms with gigantic showerheads and underfloor heating, electrically driven curtains that hide wardrobe and desk space, and recycled bamboo-board floors, with aircon, internet and mega TV as standard. Downstairs there's a DVD library freshly restocked with the naughty films the staff kept pinching, as well as a restaurant and a groovy private bar that never closes, serving their own custom-designed cocktails. Despite the glorious luxury and breathtaking rooms, Drakes believe their defining style is service: they'll prepare your room any old way you like, so it can be ready on your arrival with a hot bath drawn, *Carry on Columbus* playing on the DVD, balloons, champagne or even a special 'love hamper' from She Said erotic boutique. You don't even have to leave the room to get a haircut. Anything is possible apparently, "*as long as it's legal*". Recommended.

Doubles £100-325

Hotel Du Vin

Ship Street (01273) 718588
www.hotelduvin.com

Stunning design, beautiful rooms, friendly staff… the Hotel Du Vin just oozes style. The rooms are named after famous wine houses and some include dual-pedestal baths where you and your lover can get up to all sorts of adventures.

There are 37 bedrooms in total, thoroughly modern if not quite as large as you might expect for the price, and a fabulous carved staircase; if you come to visit, keep your eyes peeled for the gargoyles.

The restaurant comes highly recommended (see *Restaurants* chapter) but don't assume you'll get a seat unless you book in advance.

Doubles from £180, all rooms en-suite.

QUITE POSH WITH A HINT OF BOHEMIAN

Amherst

2 Lower Rock Gardens (01273) 670131
www.amhersthotel.co.uk

Amherst pride themselves on making their guests feel special. All the rooms are tasteful and modern while little touches like offering breakfast in bed, free snacks, herbal teas and broadband data points in every room show that lots of thought has gone into the place. And being located very close to the seafront, several of the rooms here have terrific sea views. What more could you ask for? A foot massage while you tuck into your bacon? If you ask nicely they'll probably do that for you too.

Singles £90-195, doubles £120-195, cooked breakfast £6 extra

Brighton Pavilions Hotel

7 Charlotte Street,
Kemp Town
(01273) 621750
www.brightonpavilions.com

Serving up a hefty portion of chintz, this is possibly the cleanest hotel I've ever seen. All the rooms are themed and beautifully decorated along the lines of Titanic staterooms or Roman villas, while the Safari room even has a mosquito net for those who prefer their protection not to come out of a foil sachet. They've spent £250,000 on this place and it shows.

A rather large American lady did then snap a toilet seat in half but, don't worry, they've replaced it.

Singles start at £40, doubles £70-100, £90-150 for a four poster

Guest and the City

2 Broad Street, Kemp Town
(01273) 698289 or 0795 866 7922
www.guestandthecity.co.uk

A relative newcomer to the new breed of guesthouses with the winning formula of friendliness, beautiful modern design and proximity to the beach. And consistently rave reviews online prove its success. As with all guesthouses, everybody prefers the sea view rooms here and who can blame them? We'd encourage whatever dirty tactics you can muster (blackmail, slander, stink bombs through the letterbox) to bag one, as the superior doubles at the front come with their own balcony and stunning stained-glass window featuring classic Brighton landmarks.

The open kitchen downstairs offers the chance for a much less formal breakfast experience (no hushed conversations and awkward rustling of newspapers), not least because owner Chris is a genial fellow. Thumbs up all round.

Doubles £70-£120

Kemp Townhouse

21 Atlingworth Street, Kemp Town
(01273) 681400
www.kemptownhouse.com

The fruition of many years' planning and the interior design dreams of its amiable owners Claas and Russell, Kemp Townhouse has avoided the fashion cliché of themed rooms in favour of a simple elegant style, matched by a soothing conviviality. Describing their look as Modern English (despite Claas and Russell being German and Scottish!), you'll find no frilly curtains or flowery duvets here. Theirs is an elegant masculine aesthetic with a hint of Art Deco, and a nod toward the seaside location with monochrome photos of Victorian families on the beach. There are some particularly nice touches that demonstrate how much care has gone into the design: the sharp red wardrobe interior, based on the lining of a Savile Row suit; the triggered indigo bathroom light for avoiding waking loved ones should you need to indulge in a spot of late-night micturation, and three ground-floor rooms discreetly set up to cater for those with mobility difficulties. And you might want to stay an extra night just to sample everything on the expansive breakfast menu from the full English to the eggs Benedict.

And I couldn't help noting that Claas' full name is Claas B Wulff. If only he'd worked a little harder at school with his howling...

Doubles £90-195

Myhotel

17 Jubilee Street (01273) 900300
www.myhotels.com

Brand spanking new and as 21st century as Gerry Anderson, myokco mputerdocumentshotel is something of a love-it-or-hate-it proposition, so singular is the vision that has created it. Aromatherapy 'zones' waft different smells up your nose as you wander through the building and an overriding zeal for feng shui has produced curves everywhere: in the walls, the carpet patterns and the funky space-age furnishings. The lobby, with its mix of Freddie Mercury and Maharishi quotes, 80s-style coloured floor lights and copies of *Wallpaper** carefully placed on the coffee tables seems, however, to be a confusion of ideas, veering from the cheesy to the stunning.

The rooms themselves are extraordinary – the floor-to-ceiling windows, luxurious window seats and fittings in white with splashes of neon conjure a Stanley Kubrick vision of the future. Privacy advocates might find themselves wondering if anyone can see in from the offices opposite (I'd suggest angling for a view of Brighton's lovely new library instead). In fact it's probably best that you're fairly intimate with your room mate as well since the bathroom doesn't have a door and

only a frosted glass one separates you from an encounter with their previous night's curry. Their ridiculously popular cocktail bar, with fishtanks embedded in the walls, is in line with all this uncompromising modernity but fortunately (or disappointingly?) the hotel staff are not robots from the future and couldn't be friendlier. They'll even give you a little connector to link your iPod to your room's invisible sound system.

Singles from £89, doubles £109-200, cooked breakfast £18

VERY BOHEMIAN

Blanch House

17 Atlingworth Street, Kemp Town
(01273) 603504
www.blanchhouse.co.uk

Blanch House probably just pips it for being the best of the old breed of fashionable themed Brighton hotels as despite its ultra-trendy decor it doesn't suffer the *Nathan Barley* factor, though the presence of ISDN lines in the rooms will be a tad bemusing to inhabitants of the current century. All twelve of the rooms are imaginative and spotless, from Boogie Nights with its 70s chocolate-brown and orange colour scheme to the smaller Alice Room with silver-embossed wallpaper, chandelier and queen-size bed. The Snowstorm room even houses a collection of snow globes to play with, and every room comes complete with DVD and flat-screen TV, chocolates and other special treats that I promised not to mention. Toss in their lovely restaurant and bar serving specialist cocktails and you might even decide to get married here – they're licensed for it thanks to the former owners, who decided that what they really wanted to do was get married at home.

Rooms £100-230, breakfast included

Hotel Neo

19 Oriental Place (01273) 711104
www.neohotel.com

Maybe owner Steph is a little short-sighted, thought it was Oriental *Palace* she was moving into and decided to take up the challenge to turn her new hotel into somewhere to rival the Pavilion. Not that Neo is all dragon motifs and koi carp; the Eastern theme is largely confined to the bedrooms, which are lavishly decorated with oriental wallpaper and artwork and come with complimentary kimonos, while the king-sized chiropractor-endorsed beds and red velvet elicit thoughts of boudoir seduction. Elsewhere the hotel is decorated with objets d'art, huge chandeliers, ornate mirrors and a giant stag's head by the entrance that adds a touch of eccentricity. And Steph clearly has a love of all things black: it's a colour that prevails throughout, from the bathroom tiles to the carpets (which, yes, they hoover every day!) adding a surprisingly sumptuous feel to the place. Even the little cocktail bar – serving toffee-apple martinis – and their breakfast menus are something out of the ordinary. Stylish without being gimmicky, Neo is a rarity in Brighton: a perfect mix of glamour, eccentricity ***and*** elegance. Highly recommended.

Singles £55-65, doubles £105-160

Hotel Pelirocco

10 Regency Square (01273) 327055
www.hotelpelirocco.co.uk

Fancy a room decorated by Jamie Reid, or sleeping surrounded by artfully displayed ladies' knickers? Here artistic heroes, record labels, clubs and trendy boutiques have transformed each space into an individual pocket of creativity. And with such fabulous, flamboyant and unique rooms as Betty's Boudoir, Modrophenia, Pussy and Cissy Mo's Magic Garden it is easy to see why the Pelirocco created such a media phenomenon when it first opened. Some may find the decor on the visually alarming side and wish they'd thought to wear shades, but you can't deny it's got personality. In traditional Brighton manner they shamelessly advertise their "dirty weekend", via the special Play Room that has an eight-foot circular bed, mirrored ceiling, stunning bathroom and even a pole for a spot of late-night cavorting. And, of course, if you have need of what my dad would call "marital aids" they'll deliver those to your room as well.

Singles £50-65, doubles £95-160, Play Room £230-300
All rooms include Sony PlayStations

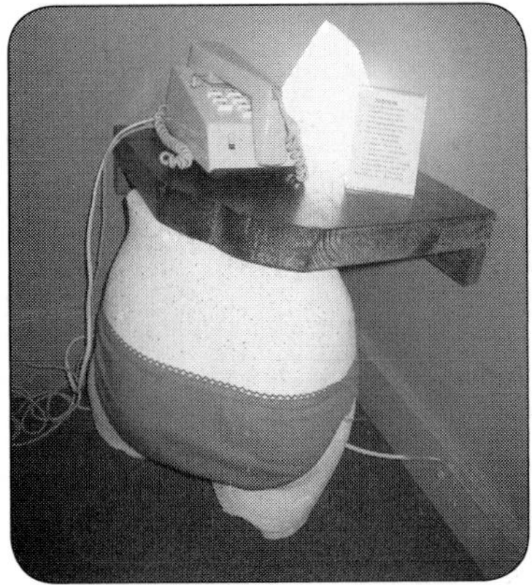

NICE & EASY DOES IT

Artist Residence

33 Regency Square (01273) 324302
www.artistresidence.co.uk

There's more than a hint of Haight-Ashbury circa 1967 in the feel and rainbow-width homemade decor splashed about this quirky little hotel, but the local artists they've unleashed on the rooms haven't been allowed into the extremely modern en suites so you can always pop in there if your eyes need a rest or, if you've got a room at the front, enjoy the fantastic sea view instead. Downstairs there's an eccentric but comfy lounge, a gallery with regular new exhibitions and they're working on a café space with a stage for open-mic nights, so don't forget to pack your euphonium. Friendly, clean and brilliant value.

Singles from £40, doubles £50-80, breakfast not available

Brighton House

52 Regency Square (01273) 323282
www.brightonhousehotel.co.uk

Newlyweds Christine and Lucho, who took over Brighton House in September 2004, have dispensed with the traditional English fry-up on grounds of health and taste and gone for an all-organic breakfast buffet which, together with stylish decor, use of environmentally-friendly cleaning products, and wi-fi internet has garnered this B&B a loyal clientele. Their dedication to sustainability also seems to have grabbed an extraordinary fistful of awards, including the 2007 Brighton & Hove Business award for responsible business, the 2007 Runners up in Tourism South East Excellence awards, the 2008 Green Tourism Business Scheme Gold standard award and the 2009 Sussex Business Award for Sustainable Business. Next year they're building an extension to the hotel to house them all.

Singles £45-55, tiny 4' wide doubles £55-85, normal doubles £85-125

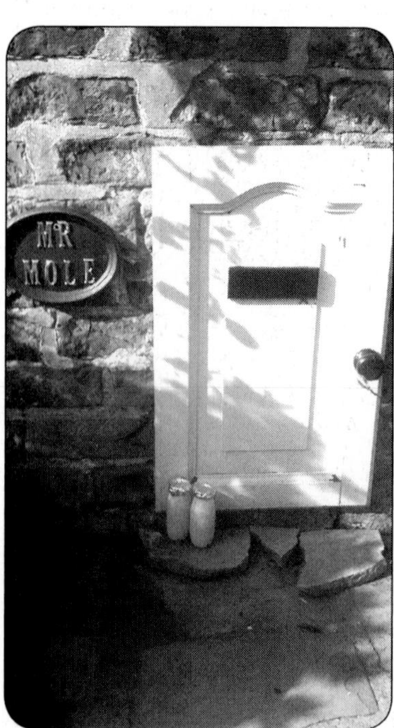

George IV Hotel

54 Regency Square (01273) 321196
www.georgeivhotel.co.uk

A tasteful period-setting B&B that manages to avoid being chintzy and has some well-priced rooms. The one to bag is Room One, with its balcony offering an unspoiled view of the sea and the dilapidated birdcage that is the West Pier. And while the views from the rooms round the back aren't exactly awe-inspiring, the ladies might get a thrill watching guys work out in the gym opposite. As well as offering continental breakfast in bed, George IV's USP has to be the old jukebox in reception, a present for owner Steve's 40th birthday. It's free to play and includes many of his favourite seven-inches (insert gag here). ***Huge*** brownie points for there still being a *Cheeky Guide* in every room!

Standard double £65-85, sea view £80-120, Room One £95-125

New Steine Hotel

10-11 New Steine, Kemp Town
(01273) 681546
www.newsteinehotel.com

Owned by the ever-smiley Herve (*"I like people"*) who also runs Gulliver's Hotel just down the road, the New Steine is understated and well maintained. Rooms are attractive and clean with fancy toiletries and complimentary mineral water. The bistro downstairs offers fine French food, and there's a natty mural of a Gallic street scene so you can amuse yourself during meals playing 'spot the oignon'.

Top tip: This is one of the few places in town that allows you to book just a Friday night without paying for the entire weekend!

Singles from £35, doubles £49-125

b
blanch house hotel
17 atlingworth st
brighton bn2 1pl
01273 603504
individually styled
en-suite rooms
restaurant
award winning
cocktail bar
private hire
www.blanchhouse.co.uk

NEW STEINE
ROOMS & FRENCH BISTRO
style bar
art food
01273
681546/695415
COMBINING, STYLE, COMFORT, ART, FOOD
AND IMPECCABLE SERVICE
AT AFFORDABLE PRICES
NEW STEINE HOTEL & BISTRO
Licensed Boutique Hotel & French Restaurant
10-11 New Steine, Brighton BN2 1PB
www.newsteinehotel.com
Tel: 01273 681546 Fax: 01273 622663
24 hours reception, 7 days a week

THE LAST CHICKEN IN THE SHOP

Abbey Hotel

Norfolk Terrace (01273) 778771

Not to be confused with the Abbey Lodge in Kemp Town, the Abbey Hotel is probably the cheapest weekly rental hotel in Brighton. The cheap, self-catering rooms are on the first three floors and on the whole are cramped and pretty hairy. If they're really all you can afford I'd rather you came and slept on my floor.

£30 for a single, doubles start at £53

GUESTHOUSE STRIPS

If you don't have any luck with the ones listed, or fancy going it alone, you will find countless B&Bs and guesthouses in the places below. In the most traditional B&B areas, like Madeira Place, prices change daily and sometimes in accordance with what they think you'll pay, so be terribly polite and dress down for the occasion and you'll get a better offer.

Madeira Place, Lower Rock Gardens & New Steine

Close to the seafront but lacking a proper sea view. Fairly cheap, plentiful and near just about everything.

Grand Parade

Right in the town centre, ten minutes' walk from the sea and close to North Laine.

Regency & Bedford Squares

These squares are found just past the West Pier and rooms overlook the sea (unless of course you get one at the back with a view of the gasworks).

OTHERS

For a wide range of Brighton hotels with independent reviews from satisfied and dissatisfied customers, try *www.activehotels.com* or *www.tripadvisor.com.*

For cheaper or mid-price B&Bs/hotels, here are a few others that don't smell of cat wee:

Alvia Hotel

36 Upper Rock Gardens (01273) 682939

Ambassador Hotel

22 New Steine (01273) 676869

Brightonwave

10 Madeira Place (01273) 676794

Funchal

17 Madeira Place (01273) 603975

Keehans

57 Regency Square (01273) 327879

Hotel 19

19 Broad Street (01273) 675529

Leona House

74 Middle Street (01273) 327309

Square

4 New Steine (01273) 691777

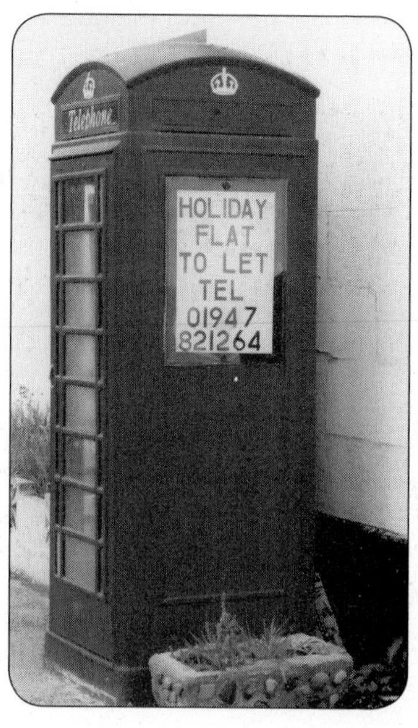

HOSTELS

Baggies Backpackers

33 Oriental Place (01273) 733740

Run by the very lovely Jem and Val, Baggies stands head and shoulders above the crowd, thanks to being run by people who genuinely care about their hostel and the visitors who come through their door. Everything here has been carefully thought out, from the free loo roll, laundry powder, tea and coffee to the two separate hangouts: a TV room with more than 1,000 videos to choose from and a TV-free chillout/ dance room with enough guitars, CDs, ashtrays and tealights to keep the most experienced backpacker happy. You may balk at being given Disney character-adorned sheets (some of which have frankly seen better days) but all rooms have built-in basins and are always clean and fresh, as are the showers and bathrooms, which is not a challenge met by many hostels. Recommended.

Dorm rooms £13 all year round

Grapevine Seafront/ Grapevine North Laine

75-76 Middle Street & 29-30 North Road (01273) 777717

www.grapevinewebsite.co.uk

What used to be Brighton Backpackers on Middle Street had, according to its manager, become *"a right shithole"* but a makeover a couple of years ago has meant that what is now the Grapevine Seafront "budget hotel" offers serviceable rooms to share with up to three other people. I'm not sure how much sleep you'll get though given the number of nightclubs opposite. There are some en-suite doubles on the seafront side which are a bit quieter but to be honest there're much better hotels available for the same money. The North Laine version is now the hostel proper and is probably a better bet for a decent snooze, if still not somewhere you'd want to take your girlfriend for a romantic getaway.

Grapevine Seafront Middle Street £15-40 per person per night, Grapevine North Laine £13-15 per night

St Christopher's/The Palace Hotel

10-12 Grand Junction, opposite Brighton Pier (01273) 202035
www.st-christophers.co.uk

This place seems to have become something of a horror show since our last rather positive review, with the breakfast reduced to stale cornflakes and a wonky toaster, the rooms falling to pieces and, in the words of *Cheeky Guide* reader John Bance: "*the staff are rude, ignorant and look totally out of it all the time on crystal meth or something*". John asked one member of staff if they had any soap or shampoo sachets and "*she said 'we don't do them' and stuck her thumbs up in a matey way! Bizarre*". Though if you just want somewhere cheapish with a view of the pier and don't mind whether the phone or TV work or the odd pubic hair in the shower then you might want to risk it.
Dorm £17-25, double room £48-100

Walkabout Backpackers

78-81 West Street (01273) 770232
www.walkabout.eu.com

Unfortunate stag and hen parties are often unwittingly booked in here on package deals, and then surprised to find that a pool of vomit on the bedroom floor has already been thoughtfully provided for them on arrival. Lowlights include the squalor, the location (sandwiched between two of Brighton's most vile nightclubs on West Street), the ridiculous levels of noise at weekends, the bar and the communal TV room that feels more like a Care in the Community waiting room. Highlights include er… erm… er…
£20-25 per night

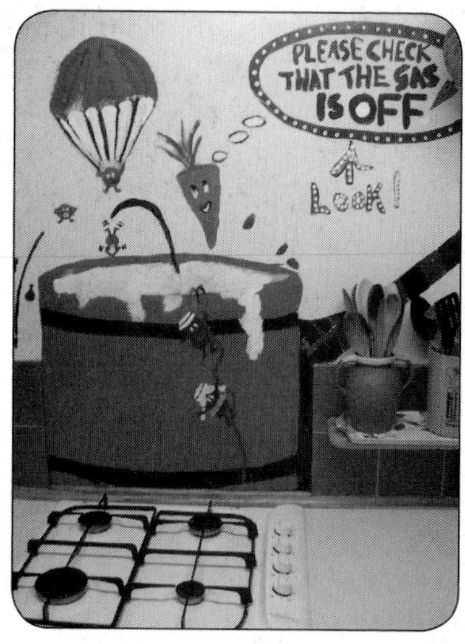

CAMPING

Sheepcote Valley Caravan Club

Behind the Marina off Wilson Avenue
(01273) 626546

Non-member peak charges – caravan from £20ish-35 a night with electric hook-up, two people in a tent (with car parking) starts at £15ish per night.

BRIGHTON PEERS

by Cool CHEESE

YOGA MUM

LIVES:- IN A BASEMENT FLAT IN HOVE WITH HER TEEN-AGE SON AND FOUR CATS

SPOTTED:- CRUISING AT INFINITY FOODS AND AT EVERY YOGA CLASS IN TOWN

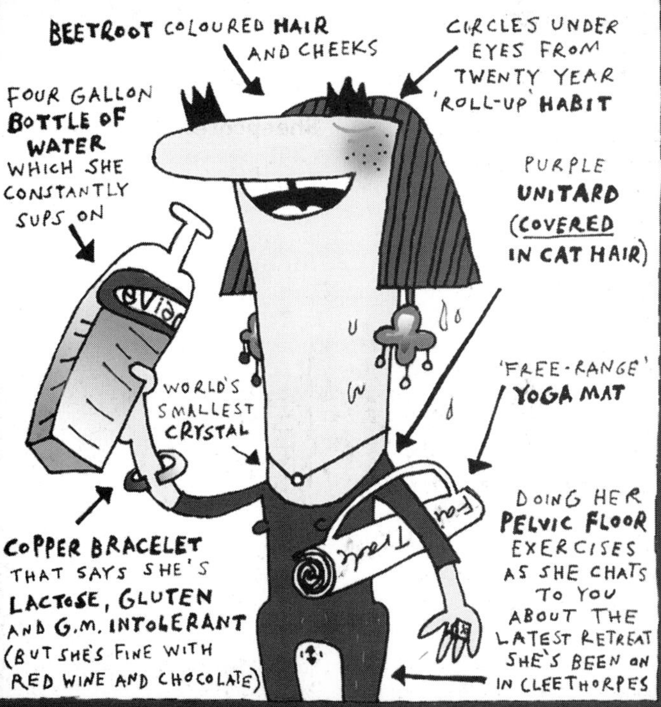

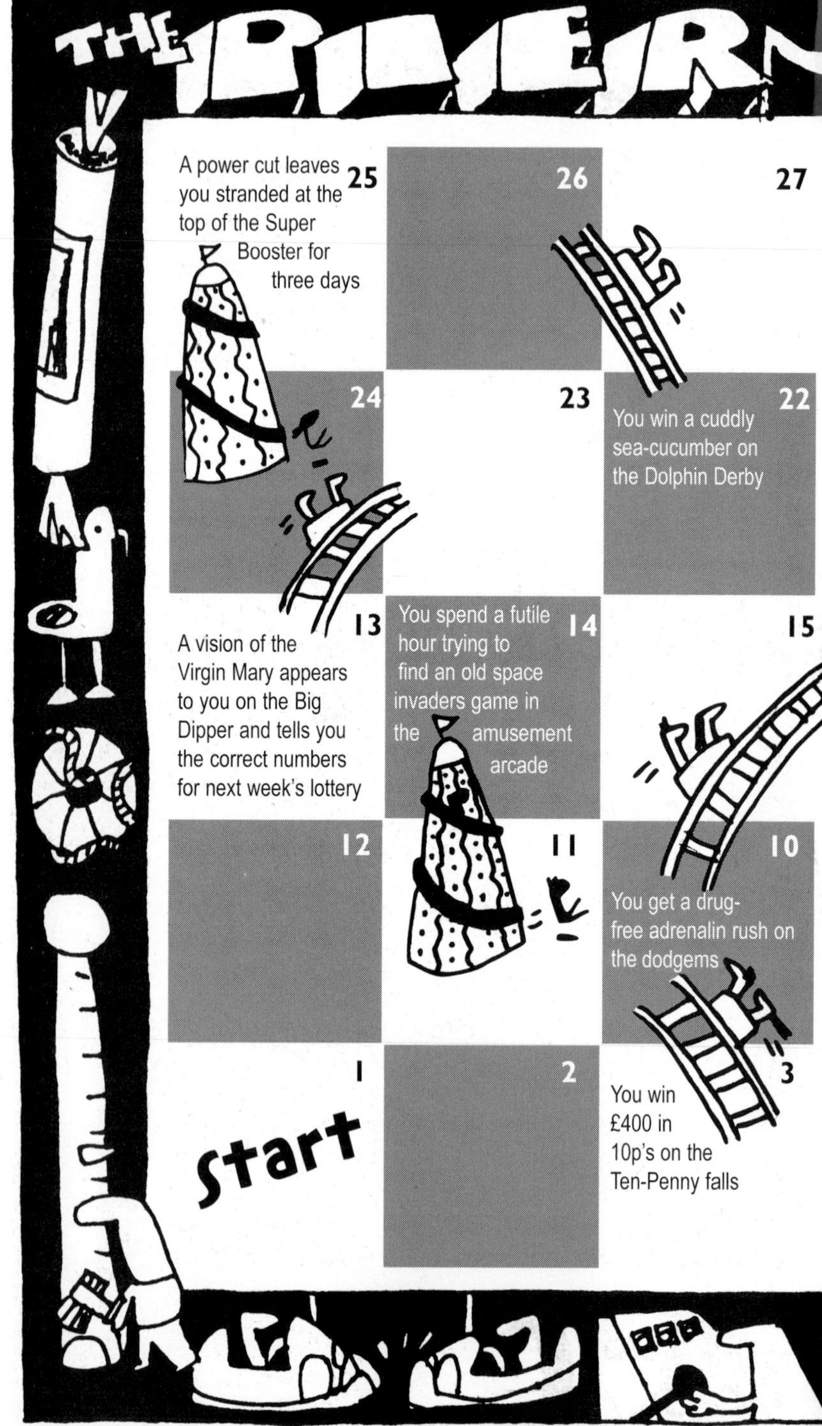
THE PIER
25
A power cut leaves you stranded at the top of the Super Booster for three days
26
27
24
23
22
You win a cuddly sea-cucumber on the Dolphin Derby
13
A vision of the Virgin Mary appears to you on the Big Dipper and tells you the correct numbers for next week's lottery
14
You spend a futile hour trying to find an old space invaders game in the amusement arcade
15
12
11
10
You get a drug-free adrenalin rush on the dodgems
1
Start
2
3
You win £400 in 10p's on the Ten-Penny falls

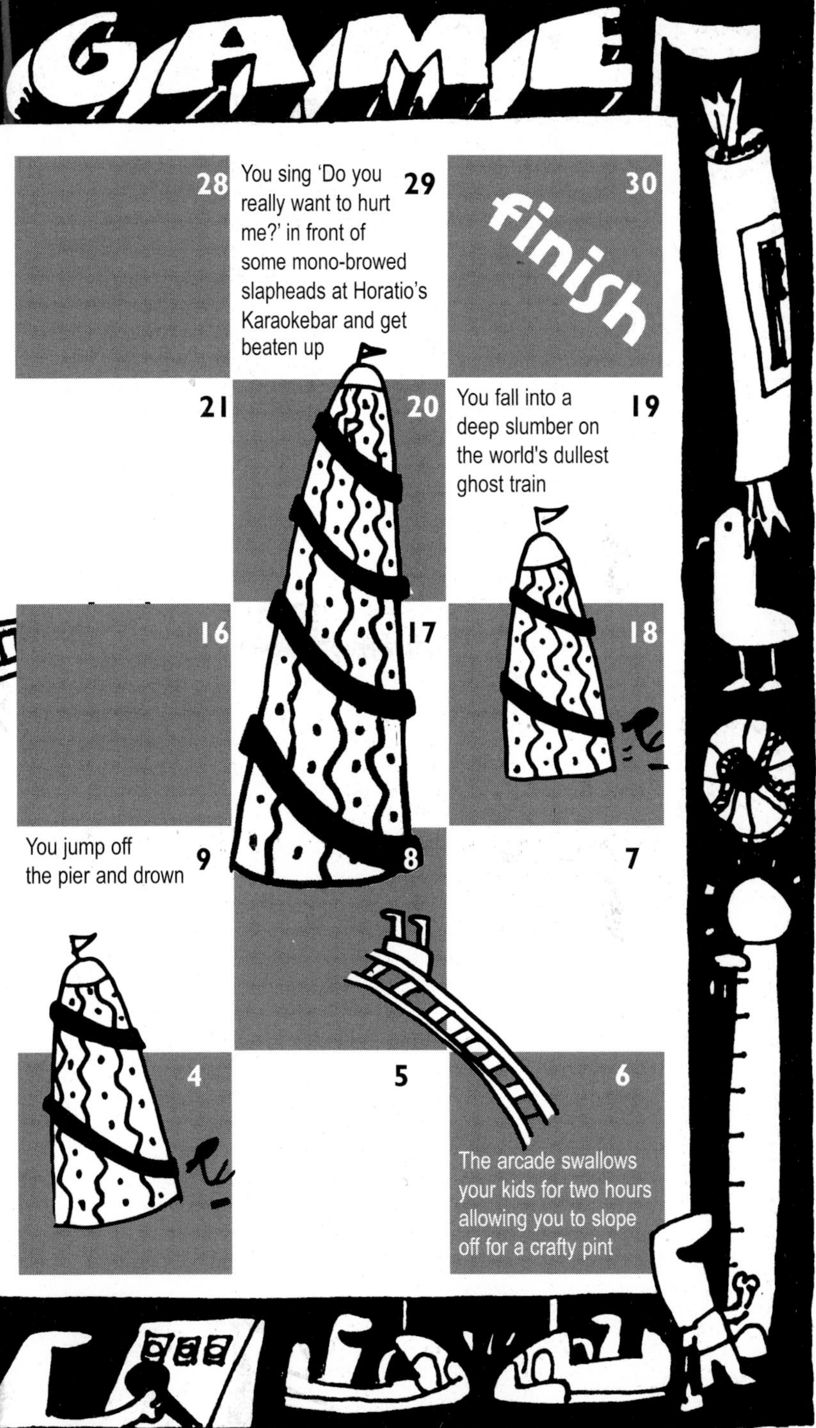
GAME
28
You sing 'Do you really want to hurt me?' in front of some mono-browed slapheads at Horatio's Karaokebar and get beaten up
29
30
finish
21
20
You fall into a deep slumber on the world's dullest ghost train
19
16
17
18
You jump off the pier and drown
9
8
7
4
5
6
The arcade swallows your kids for two hours allowing you to slope off for a crafty pint

Outside Brighton

Beachy Head

This notorious suicide spot has featured in the closing scenes of *Quadrophenia* and several Monty Python sketches and is also a popular spot for birders as plenty of migrant oddities that get blown over the water stop here to catch their breath and visit the 24-hour All You Can Eat Worm Café. It can get pretty windy up here so be careful near the edge but do look out for the red-and-white striped lighthouse and the spooky old burned-out car halfway down the cliffs. It takes about 45 minutes to reach Beachy Head from Brighton and, while there's not much else around, it's worth the visit for the spectacular views and having your head blown off. There's also a pub nearby if you get thirsty, though the Samaritans adverts ***can*** have a sobering effect on your spirits.
(Leave Brighton and continue heading east along the coast to Eastbourne)

Devil's Dyke

So the story goes that the devil started to dig a deep chasm to let the sea in to drown all the pious villagers of the Weald but an old lady – on hearing the sound of the devil's mechanical digger – lit a candle in her window, held it in front of a colander and tricked him into believing it was sunrise. The devil scarpered but his unfinished business – a 300-foot valley in the heart of the South Downs – remained. Now I know there are several flaws in this local myth (like what kind of idiot mistakes a colander and candle for the sunrise, and why didn't the devil just come back the following night anyway?), but we'll let it pass as it's a good yarn.

A visit to the Dyke is heartily recommended; this striking geographical feature offers plenty of opportunity for long walks, terrific views across the Downs and a shortcut down the steep hill to the Shepherd and Dog in Fulking for steak-and-ale pie, chips, a few pints and a heart attack as you attempt the journey back. The Dyke is a fifteen-minute drive out of Brighton and in summer you can even catch an open-top bus there from the city centre. Be prepared for crowds at the weekend and dogging in the car park at night.
(Take Dyke Road out of Brighton, cross the motorway and follow signs)

Ditchling

A quintessential English village with a few famous inhabitants, good pubs and a cake shop with the best treacle tart in the world. Past the strange little museum and village pond as the road bends to the left there's a stile and a very agreeable walk offering excellent views of the Downs. Go up the hill, take a picnic, enjoy the view and expect to share your field with a few friendly cows.

(Take Dyke Road out of Brighton, join the motorway going east, and follow signs for Ditchling Beacon.)

Eastbourne

To many Brightonians, Eastbourne is the world's largest open-plan hospice, offering more hearing-aid shops than cafés, a neat line in poodle parlours, and a population of the walking dead. And while this isn't too far from the truth (OK – it is the truth), this sedentary coastal town still has enough tricks up its sleeve to merit a visit, even if you ***are*** under 60. For as well as the very pretty area known as the Old Town (for obvious reasons), Eastbourne has a surprisingly attractive seafront. Lacking the naff commercialism of Brighton's front, Eastbourne's is – rather refreshingly – adorned with lush greenery. In summer the promenade teems with palm trees, flowerbeds, bushes and trees, brass bands are in full swing and old couples in cardies and blazers stroll along arm in arm. Add to this the facts that the beach is infinitely cleaner than Brighton's, the pebbles are smaller and the pier and seafront aren't rammed with drunk Londoners and hen parties, and the prospect of spending a lazy day here sloping around, lounging on the beach and swimming can be very appealing.

Of course one shouldn't get too carried away. Eastbourne's town centre could rival that of Doncaster's for grimness, but when the grime and chaos of Brighton get too much for you, a day out here ***can*** feel like a nice long soak in the bath. Just don't stay too long – you might end up all wrinkly.

(Take the eastern coastal road out of Brighton, or the A27 for a quicker inland route, and you'll be there in 45 minutes)

Lewes

On the surface Lewes is a cosy little town, ideal for taking your parents to for an afternoon stroll round the castle and a nose through some old bookshops. Below the surface the town has more than its share of occultists, witches and eccentrics and is host to the largest fireworks event in the UK (see diary of events), which is the closest you'll ever get to feeling you're in *The Wicker Man*.

The best pub here, without a doubt, is the Lewes Arms, a wonderful little boozer tucked away down one of the many side streets. Host to a number of bizarre games, including 'Toads' and an annual Pea Throwing Competition (the rules of which are very amusing), it's probably your best port of call for a real taste of Lewes and a chance to meet some of the town's fruitier characters.

(Fifteen minutes' drive from Brighton, east along the A27)

Stanmer Park

Head out of Brighton towards Sussex University and you'll find this large park. There's ample room here for big footie games, frisbee throwing and a chance to take some long rambles in the woods. There's also an organic farm, a small church and a great teashop, (though it's unfortunately located next to a stableful of cows, so if you sit outside be ready for some fruity odours and flies dive-bombing your baked potato). This is possibly the closest place to Brighton where you can forget the crowds, especially if you take the walk past the village and continue up the hill. (Go far enough and you'll reach a gate by a pylon that gets mentioned in *The Day of the Triffids*!) Look out for the tree trunk carved into badgers behind Stanmer House and extra brownie points if you get to see the Earth Ship, a startling demonstration of how much cash you could stop giving EDF and Southern Water if you built your house out of old tyres, crisp packets and mud.

(Ten minutes' drive from Brighton, on the A27 towards Lewes)

PLEASE BE GENTLE DON'T BE BOLD THE MONKEY BAND IS VERY OLD THANK YOU

Worthing & Goring

www.sistinechapeluk.co.uk

Those who find the pace of life in Eastbourne too soporific will doubtless find Worthing catatonic, bringing to mind the lyrics of the old Morrissey song *Every Day is Like Sunday*. This once-popular seaside resort has barely changed in 50 years but therein lies its (limited) appeal. When you've spent enough time in Brighton to grow a little weary of every day being like Saturday, a day trip to a faded, sleepy seaside town can be a refreshing reminder of a gentler pace of life.

Visit Worthing on a warm summer's day (any other time would be foolhardy) and you can enjoy a stroll along a seafront that time forgot: a movie at the old Art Deco cinema, the old pier with many amusement games still only 2p (including the charming Monkey Band at the back that kids will love despite the drummer having apparently died), a coffee at Coast, the open-air hexagonal café five minutes from the pier, or liver and bacon at the fantastic 1950s cafeteria opposite (frequented by Harold Pinter when he lived here in the 60s).

And if you need a few oohs and aaaahs prompted by local landmarks, seek out the Martyrs Church in Goring where a local artist has lovingly (and rather astonishingly) recreated the ceiling of the Sistine Chapel. Or head up to Lancing College, the impressive Pratchett-esque Gothic building you can see from the A27 when travelling west; the church and crypt are open to the public, while the grounds have a commanding view of the Downs, the beach and Shoreham Airport and are a good spot for a quiet picnic.

Forget good shopping, nightlife and excitement in Worthing: they barely exist, but for a spot of irony-free retro and a bit of peace and quiet (as once found here by Oscar Wilde, hence Mr Worthing in *The Importance of Being Earnest*), an afternoon in Worthing in the summer can be a tonic for the nerves.

Useful Info

ARRIVING BY RAIL

National Rail Enquiries
08457 48 49 50
www.thetrainline.com
www.southernrailway.com

Trains from London leave Victoria and Kings Cross Thameslink about twice an hour. The Victoria link is usually quicker – about 50 minutes for the fast train. Be careful when returning to London late at night however, the last train usually leaves well before midnight, even at weekends. There are also direct train services along the coast if you are not coming via London.

Top tip: You can buy train tickets to and from London at a fraction of the price from One Stop Travel at 16 Old Steine just at the bottom of St James' Street but expect a bit of a queue! Alternatively you can buy single tickets in advance from Southern's website (see above) or at the station the day before for as little as £3.

Sunday trains

Irritatingly, Railtrack (or whoever) have been 'repairing' the line between Brighton and London now for more than 300 years. Why it is taking them so long to fix 40-odd miles of track is a mystery but it does mean that if you catch the London-to-Brighton train on a Sunday your journey could take several hours as you find yourself rerouted via Littlehampton, Eastbourne and Barnsley, shoved onto a bus for half your journey and then fined £50 on arrival for your ticket being an awaydaysupersaver instead of a superdayawaysaver. I kid you not, I have spent some miserable Sunday evenings dreaming of being at home by the fire sipping fine wines, when instead I'm standing in the rain in the middle of sodding nowhere, waiting for some surly driver who turns up an hour late and doesn't seem to know where he's going. And to top it all, after five minutes the bloody bus breaks down. And there're no free seats. And yes, this has happened more times than I care to mention. Now that's off my chest I feel much better. Ignore this at your peril!

ARRIVING BY PLANE

From Gatwick

A train will get you to Brighton in twenty minutes. If there are four of you a taxi may actually cost less. The cheapest option is to get a coach or walk.

From Heathrow

It's a drag, to be honest. The simplest option is a coach that'll go via every Heathrow terminal and Gatwick and take about three hours. Otherwise it's tubes and trains via London, which is quicker but a pain if you've got heavy cases.

If you can persuade someone to collect you from/take you to Heathrow and you're both single, the least you can do is ask them to marry you.

ARRIVING BY COACH

National Express

08709 013 190

www.gobycoach.com

While they do takes twice as long as the train and often reek of chemical loos, if you're flying in or out of Gatwick in the small hours (courtesy of a cheapo EasyJet flight) this is a better bet than a £50 cab fare.

ARRIVING BY ROAD

Once you've packed your sandwiches, toothbrush, bucket and spade, make your way to the London orbital then take the M23/A23 all the way to Brighton. It shouldn't take more than 45 minutes once you've left the M25. It's as simple as that. To avoid the London rush hour it's best to stay off the M25 any time between 7am and 11pm. If you're lucky enough not to be coming via London you'll probably be taking the coastal route along the A27.

ARRIVING BY HELICOPTER

You'll get as far as Shoreham Airport and then it's a two-hour walk to Brighton along the seafront. What do you mean you haven't got a helicopter?

BUSES

Brighton & Hove Bus Company

(01273) 886200
www.buses.co.uk

The Big Lemon

(01273) 681681
www.thebiglemon.com

Buses in Brighton are frequent and plentiful. So plentiful in fact that Western Road is chockablock with them day and night, resulting in the world's first ever bus-only gridlock which lasted for more than eighteen hours in 2007. There used to be a flat fare of £1.80 which was only economical if travelling long distances like Worthing to Peacehaven, but you can now travel for £1.50 within the city centre and some short-hop routes like the station to the pier are just £1.

Also worth celebrating is The Big Lemon, a local company whose buses are run entirely on used cooking oil. Unfortunately they don't run all over town but do have a regular five-day service that operates between the town centre and Falmer at the far end of Lewes Road by the universities. No surprise that the students champion this service – it's ethical, runs until 4am and the engines are cleaner than those on the Brighton and Hove service.

Top tip: The Big Lemon buses are available for private hire and also run a service to Glastonbury each year.

Open-Top Bus Tour

May-September, tours daily from 10am
www.city-sightseeing.com

Brighton for lazybones. Do the lot in one hour for £8. Meet opposite the Pool Valley coach station on Brighton seafront.

TAXIS

(01273) 202020 • 204060 • 747474 • 205205

There are plenty to choose from and all the services are pretty much the same. Only two types of Brighton taxi driver seem to exist: the friendly cabby who chats amiably all the way to your destination and the silent, morose type whose only words are "*fucking idiot*", which he shouts at every other driver on the road. Typically, taxi fares in Brighton are among the highest in the country and more expensive per mile than flying Concorde (RIP). Taxi drivers in Brighton are required by law to carry inflatable life jackets under their seats so check when you get in. If there isn't one you should be able to blag a free ride.

CITY CAR CLUB

0845 330 1234
www.citycarclub.co.uk

A cracking idea for a town with nowhere to park (and sinking into the sea under the weight of traffic and Eubank's monster truck), City Car Club is a pay-as-you-go car-hire service with designated parking bays close to where you live. It's dead easy to join: go online, book it for a minimum of an hour, open the doors with a smart card, punch in your PIN number and you're off! Brrm Brrm!!

BRIGHTON SUBWAY

Closed because of subsidence and waterlogging, Brighton's once-famous Metro line used to stretch as far as Eastbourne, Worthing and London. Nowadays it is notable for Brighton's expanding subterranean community, several fight clubs and occasional sightings of the Brunswick Yeti.

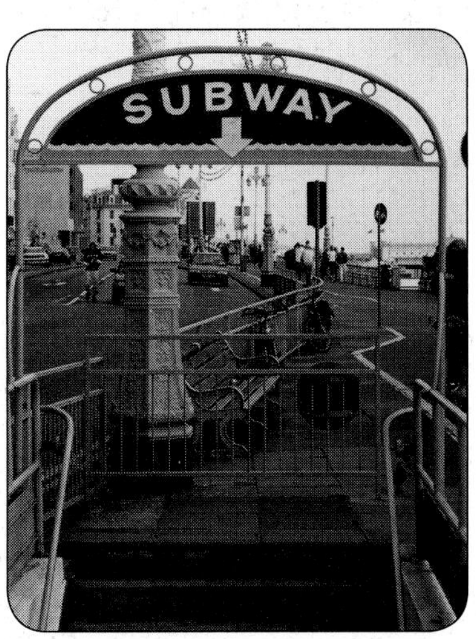

WALKING

Visitors from LA might be interested to learn that this mode of transport is still immensely popular in Brighton.

BIKES

Along with *The Simpsons* (series three to nine), cheese on toast and iPods, bikes remain one of our greatest achievements. And despite the hills, Brighton is ideal for cyclists; you can be just about anywhere in under fifteen minutes (provided you smoke less than 40 a day). Unfortunately the council's botch-job cycle lanes are far from ideal. You'll be taking your life in your hands cycling along Western Road and North Street, where there aren't ***any*** cycle lanes and the constant cavalcade of buses squeezes you off the road onto the busy pavement. Elsewhere – such as parts of North Laine where cyclists can go the wrong way down one-way streets – things are equally hazardous. While contraflows work in a cyclist's favour in theory, in practice drivers do not seem to respect or realise cyclists have the right of way here and will often just drive at you, forcing you off the road or worse. And don't get me started on the Seven Dials roundabout.

To end on a more positive note, I've been cycling round Brighton for fifteen years and lived to tell the tale, and the seafront really is great for bikes – it's long and flat and you can go all the way from Hove to the Marina and Rottingdean via the undercliff pass. In summer though, invest in a horn; you'll be spending half your time dodging the dozy gits who walk in the seafront cycle lanes.

Suicycle!!

Weird Cycle Lanes

by freewheelin' cyclin' spokes-man Alan 'Fred' Pipes

Flabike-asting!!

Brighton & Hove, which in October 2005 received £3 million of government money as a Cycling Demonstration Town, has lots and lots of cycle lanes. However, they don't all join up. In fact, few do, and there are many strange short ones here and there to mystify urban cyclists, who are forever told to dismount, walk a couple of feet along wide pavements, and then remount.

These have been documented in *www.weirdcyclelanes.co.uk*, a website started in 2000 that grew out of an article in *The Guardian* claiming that some cycle lane Up North was the shortest in Britain. The shortest in Brighton at the time was by the Gloucester nightclub and led into North Laine, but stopped after about a car's length. As time went by, even shorter and weirder ones began appearing!

This town (er, city) has a love/hate relationship with cyclists and the letters page of *The Argus* is filled with apoplectic correspondents from Hove banging on about demon cyclists jumping red lights, going down St James's Street the wrong way, cycling on pavements and not paying 'road tax'. Hove Esplanade, in particular, although about a mile wide, is festooned with No Cycling signs and guarded by impenetrable barriers each end.

The problem is that the land for cycle lanes is either stolen from the roads, thus annoying motorists who need to park on them, or from the pavements, thus incurring the wrath of pedestrians who like nothing better than to stroll nonchalantly along the seafront cycle lanes between the piers. Should a cyclist swerve to avoid any of them, they are liable for an instant thirty-quid fine for cycling on the pavement from one of our growing number of cycle bobbies!

PARKING

Devilishly tricky ***and*** expensive. Parking meters have been phased in for most streets close to the city centre (and many that aren't). There are, however, several multi-storey car parks in the town, which are all signposted. One of the cheapest places to leave your car is the car park near the bottom of Trafalgar Street, just down from Brighton Station. If you want my advice though, park out of town and walk or get a bus: it's never that far to anywhere in Brighton and should you park illegally and leave the car for more than ten minutes you ***will*** get a thirty-quid fine.

A few hard facts

1. Brighton & Hove traffic wardens once issued a ticket to a hearse (the undertakers were moving a body), thus breaching the city's own parking laws.

2. The council has fitted solar-powered pay-and-display meters across most of the town. Stop anywhere for more than three seconds and you'll be expected to cough up anything from 50p to £3 for just five minutes' parking. It is interesting to note, however, that if a black piece of card is placed over the solar panel on the top of the meter, the meter ceases to function after three days. Erm, allegedly.

3. Parking tickets are issued at a rate of one every two minutes in Brighton and generate more than £1 million profit for the council. (Ticket issuers are contracted to NCP, but both NCP and the council share the profits.)

4. Traffic wardens should receive our pity and ***not*** our contempt, being, as they are victims of a loveless childhood.

An illegally parked café A-board gets its third ticket of the day

TOURIST INFORMATION

Royal Pavilion Shop & Brighton Toy Museum

4-5 Pavilion Buildings 09067 112 255 &
Top of Trafalgar Street
(but at 50p perminute, it's not cheap!)
Textphone (01273) 292595
Mon-Fri 9am-5pm, Sat 10am-5pm, Sun 10am-4pm
www.tourism.brighton.co.uk
www.visitbrighton.com

While most tourist info centres seem to stock the ubiquitous flyers featuring kids screaming on a rollercoaster and waxworks dummies dressed as Victorian chimney sweeps, Brighton's is stuffed with fascinating books, well-informed staff and good offers. I even found an out-of-print book here recently that I'd been searching for in vain for months (*Sherlock Holmes and the Brighton Pavilion Mystery*). If it's information you're after they can sort out on-the-day bookings for B&Bs and hotels, as well as for National Express coaches and day trips. You'll also find all the customary gubbins about local tours, museums and places to visit.

DRUGS

Because drug use is widespread in Brighton, the clubs have very strict policies. You might see a club night called Spliff whose advertising features PVC-clad models smoking huge reefers but one whiff of grass in their special smoking area and you'll be chucked out. If you want to purchase legal highs check out the Guarana Bar or Organic Shamanic. If you want to purchase illegal highs ask around for the bloke who plays table tennis.

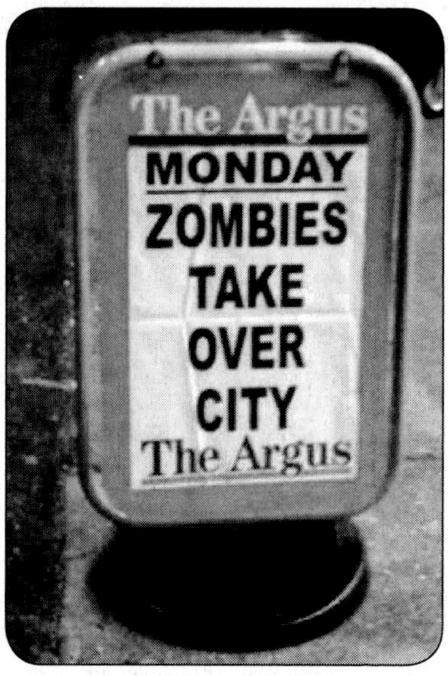

And on Tuesday, vampires opened up a new garden centre

CRIME

As with any UK city, don't walk around with your wallet hanging out of your back pocket and you should be fine. Hang around on West Street at the weekend for long enough however and you will be robbed by junkies, stripped naked by loose women, beaten up by lager louts and pecked to death by seagulls.

NEW TO BRIGHTON?

If you've just arrived in Brighton from a different city, are working here temporarily, realise that all your friends have settled down/moved away, want to try something new or just like meeting new people, My Brighton are a social group in Brighton who meet for a drink at the pub and organise other events during the week. Check out their website *www.my-brighton.org.*

WANT TO GET YOUR OWN BACK ON AN UNCARING WORLD THAT PUSHES YOU AROUND AND TRAMPLES ON YOUR NAUGHTY BITS?

THEN ENROL TODAY AS A...

BRIGHTON TRAFFIC WARDEN!

FEEL POWERFUL IN A UNIFORM!!

BRING MISERY TO THE LIVES OF OTHERS... EVERY DAY!!

VICTIMISE PILLARS OF THE LOCAL COMMUNITY AS YOU SLAP TICKETS WILLY-NILLY ON BUILDERS' VANS, HEARSES, AMBULANCES, FIRE-ENGINES, AND EVEN THE VEHICLES OF THE POOR FOOLS WHO PAY £1,000 A YEAR FOR A RESIDENT PARKING PERMIT BUT **STILL CAN'T FIND ANYWHERE TO PARK!!!!!!**

LAUGH MANIACALLY AT THE INJUSTICE OF IT ALL AS THE SCUMBAG COUNCILLORS WHO DREAMT UP THE SCHEME, DRIVE BACK TO THEIR £500,000 HOMES AND PRIVATE GARAGES!!!!

SCREAM DEMONICALLY AS YOU DRINK THE BLOOD OF A FRESHLY CULLED NAKED VIRGIN AND INVOKE BEELZEBUB TO TAKE YOUR SOUL AND TRANSFORM YOU INTO ***A CREATURE OF THE NIGHT!***

APPLICANTS WITH A CONSCIENCE NEED NOT APPLY

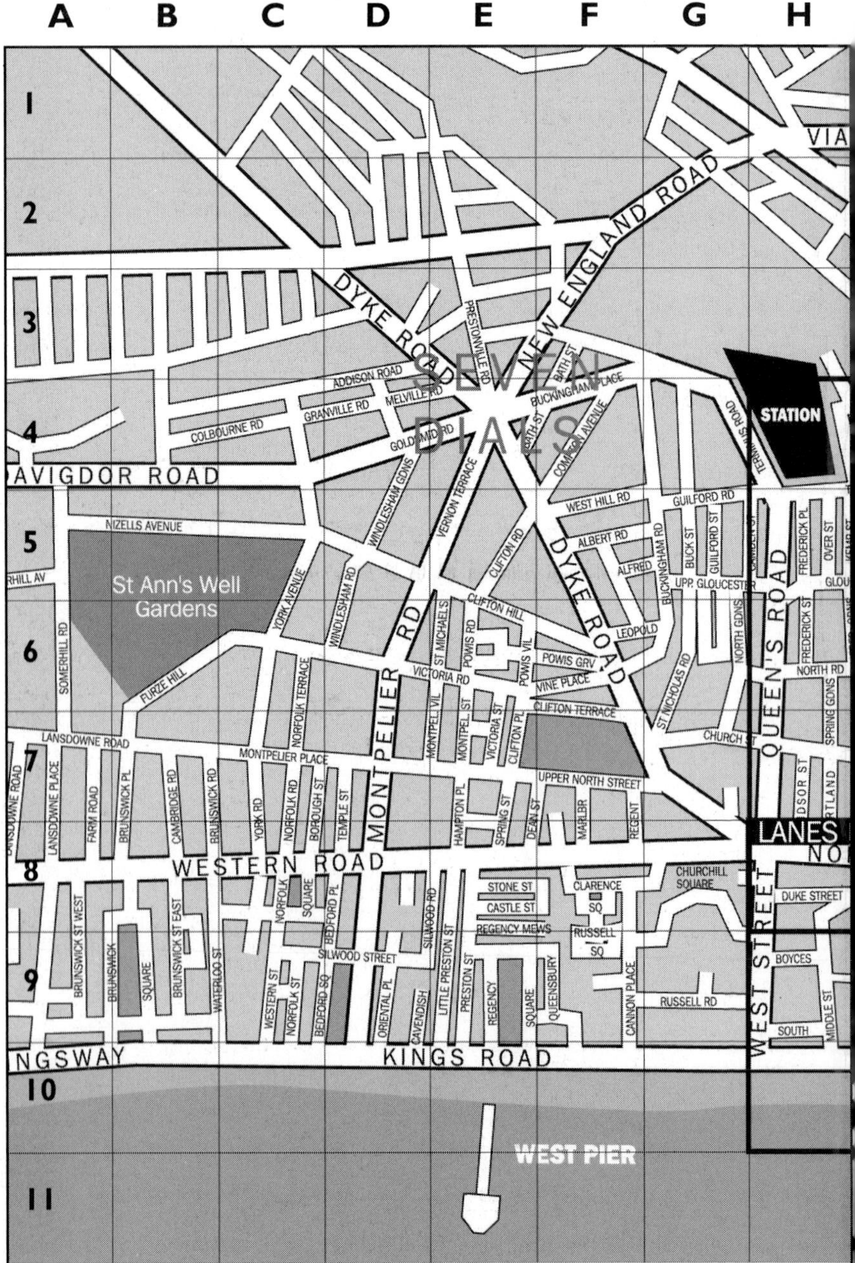
A
B
C
D
E
F
G
H
1
2
3
4
5
6
7
8
9
10
11
NEW ENGLAND ROAD
DYKE ROAD
SEVEN DIALS
STATION
ADDISON ROAD
GRANVILLE RD
MELVILLE RD
COLBOURNE RD
PRESTONVILLE RD
BATH ST
BUCKINGHAM PLACE
COMPTON AVENUE
TERMINUS ROAD
DAVIGDOR ROAD
NIZELLS AVENUE
WINDLESHAM GDNS
VERNON TERRACE
WEST HILL RD
GUILFORD RD
ALBERT RD
ALFRED
BUCKINGHAM RD
BUCK ST
GUILFORD ST
FREDERICK PL
QUEEN'S ROAD
UPP. GLOUCESTER
St Ann's Well Gardens
YORK AVENUE
WINDLESHAM RD
CLIFTON RD
CLIFTON HILL
LEOPOLD
SOMERHILL RD
FURZE HILL
MONTPELIER RD
ST MICHAEL'S
POWIS RD
POWIS VIL
POWIS GRV
VICTORIA RD
VINE PLACE
ST NICHOLAS RD
NORTH GDNS
FREDERICK ST
NORTH RD
NORFOLK TERRACE
CLIFTON TERRACE
SPRING GDNS
LANSDOWNE ROAD
MONTPELIER PLACE
MONTPEL VIL
MONTPEL ST
VICTORIA ST
CLIFTON PL
CHURCH ST
UPPER NORTH STREET
LANSDOWNE PLACE
FARM ROAD
BRUNSWICK PL
CAMBRIDGE RD
BRUNSWICK RD
YORK RD
NORFOLK RD
BOROUGH ST
TEMPLE ST
HAMPTON PL
SPRING ST
DEAN ST
MARLBR
REGENT
LANES
WESTERN ROAD
STONE ST
CLARENCE SQ
CHURCHILL SQUARE
CASTLE ST
REGENCY MEWS
RUSSELL SQ
DUKE STREET
WEST STREET
BRUNSWICK ST WEST
BRUNSWICK SQUARE
BRUNSWICK ST EAST
WATERLOO ST
NORFOLK SQUARE
BEDFORD PL
SILWOOD RD
SILWOOD STREET
WESTERN ST
NORFOLK ST
BEDFORD SQ
ORIENTAL PL
CAVENDISH
LITTLE PRESTON ST
PRESTON ST
REGENCY SQUARE
QUEENSBURY
CANNON PLACE
RUSSELL RD
BOYCES
MIDDLE ST
SOUTH
KINGS ROAD
WEST PIER

I J K L M N O P
DUCT RD
ELM GROVE
HANOVER
ISLINGWORD RD
LONDON RD
The Level
LEWES ROAD
HANOVER ST
HANOVER TERR.
COLEMAN ST
WASHINGTON ST
LINCOLN ST
EWART ST
ISLINGWORD ST
SOUTHAMPTON ST
FINSBURY RD
SOUTHOVER ST
NEWHAVEN ST
LEWES ST
BELGRAVE ST
NEWARK PL
JERSEY ST
GROVE ST
HOLLAND ST
SCOTLAND ST
QUEBEC ST
MONTREAL RD
TORONTO TER
ALBION HILL
NORTH LAINE
ALBION ST
GROVE HILL
TRAFALGAR ST
TRAFALGAR LA
KENSINGTON PL
TIDY ST
SYDNEY ST
GLOUCESTER ST
RICHMOND ST
NORY PLACE
ASHTON RISE
JOHN ST
QUEEN'S PARK ROAD
WEST DRIVE
Queen's Park
EAST DRIVE
FOUNDRY ST
QUEENS GDNS
UPPER GDNR
KENSINGTON
KENS. ST
ROBERT ST
VINE ST
CHELTENHAM
GRAND PARADE
SUSSEX ST
NORTH RD
CIRCUS ST
SOUTH AVENUE
PARK HILL
FRESHFIELD PLACE
STEVENSON
ROAD
FRESHFIELD ROAD
SUTHERLAND ROAD
TITCHBORNE
GARDNER ST
REGENT ST
KINGSWOOD
CARLTON HILL
CHURCH STREET
WILLIAM ST
WHITE ST
BLAKER ST
MT PLEASANT ST
EGREMONT PLACE
LEICESTER ST
TILLSTONE ST
PARK ST
EDWARD ST
BOND ST
NEW RD
PAVILION
PRINCES ST
GEORGE ST
DORSET GDNS
HIGH ST
CHAPEL ST
DEVONSHIRE PL
ST JAMES AVE
UPP. ROCK GDNS
HEREFORD ST
SOMERSET ST
SUTHERLAND RD
COLLEGE RD
VERONICA
UPP. BEDFORD
MONTAGUE ST
BRISTOL ST
KEMP TOW
STREET
LANES
OLD STEINE
ST JAMES'S ST
EAST ST
PRINCE ALBERT ST
STEINE ST
MANCHESTR
CHARLES
BROAD
MADEIRA
CAMFRDS
MARGRT
WNTWTH
NW STEINE
ROCK PL
LR RCK GDN
ATLNGWTH
GRAFTON
WYNDHM
CHARLES
MARINE
BEDFORD
ROYAL CR
BURLINGTON
CRESCENT PL
BLOOMSBURY
MARINE PARADE
SHIP ST
LION ST
POOL
VALL
MADEIRA DRIVE
PALACE PIER

INDEX FOR MAP